I0651471

Florian Cajori

A History of Physics in its Elementary Branches

Including the Evolution of Physical Laboratories

Florian Cajori

A History of Physics in its Elementary Branches
Including the Evolution of Physical Laboratories

ISBN/EAN: 9783337276140

Printed in Europe, USA, Canada, Australia, Japan

Cover: Foto ©ninafisch / pixelio.de

More available books at **www.hansebooks.com**

A

HISTORY OF PHYSICS

IN ITS ELEMENTARY BRANCHES

INCLUDING THE

EVOLUTION OF PHYSICAL LABORATORIES

BY

FLORIAN CAJORI, Ph.D.

PROFESSOR OF PHYSICS IN COLORADO COLLEGE

New York
THE MACMILLAN COMPANY
LONDON: MACMILLAN & CO., Ltd
1917

Set up and electrotyped. Published January, 1899. Reprinted
July, 1906 ; January, July, 1909 ; January, 1914; March, 1916 ;
October, 1917.

Norwood Press
J. S. Cushing & Co. — Berwick & Smith Co.
Norwood, Mass., U.S.A.

PREFACE

This history is intended mainly for the use of students and teachers of physics. The writer is convinced that some attention to the history of a science helps to make it attractive, and that the general view of the development of the human intellect, obtained by reading the history of science, is in itself stimulating and liberalizing.

In the announcement of Ostwald's *Klassiker der Exakten Wissenschaften* is the following significant statement: "While, by the present methods of teaching, a knowledge of science in its present state of advancement is imparted very successfully, eminent and far-sighted men have repeatedly been obliged to point out a defect which too often attaches to the present scientific education of our youth. *It is the absence of the historical sense and the want of knowledge of the great researches upon which the edifice of science rests.*"

It is hoped that the survey of the progress of physics here presented may assist in remedying this defect so clearly pointed out by Professor Ostwald.

As it seems best not to increase the size of the book beyond the limit originally intended, it is necessary to omit a few subjects which properly belong to elementary physics.

It gives me great pleasure to acknowledge my obligations to Mr. S. J. Barnett, Ph.D., and Mr. P. E. Doudna, A.M., of Colorado College, for assistance in proof-reading and for important suggestions and criticisms.

FLORIAN CAJORI.

COLORADO COLLEGE, COLORADO SPRINGS,
November, 1898.

CONTENTS

A HISTORY OF PHYSICS

—◦○;◦;○◦—

THE GREEKS

In mathematics, metaphysics, literature, and art the Greeks displayed wonderful creative genius, but in natural science they achieved comparatively little. It would not be correct to say that they possessed little or no aptitude for observing natural phenomena, but it is true that, as a rule, they were ignorant of the art of experimentation, and that many of their physical speculations were vague, trifling, and worthless. As compared with the vast amount of theoretical deduction about nature, the number of experiments known to have been performed by the Greeks is surprisingly small. Little or no attempt was made to verify speculation by experimental evidence. As a conspicuous example of misty philosophizing we give Aristotle's proof that the world is *perfect:*[1] "The bodies of which the world is composed are solids, and therefore have three dimensions. Now, three is the most perfect number, —it is the first of numbers, for of *one* we do not speak as a number, of *two* we say both, but *three* is the first number of which we say *all*. Moreover, it has a beginning, a middle, and an end."

MECHANICS

Mechanical subjects are treated in the writings of Aristotle. The great peripatetic had grasped the notion of the parallelo-

[1] *De Cœlo*, I. 1, as translated by Whewell.

1

gram of forces for the special case of the rectangle. He attempted the theory of the lever, stating that a force at a greater distance from the fulcrum moves a weight more easily because it describes a greater circle. He resolved the motion of a weight at the end of the lever into tangential and normal components. The tangential motion he calls *according to nature;* the normal motion *contrary to nature.* The modern reader will readily see that the expression *contrary to nature* applied to a natural phenomenon is inappropriate and confusing.

Aristotle's views of falling bodies are very far from the truth. Nevertheless they demand our attention, for the reason that, during the Middle Ages and Renaissance, his authority was so great that they play an important rôle in scientific thought. He says: "That body is heavier than another which, in an equal bulk, moves downward quicker."[1] In another place he teaches that bodies fall quicker in exact proportion to their weight.[2] No statement could be further from the truth.

A modern writer endeavours to exonerate Aristotle as a physicist. "If he could have had any modern instrument of observation — such as the telescope or microscope, or even the thermometer or barometer — placed in his hands, how swiftly would he have used such an advantage!"[3] But in the case of falling bodies, the experiment was within his reach. If it had only occurred to him, while walking up and down the paths near

---

[1] *De Cœlo*, IV. 1, p. 308.

[2] This law is assumed by him in the following reasoning: ". . . suppose α without weight, but β possessing weight; and let α pass over a space γδ, but β in the same time pass over a space γε, — for that which has weight will be carried through the larger space. If now the heavy body be divided in the proportion that space γε bears to γδ, . . . and *if the whole is carried through the whole space γε, then it must be that a part in the same time would be carried through γδ.* . . ." — *De Cœlo*, Book III., Ch. II.

[3] Article "Aristotle" in *Encyclopædia Britannica*, Ninth Edition.

his school in Athens, to pick up two stones of unequal weight and drop them together, he could easily have seen that the one of, say, ten times the weight did not descend ten times faster.

Immeasurably superior to Aristotle as a student of mechanics is Archimedes (287(?)–212 B.C.).[1] He is the true originator of mechanics as a science. To him we owe the theory of the centre of gravity (centroid) and of the lever. In his *Equiponderance of Planes* he starts with the axiom that equal

FIG. 1.

weights acting at equal distances on opposite sides of a pivot are in equilibrium, and then endeavours to establish the principle that "in the lever unequal weights are in equilibrium only when they are inversely proportional to the arms from which they are suspended." His appreciation of its efficiency is echoed in the exclamation attributed to him: "Give me a fulcrum on which to rest, and I will move the earth."

We reproduce from a mechanical work of Varignon, published in Paris in 1687, a figure (Fig. 1) illustrating this saying. The Latin motto in the figure may be rendered thus: "Touch it and you will move it."

[1] Consult *The Works of Archimedes*, edited in modern notation, with introductory chapters, by T. L. HEATH. Cambridge, University Press.

While the *Equiponderance* treats of solids or the equilibrium of solids, the book on *Floating Bodies* treats of hydrostatics. His attention was first drawn to the subject of specific gravity when King Hieron asked him to test whether a crown, professed by the maker to be pure gold, was not alloyed with silver. The story goes that our philosopher was in a bath when the true method of solution flashed on his mind. He immediately leaped from the bath and ran home, shouting, "I have found it!" To solve the problem he took a piece of gold and a piece of silver, each weighing the same as the crown. According to one author,[1] he determined the volume of water displaced by the gold, silver, and crown respectively, and calculated from that the amount of gold and silver in the crown. According to another writer,[2] he weighed separately the gold, silver, and crown, while immersed in water, thereby determining their loss of weight in water. From these data he easily found the solution. It is possible that Archimedes solved the problem by both methods.

In his *Floating Bodies* Archimedes established the important principle, known by his name, that the loss of weight of a body submerged in water is equal to the weight of the water displaced, and that a floating body displaces its own weight of water. Since the days of Archimedes able minds have drawn erroneous conclusions on liquid pressure. The expression "hydrostatic paradox" indicates the slippery nature of the subject. All the more must we admire the clearness of conception and almost perfect logical rigour which characterize the investigations of Archimedes.[3]

---

[1] VITRUVIUS, IX. 3.

[2] *Scriptores metrologici Romani* (ed. HULTSCH, pp. 124–208).

[3] A valuable paper with numerous extracts from authors is CH. THUROT's *Recherches Historiques sur le Principe d'Archimède*, Paris, 1869 (extrait de la *Revue Archéologique*, Années 1868–1869).

Archimedes is said to have shown wonderful inventive genius in various mechanical inventions. It is reported that he astonished the court of Hieron by moving heavy ships by aid of a collection of pulleys. To him is ascribed the invention of war engines, and the endless screw ("screw of Archimedes") which was used to drain the holds of ships.

About a century after Archimedes, there flourished *Ctesibius* and his pupil *Heron*, both of Alexandria. They contributed little to the advancement of theoretical investigation, but they displayed wonderful mechanical ingenuity. The force-pump is probably the invention of Ctesibius. The suction pump is older and was known in the time of Aristotle. According to Vitruvius, Ctesibius designed the ancient fire-engine, consisting of the combination of two force-pumps, spraying alternately. The machine had no air-chamber, and therefore could not produce a steady stream. Heron describes the fire-engine in his *Pneumatica*. During the Middle Ages the fire-engine was unknown. It is said to have been first used in Augsburg in 1518.[1] Ctesibius is credited with the invention of the hydraulic organ, the water-clock, and the catapult. Heron showed the earliest application of steam as a motive power, in his toy, called the "eolipile" (Fig. 2). It consisted of a hollow sphere with two arms at right angles to its axis and bent in opposite directions at its ends. When steam was generated in the sphere, it escaped through the arms and caused the sphere to rotate. It was the forerunner of Barker's water-mill and the

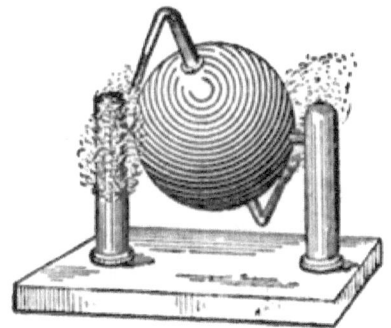

FIG. 2.

---

[1] A. DE ROCHAS in *La Nature*, Vol. XI., pp. 13, 14 ; 1883.

modern turbine. Heron wrote an important book on geodesy, called *Dioptra*.[1]

The Greeks invented the hydrometer, probably in the fourth century A.D. There appears to be no good evidence for attributing its origin to Archimedes. The hydrometer is described in full by Bishop *Synesius* in a letter to Hypatia. It consisted of a hollow, graduated, tin cylinder, weighted below. It was first used in medicine, to determine the quality of drinking-water, hard water being at that time considered unwholesome. According to Desaguliers it was used for this purpose as late as the eighteenth century.[2]

LIGHT

The fragment of a Greek document, found in Egypt, speaks of various optical illusions; for instance, that the sun appears larger when at the horizon than when near the zenith.[3] Optics is, indeed, one of the oldest branches of physics. A converging lens of rock crystal is said to have been found in the ruins of Nineveh.[4] In Greece, burning-glasses seem to have been manufactured at an early date. Aristophanes, in the comedy of *The Clouds*, Act II. (performed 424 B.C.), introduces a conversation about "fine transparent stone (glass) with which fires are kindled," and by which, standing in the sun, one can, "though at a distance, melt all the writing" traced on a surface of wax. The Platonic school taught the rectilinear propagation of light

[1] For a full account of Heron, "the first engineer," see W. A. TRUES-DELL in *Jour. of the Ass. of Engin. Soc.*, Vol. XIX., Philadelphia, 1897, pp. 1-19.

[2] E. GERLAND in *Wiedemann's Annalen*, Vol. 1, New Series, 1877, pp. 150-157. See also his *Gesch. d. Physik*, p. 40.

[3] See K. WESSELY in *Wiener Studien*, Vol. 13, 1891, pp. 312-323. Abstracted in *Wiedemann's Beiblätter*, Vol. 17, 1893.

[4] E. GERLAND, *Geschichte der Physik*, Leipzig, 1892, p. 9.

and the equality of the angle of incidence to that of reflection. The astronomer, *Claudius Ptolemy*, who flourished in Alexandria in 139 A.D., measured angles of incidence and of refraction, and arranged them in tables.

Metallic mirrors seem to have been manufactured in remote antiquity. "Looking-glasses" are referred to in *Exodus* 38 : 8, and in *Job* 37 : 18; they have been found in graves of Egyptian mummies. Spherical and parabolic mirrors were known to the Greeks. To *Euclid* (about 300 B.C.) is attributed a work on *Catoptrics*, dealing with phenomena of reflection. In it is found the earliest reference to the focus of a spherical mirror. In Theorem 30 it is stated[1] that concave mirrors turned toward the sun will cause ignition. In the "fragmentum Bobiense," a document written, perhaps, by Anthemius of Tralles, the focal property of parabolic reflectors is demonstrated. Several Greek authors appear to have written on concave mirrors. The story that, when the Romans were besieging Syracuse, *Archimedes* defended his native city by the use of mirrors reflecting the sun's rays, and setting on fire the ships when they came within bowshot of the walls, is probably a fiction.

The Greeks elaborated several theories of vision. According to the *Pythagoreans, Democritus*, and others vision is caused by the projection of particles from the object seen, into the pupil of the eye. On the other hand, *Empedocles* (about 440 B.C.), the *Platonists*, and *Euclid* held the strange doctrine of ocular beams, according to which the eye itself sends out something which causes sight as soon as it meets something else emanated by the object.[2]

---

[1] *Euclidis Opera Omnia*, Vol. 7, Edidit I. L. HEIBERG, Lipsiæ, 1895. See also E. WIEDEMANN in *Wied. Annalen*, Vol. 39, 1890, p. 123.

[2] For Plato's theory, see *The Dialogues of Plato*, Vol. II., translated by B. JOWETT, C. Scribner's Sons, New York, pp. 537 *et seq.*

ELECTRICITY AND MAGNETISM

To the Greeks we owe a few isolated observations on electricity and magnetism. *Thales of Miletus* (640–546 B.C.), one of the "seven wise men" of early Greece, is credited with the knowledge that amber, when rubbed, will attract light bodies, and that a certain mineral, now called magnetite, or loadstone, possesses the power of attracting iron. Amber—a mineralized yellowish resin—was used in antiquity for decoration. In common with the bright shining silver-gold alloys, and gold itself, it was called "electron"; hence the word "electricity." About three centuries after Thales, *Theophrastus*, in his treatise *On Gems*, mentions another mineral which becomes electrified by friction. We know now that all bodies can be thus electrified. Pliny says that ignorant people called the loadstone "quick-iron." The large extent to which this phenomenon of magnetic attraction excited the imagination of men is shown by the fable of the shepherd Magnes, who, on Mount Ida (on the island Crete), was so strongly drawn to earth by the tacks in his sandals and the iron tip of his staff, that he could hardly pull himself away. He dug to ascertain the cause, and discovered a wonderful stone (magnetite). Another fable speaks of a powerful magnetic mountain, which pulled the nails out of ships, even when the latter were at considerable distance from it.[1]

Pliny tells another story concerning the loadstone. At Alexandria the construction of a vaulted roof of magnetite in the temple of Arsinoe was undertaken for the purpose of suspending in the air the iron statue of the queen. As time went on, the story was greatly embellished. Thus, according

[1] This story recurs frequently in literature; for instance, in the tale of the third mendicant in the *Arabian Nights*.

to the Venerable Bede, the horse of Bellerophon, on the island of Rhodes, weighed 5000 pounds, and was suspended by magnets.[1] A similar story is told of Mohammed's coffin. Of course, such a suspension in air is mechanically impossible.

During antiquity iron was mined chiefly along the coasts of the Ægean Sea and on the Mediterranean islands. Magnetic iron ore is said to have been found also near Magnesia in Asia Minor. According to Lucretius the term "magnet" is derived from "Magnesia." There were iron mines on the island of Samothrace. The miners of that locality showed the action of the loadstone in connection with the so-called Samothracian rings. Says Socrates: ". . . that stone not only attracts iron rings, but also imparts to them a similar power of attracting other rings; and sometimes you may see a number of pieces of iron and rings suspended from one another so as to form quite a long chain: and all of them derive their power of suspension from the original stone."[2]

The polarity of magnets and the phenomenon of repulsion which may exist between electric charges or magnetic poles were unknown to Greek antiquity.

METEOROLOGY

Previous to the middle of the fifteenth century no systematic meteorological records are known to have been kept anywhere.[3] Yet the Greeks paid some attention to meteorology. It is in Athens that we find the oldest contrivance for observing the direction of the wind. There, in its essential

[1] BEDA, *De Sept. Mirac. Mundi;* quoted by PARK BENJAMIN in *The Intellectual Rise in Electricity,* New York, 1895, p. 46. (Hereafter this work will be referred to as BENJAMIN.)

[2] JOWETT, *Dialogues of Plato,* Vol. I., p. 223. (Ion.)

[3] G. Hellmann, *Himmel und Erde,* Vol. II., 1890, p. 113.

parts standing to this day, is the "tower of the winds," built about 100 B.C. Upon an octagon of marble was a roof, the highest part of which carried a weather-vane in form of a triton. It is improbable that weather-vanes were ever common in Greece or Rome, for there is no Greek or Latin name to designate the instrument.[1] Among the Greeks meteorology can hardly be said to have risen to the dignity of a science. *Theophrastus of Eresus* (371–286 B.C.), a disciple of Aristotle, wrote a book *On Winds and on Weather Signs*,[2] but like most other Greek philosophers, he was hardly the man to adopt patient and exact observation in place of dogmatic assertion and the teaching of authority. *Aristotle* makes a good observation on the formation of dew; viz. dew is formed only on clear and quiet nights.[3]

Aratus of Soli, who lived about 275 B.C., wrote a book of *Prognostics*, giving predictions of the weather from observation of astronomical phenomena, and various accounts of the effect of weather on animals. Several editions of this and other works of Aratus were printed; one edition was brought out by Melanchthon.

SOUND

The pyramids of Egypt and the ruins of ancient cities bear testimony to the fact that practical geometry and practical mechanics antedated by many centuries the earliest records which we possess on abstract geometry and theoretical mechanics. In the same way, the knowledge of vocal and instrumental music, said to have been possessed by nations of great

---

[1] HELLMANN, *op. cit.*, p. 119.

[2] Translated by J. G. WOOD, London, 1894, with an introduction and an appendix of historical interest and value.

[3] J. C. POGGENDORFF, *Geschichte der Physik*, Leipzig, 1879, p. 42. (Hereafter this work will be quoted as POGGENDORFF.)

antiquity, demonstrates that the art of music is incomparably older than the theory of acoustics. The beginning of the theory of harmonics reaches back to *Pythagoras* (580?–500? B.C.), but the accounts of his researches are so intertwined with fable and with error, that it is difficult to ascertain just what Pythagoras did. Passing by a blacksmith's shop, he is said to have noticed that the hammers as they struck the anvil produced sounds having the intervals a "fourth," a "fifth," and an "octave." He found the weights of the hammers[1] to be, respectively, as $1 : \frac{3}{4} : \frac{2}{3} : \frac{1}{2}$. Subsequent experimentation with musical strings of the same material and equal lengths and thicknesses showed that weights proportionate to $1, \frac{3}{4}, \frac{2}{3}, \frac{1}{2}$, would give the above intervals. This research pointed to an arithmetical relation between musical intervals, and established a close connection between subjects so far apart as arithmetic and music.

It will readily be seen that the above account contains two errors. Hammers of the weights given above will not yield the sounds in question. Nor is the law of weights for strings stated correctly; the pitch of tones varies, not as the weights, but as the square roots of the weights.

Some modern writers have been led to surmise that Pythagoras did not base his opinions upon experiment, that the smithy in which he got his information was the land of Egypt, whence he imported his knowledge.[2] Other writers assume that Pythagoras really did not vary the tensions of the strings, but varied their lengths, thereby arriving at the correct law that pitch changes inversely as the lengths of the strings.[3] It

---

[1] NICOMACHUS, *Harmonices*, I., p. 10 (Ed. Meibomius); PORPHYRY, *Ptol. Harm.*, c. 3, p. 213 ; DIOGENES LAERTIUS, VIII., 12.

[2] See article "Music" in *Encycl. Brit.*, 9th ed. This article contains much information on Greek musical scales.

[3] HELMHOLTZ, *Sensations of Tone*, trans. by A. J. ELLIS, London, 1885,

is said that Pythagoras was the first to establish the eight complete degrees in the diatonic scale.[1]

His speculations on harmony and musical intervals were uncontrolled by further inquiry into the facts. The seven planets are the seven strings of the lyre, which give us a beautiful "harmony of the spheres."[2] This idea was not advanced as poetry, but as physical philosophy. The fact that the human ear cannot detect such interplanetary music did not seem to weaken his belief in its existence!

The theory of sound was touched upon by Aristotle, who entertained correct ideas on the character of the motion of air constituting sound, and who knew that, if the length of a pipe is doubled, a vibration in it occupies double the time.

ATOMIC THEORY

It is worthy of notice that the atomic theory finds its earliest advocates in Greece. That the theory of the atomic constitution of matter is far from being a self-evident truth follows at once from the fact that the two thinkers who have swayed philosophic thought most powerfully, Aristotle and Kant, teach that space is continuously filled.[3] The great ancient expositor of the atomic theory is *Democritus of Abdera* (about 460–370 B.C.). He taught that the world consists of empty space and an infinite number of indivisible, invisibly small atoms. Bodies appear and disappear only by the union

p. 1. For fuller references and details regarding Pythagoras, see E. ZEL-LER, *History of Greek Philosophy*, trans. by S. F. ALLEYNE, London, 1881, Vol. I., pp. 431–433. Consult also C. H. H. PARRY, *The Evolution of the Art of Music*, New York, 1896, "Scales," pp. 15–47.

[1] HELMHOLTZ, *op. cit.*, p. 266.

[2] NICOMACHUS, *op. cit.*, I., p. 6, II., p. 33 ; PLINY, H. N., II., p. 20 ; Simpl. in ARIST. *de Cœlo. Schol.*, p. 496, 11.

[3] KURD LASSWITZ, *Geschichte der Atomistik*, Vol. I., p. 2.

and separation of atoms. Even the phenomena of sensation and thought are the result of their combination. The atomic theory did not play any great rôle in scientific progress until after the discovery by *Dalton* of the chemical law of multiple proportions.

CAUSES OF THE FAILURE OF GREEK PHYSICAL INQUIRY

While the Greeks achieved more in physical research than did other nations of antiquity, they nevertheless accomplished infinitely less in this field of intellectual activity than in other directions. The question why the Greeks made no progress in physics is an old puzzle, and is not easily answered. Francis Bacon says that "the proceeding has been to fly at once from the sense and particulars up to the most general propositions, as certain fixed poles for the argument to turn upon, and from these to derive the rest by middle terms: a short way, no doubt, but precipitate; and one which will never lead to nature, though it offers an easy and ready way to disputation." "The ancients proved themselves in everything that turns on wit and abstract meditation, wonderful men."[1] According to Whewell, "the defect was, that though they had in their possession facts and ideas, *the ideas were not distinct and appropriate to the facts.*"[2] Consider, for example, Aristotle's motions "according to nature," and "contrary to nature," attributed to the lever. Neither Bacon's nor Whewell's explanation seems satisfactory. Each endeavours to explain *how* the thing took place, rather than *why*. The question still remains to be

---

[1] F. BACON, in Preface to the "Novum Organum" (*Works*, New York, 1878, Vol. I., pp. 42, 32.)

[2] W. WHEWELL, *History of the Inductive Sciences*, New York, 1858, Vol. I., p. 87. (To be quoted hereafter as WHEWELL.)

answered, why did people of such great penetration "fly at once from the sense and particulars up to the most general propositions," or why did they come to apply ideas "not distinct and appropriate to the facts"? What causes led keen minds thus to blunder? Perhaps a more satisfactory answer is given in Mill's *System of Logic:* The Greeks "were not content merely to know that one phenomenon was always followed by another; they thought that they had not attained the true aim of science, unless they could perceive something in the nature of the one phenomenon, from which it might have been known or presumed *previous to trial*, that it would be followed by the other. . . . [They] not only sought for causes which should carry in their mere statement evidence of their efficiency, but fully believed that they had found such causes."[1] "When Thales and Hippo held that moisture was the universal cause and eternal element, of which all other things were but the infinitely various sensible manifestations;[2] when Anaximenes predicated the same thing of air,[3] Pythagoras of numbers, and the like, they all thought that they had found a real explanation, and were content to rest in this explanation as ultimate."[4]

---

[1] J. S. Mill, *System of Logic*, London, 1851, Vol. I., p. 367, where Mill adopts the view of a writer in the *Prospective Review*, February, 1850.

[2] Moisture is the necessary constituent of food ; it is essential to germination ; the fertility of land depends on it.

[3] All creatures breathe air, live on it, and lastly, are transformed into it.

[4] Besides the works already quoted, the reader interested in Greek science may consult August Heller, *Geschichte der Physik*, Stuttgart, 1882, Vol. I., pp. 1-157; G. Milhaud, *Origines de la Science Grecque*, Paris, 1893.

THE ROMANS

THE genius of the Roman people was exercised in war, conquest, government, and law, but no effort was put forth for the advancement of pure mathematics or science. The Roman scientific writers were contented to collect the researches of Greek predecessors. Among these are *Marcus Vitruvius Pollio* (85–26 B.C.), the architect of Emperor Augustus; *Titus Carus Lucretius* (95–52 (?) B.C.), the author of *De Rerum Natura;* *Lucius Annœus Seneca* (2–66 A.D.), the tutor of Emperor Nero; *Pliny* (23–79 A.D.), the compiler of a large work on natural history; and *Anicius Manlius Severinus Boethius* (480 ?–524), at one time a favourite of King Theodoric.

Boethius wrote a work on *Music* which contains much information on Greek theories of harmony. Seneca taught the identity of rainbow colours with those formed by the edge of a piece of glass. He observed that a globular glass vessel, filled with water, magnifies objects, but he was led by this observation no further than to remark that nothing is so deceptive as our sight. His writings are replete with moral sentiment. This accounts, perhaps, for the fact that his *Naturalium quaestionum libri* VII was used for so long, during the Middle Ages, as a text-book of physics.[1] His grasp of mechanics is illustrated by the story which he gravely tells of a fish, less than a foot long, which, by clinging to a ship, completely stops its motion even in a gale. He claimed that,

---

[1] F. ROSENBERGER, *Geschichte der Physik*, Part I., 1882, p. 45. (This work will be quoted after this as ROSENBERGER.)

during the battle of Actium, Antonius's largest vessel was thus bound fast.

Cleomedes, whose place and time of birth are unknown, probably flourished about the time of the Emperor Augustus. He noticed, as did Archimedes and Euclid, that a ring on the bottom of an empty vessel, just hidden by the edge, becomes visible when the vessel is filled with water. But he goes further and suggests that in the same way the sun may be in sight when, as a matter of fact, it is a little below the horizon. Thus he is the first to consider atmospheric refraction.

Lucretius is the first ancient writer who refers to the *repulsive* effect of a magnet and to the experiment with iron filings. The latter "will rave within brass basins," when the loadstone is placed beneath.

THE ARABS

THE growth of the Arabic nation presents an extraordinary spectacle in intellectual history. Scattered barbaric tribes were suddenly fused in the furnace blast of religious enthusiasm into a powerful nation. A career of war and conquest was followed by a period of intellectual activity. About the eighth century A.D. the Mohammedans began to figure as the intellectual leaders of the world. With wonderful celerity they acquired the scientific and philosophic treasures of the Hindus and Greeks. Old books were translated from the Greek into Arabic. Chemistry, astronomy, mathematics, and geography became favourite subjects of study. In a few instances the Arabs made original contributions to science, but as a rule they did not distinguish themselves in original research; they were learned rather than creative.

So far as we know, there was only one branch of physics which was successfully cultivated on Arabic soil and but one man prominently identified with it. The branch was optics, and the man was *Al Hazen* (965?-1038). His full Arabic name is Abû 'Alî al Hasan ibn al Hasan ibn Al Haitam. He was born in Bosra on the Tigris and rose to the position of vizier. He was then called to Egypt by one of the caliphs who had heard that Al Hazen had thought out plans for so regulating the flow of the Nile that each year there should be plenty of water for irrigation. Closer inspection of the grounds compelled him to abandon the project. He committed other errors which brought him into disfavour with the caliph.

17

He feigned insanity and sought concealment until after the
death of the caliph.   Subsequently he made his living by
copying manuscripts.   He wrote on astronomy, mathematics,
and optics.

His *Optics* was translated into Latin and printed at Bâle in
1572.   To the law of the equality of the angles in reflection,
which he learned from the Greeks, he added the law that both
angles lie in the same plane.   He made a study of spherical
and parabolic mirrors.   The greater the number of rays which
pass through a point, the more intense is the heat there.   Rays
incident upon a spherical mirror, and parallel to the principal
axis, are reflected to this axis.   All the rays reflected from
points in the mirror lying on the circumference of a circle
which is perpendicular to the axis (and these rays only) pass
through one and the same point on the axis.   He constructed
a mirror out of a number of separate spherical rings, of which
each has its own radius and its own centre, but so chosen that
all rings reflect all the rays accurately to one and the same
point.   The following is known as "Al Hazen's problem":
Given the position of a luminous point and of the eye, to find
the point on the spherical, cylindrical, or conical mirror at
which the reflection takes place.   The beginnings of this
problem are found in Ptolemy's optics; after Al Hazen's
masterly but complicated discussion of it, it became famous in
Europe on account of the geometrical difficulties to which the
general problem gave rise.[1]

In repetition of what had been done by Ptolemy, Al Hazen

---

[1] For Al Hazen and his researches see PAUL BODE, "Alhazensche
Spiegel-Aufgabe," Separat-Abdruck aus dem *Jahresbericht des Physi-
kalischen Vereins zu Frankfurt a. M.*, 1891–92 ; LEOPOLD SCHNAASE, *Die
Optik Alhazens*, Pr. Stargard, 1889 ; BAARMAN in *Zeitschr. d. deutschen
Morgenl. Gesellschaft*, 36, 1882, p. 195 ; E. WIEDEMANN, in *Wiedemann's
Annalen*, N. F., Vol. 39, pp. 110–130 ; also Vol. 7, p. 680.

took measurements of angles of incidence and of refraction, but, like his predecessor, he failed to discover the true law of refraction. His apparatus consisted of a graduated circular copper ring, supported in a vertical position, and dipped half way into water. The incident ray passed through a hole in the rim of the ring and through a perforated disk at the centre. The apparatus closely resembles that utilized at the present time in elementary instruction, and has the great advantage of permitting the angles of incidence and refraction to be read directly.

The apparent increase in diameter of sun and moon, when near the horizon, he declares to be an illusion due to the fact that their size is estimated by that of the less distant terrestrial objects. This explanation has held its ground to the present day, but is not accepted by all. Al Hazen arrived at the conclusion that the planets and fixed stars do not receive their light from the sun, but are self-luminous.[1]

Al Hazen is the first physicist to give a detailed description of the human eye. He says that he took his account from works on anatomy. Some of his Arabic predecessors and contemporaries, as well as he himself, stoutly combat the theory of Euclid and the Platonists, that vision is due to rays given out by the eye; they supported the view of Democritus and Aristotle that the cause of vision proceeds from the object seen.[2]

The Arabs developed the notion of "specific gravity," and gave experimental methods for its determination. *Al Biruni* used for this purpose a vessel with a spout slanting downwards. It was filled with water up to the spout, then the solid

---

[1] His paper on this subject is published in German translation by E. WIEDEMANN in *Wochenschr. f. Astr., Meteor., u. Geogr.*, 1890, No. 17.

[2] E. WIEDEMANN in *Wied. Annalen*, Vol. 39, 1890, p. 470.

was immersed, and the weight of the overflow determined. This, together with the weight of the solid in air, yielded the specific gravity. *Al Khazini*, in his *Book of the Balance of Wisdom*, written in 1137,[1] describes a curious beam balance, with five pans, for weighing in air and in water. One pan was movable along the graduated beam. He points out that air, too, must exert a buoyant force, causing bodies to weigh less.[2]

---

[1] Extracts are translated in *Journal of American Oriental Society*, VI., pp. 1–128; consult also F. Rosenberger, Part I., pp. 81–86.

[2] Readers interested in water-clocks among the Arabs may consult A. Wittstein, " Ueber die Wasseruhr und das Astrolabium des Arzachel," in *Schlömilch's Zeitschr.*, Vol. 39, 1894, Hist. Lit. Abtheilung, p. 43.

EUROPE DURING THE MIDDLE AGES

With the third century of our era there began a migration of barbaric nations in Europe. The powerful Goths from the north swept onward in a southwesterly direction, crossing into Italy and shattering the Roman Empire. The Dark Ages which followed were the germinating season of the institutions and nations of Europe. Christianity was introduced, and Latin became the language of intercourse in ecclesiastical and learned circles.

Obscurity and servility of thought, indistinctness of ideas, and mysticism characterize the Middle Ages. Writers on science were mainly commentators, and never thought of bringing the statements of ancient authors to the test of experiment. At first the science of the Middle Ages was drawn largely from Latin sources. The insignificance of Roman science has been already pointed out. But Roman writers frequently refer to Greek authors, and the desire naturally arose to read Greek authors directly. This craving was partly satisfied by the acquisition, in the twelfth century, of Arabic translations of Greek treatises. The writings of Aristotle became well known and began to assume supreme authority. Woe unto him who dared to contradict a statement made by Aristotle! Witness *Petrus Ramus* (1515–1572), who in Paris was forbidden on pain of corporal punishment to teach or write against the great philosopher. In physics, Aristotle's authority remained unshaken until the time of Galileo.

GUNPOWDER AND MARINER'S COMPASS

The Europeans of this period came into possession of two inventions which have greatly influenced the progress of civilization, viz. gunpowder and the compass. Their origin is shrouded in darkness. The preparation of gunpowder out of sulphur, saltpetre, and charcoal was known to *Marcus Græcus* in the eighth (?) century, and to *Albertus Magnus* about 1250. It is said to have been used in Europe for blasting in the twelfth century. Firearms do not appear to have been manufactured before the close of the fourteenth century.[1] It is probable that both gunpowder and the compass were known to the Chinese and the Hindus long before the thirteenth century.

There is no explicit evidence that the Chinese had any knowledge of the magnet earlier than 121 A.D.,[2] but there are obscure passages in Chinese legends regarding south-pointing chariots which have been believed by some to prove that the land compass was used in remotest antiquity.[3] No definite testimony concerning the land compass occurs before the close of the eleventh century. A Chinese author of that time says that "the soothsayers rub a needle with the magnet stone, so that it may mark the south; however, it declines constantly a little to the east. It does not indicate the south exactly."[4] This passage discloses a knowledge of magnetic declination.

As to the mariner's compass, an old Chinese encyclopædia says that "under the Tsin dynasty [265 to 419 A.D.] there were also ships indicating the south." This sentence is inconclusive; in fact, no truly reliable passage has been found to

[1] ROSENBERGER, Part I., p. 97.

[2] KLAPROTH, *Lettre à M. le Baron Humboldt sur l'invention de la Boussole*, Paris, 1834, p. 66.

[3] BENJAMIN, pp. 63–74.   [4] Quoted by BENJAMIN, p. 75.

show its use on Chinese waters prior to the close of the thirteenth century.

There is no good evidence to support the claim that the compass was brought from China to Europe by the Arabs. Moreover, there is reason for believing "that the Orient received the better arrangement of the compass from Europe."[1]

In Europe, the first mention of the mariner's compass is made in the twelfth century by *Alexander Neckam* of St. Albans, England. Another reference occurs in a poem published about the close of that century by the Frenchman *Guyot de Provins*, who speaks of the ugly brown stone to which iron turns, through which navigators possess an art that cannot fail them. A bishop of Palestine in 1218 says that the needle is "most necessary for such as sail at sea."

The old mariner's compass was operated in a very primitive manner. In a work of 1282 an Arabic writer says that the needle was floated in a basin of water by being placed inside a reed or upon a splinter of wood. When brought to rest the magnet pointed north and south. A similar practice seems to have prevailed among the early Italians.

Remarkable progess in the knowledge of magnetism and the construction of the compass is indicated in a letter written August 12, 1269, by Master Peter de Maricourt of France, commonly called *Peregrinus*. This man was greatly admired by Roger Bacon, and for good reason. His letter discloses a knowledge of magnetic polarity, states that the fragments of a divided magnet have each two poles, gives the law that unlike poles attract each other, and mentions that a strong magnet will reverse the polarity of a weaker magnet. Peregrinus invented a compass with a graduated scale and pivoted needle. He designed perpetual-motion machines based on magnetic

---

[1] A Schück in *Wiedemann's Beiblätter*, Vol. 17, 1893, p. 1107.

attraction, but was very politic, throwing the burden of success or failure upon the makers. He himself was at that time a soldier and probably had no tools for the construction of complicated machines. His letter was written from the trenches in front of Lucera (a town in southern Italy, then besieged by Charles of Anjou).[1]

After Peregrinus the graduated circle was replaced by the "Rose of the Winds," consisting of a star of, usually, thirty-two points.[2] In recent years there has been a tendency to return to Peregrinus's circle, graduated in degrees.

In the Exchange in Naples is a brass statue erected to *Flavio Gioja* as the inventor of the compass in 1302. This man, a resident of Amalfi in southern Italy, has long been considered its originator. We know now that it was used in Europe before his day, but he probably identified himself with it by introducing improvements in its construction.

An important innovation was the suspension of the magnet in gimbal rings, known as "Cardan's suspension." But *Cardan* (1501–1576) does not claim the invention, nor was it first designed for use with the compass. He describes a chair which had been constructed for an emperor, permitting that royal personage to sit in it during a drive without experiencing the least jolting. Cardan remarks that the same arrangement had been used previously in connection with oil lamps.[3]

---

[1] Peregrinus's letter was printed in 1558. It is reprinted in HELLMANN's *Neudrucke von Schriften u. Karten über Meteor. u. Erdmagn*, No. 10, Berlin, 1898. See also BENJAMIN, pp. 165–187.

[2] For their various forms consult A. BREUSING, *Die Nautischen Instrumente bis zur Erfindung des Spiegelsextanten*, Bremen, 1890, pp. 5–24.

[3] BREUSING, *op. cit.*, p. 16; CARDAN, *De subtilitate, Lib. XVII., de artibus artificiosisque rebus*, Basil, 1560, p. 1028. A remarkable form of compass was patented in 1876 by Sir William Thomson. See article "Compass" in the *Encyclopædia Britannica*, 9th ed.

HYDROSTATICS

The application of the principle of Archimedes to the famous problem of the crown alleged by its maker to be pure gold, though really alloyed with silver, is explained in a manuscript of the tenth century.[1] A treatise, prepared perhaps in the thirteenth century, explains how to find the volume of irregular bodies by the method of Archimedes, and emphasizes the practical value of this procedure by pointing out that the prices of some kinds of merchandise depend upon size. In this manuscript for the first time, says Thurot, occurs the name "specific gravity."

The Archimedean principle and the crown problem became favourite subjects with mathematicians, but received less attention from philosophers. As late as 1614 *Keckerman*, a prominent student of Aristotle, promulgated absurdities like the following: "Gravity is a motive quality, arising from cold, density, and bulk, by which the elements are carried downwards." "Water is the lower, intermediate element, cold and moist." [2] It was taught by the philosophers that water has no gravity in or on water, since it is in its own place, that air has no gravity on water, that water rises in a pump, because nature abhors a vacuum.[3] So firmly established were these false maxims regarding pressure that when Boyle published his experimental results on the mechanics of fluids, which contradicted Aristotelian opinions, he felt constrained to advance his views under the title of "hydrostatic paradoxes." [4]

[1] CH. THUROT, *Principe d'Archimède*, p. 27.
[2] WHEWELL, Vol. I., 1858, p. 236.   [3] *Ibidem*, p. 236.
[4] *Ibidem*, pp. 189, 236.

LIGHT

In the thirteenth century Europe was assimilating the science of optics as obtained from the Arabs. *Wilhelm von Moerbeck,* in 1278 Archbishop of Corinth, translated into Latin Al Hazen's treatise on parabolic mirrors. About 1270 his friend *Witelo,* or *Vitellio,* a Thuringian monk, prepared a work on optics less diffuse and more systematic than that of Al Hazen, on which it was based. *Witelo* explained the twinkling of stars as due to the motion of the air, and showed that the effect was intensified, if the star was viewed through water in motion. He pointed out that the rainbow was not formed by reflection alone, as was taught by Aristotle, but was due to both reflection and refraction.

Prominent among writers of the Middle Ages who drew from Arabic sources was *Roger Bacon* (1214?–1294). He wrote on optics, and by mistake has been credited with the invention of the refracting telescope. No doubt, Bacon suspected the possibility of designing an instrument which should enable one to "read the smallest writing at enormous distances" from the eye. But Bacon never constructed, or tried to construct, such an instrument. The claim set up for him grew out of a mistranslation of a passage in his works.[1]

Bacon was one of the most gifted minds of the Middle Ages. Educated at Oxford and Paris, he became famous as professor at Oxford. His open contempt for scholasticism and for immorality among the clergy led to the charge of heresy and to imprisonment. From his Oxford cell he sent out an appeal for *experimental science* which nearly converted his old friend Pope Clement IV. But Bacon's ideas were in advance of his time and bore no immediate fruit. In Paris he was imprisoned a second time for a period of ten years. Thus the genius of this remarkable man was crushed by the political and mental despotism of his time.

[1] E. WIEDEMANN in *Wiedemann's Annalen,* Vol. 39, 1890, p. 130.

THE RENAISSANCE

THE sixteenth century was a period of intense intellectual activity. The minds of men were cut adrift from their ancient moorings and launched forth on the wide sea of inquiry.

The movement was of great breadth. Here we witness the revival of classic learning, there the production of masterpieces in art by Michel Angelo, Raphael, and Da Vinci. Yonder we behold the stupendous struggle against Church authority, known as the Reformation. The secluded mathematician infuses new life into algebra and trigonometry. The astronomer gazes at the stars and creates a new system of the universe. The physicist abandons scholastic speculation and begins to study nature in the language of experiment.

THE COPERNICAN SYSTEM

The first great scientific victory during the Renaissance was the overthrow of the Ptolemaic and the establishment of the Copernican System. We shall pause a moment to consider briefly this great epoch in the development of our sister science, astronomy.

The Greek astronomers, Eudoxus and Hipparchus, explained planetary motions by the famous theory of epicycles and eccentrics. The apparent sweep of the planet around the earth was represented by the combination of two motions: (1) the yearly motion of the planet along the circumference of a small circle, called the *epicycle;* (2) the motion of the centre of that

27

epicycle along the circumference of a second circle which surrounds the earth. We know now that the latter circle represents approximately the true orbit of the planet around the sun and that the epicyclic motion is only apparent. This apparent motion is due to the real motion of the earth itself. If an observer is carried around in a circle, then an object at rest will appear to him to move in a circle of equal size. The ancient theory is, therefore, approximately correct, the main error lies in attributing to the planets oscillations which do not really exist, but which the planets seem to have on account of the orbital motion of the earth. Hipparchus observed that the theory of epicycles could not explain the motions of the planets, if the earth must be assumed to be exactly in the centre of the second circle mentioned above. This led him to establish the theory of the *eccentric*.

This ancient system was elaborated by and named after the distinguished Alexandrian astronomer *Claudius Ptolemy*. It made the earth immovable at the centre of the universe. Around it revolved in successively wider spheres the Moon, Mercury, Venus, Sun, Mars, Jupiter, Saturn, and lastly the eighth sphere of the fixed stars.

This geocentric theory of the universe has always had its opponents, but it was first vigorously attacked by *Nicolaus Copernicus* (1473–1543). He was probably of Polish descent and was born at Thorn, in Prussia, near the Polish boundary. For twenty-three years he was engaged in the threefold occupation of discharging ecclesiastical duties, practising medicine, and studying astronomy. With the hope of finding an explanation of less complexity than that offered by the Ptolemaic system, he zealously studied all sources of information at his command. He found that all sorts of *opinions* had been advanced. Thus, the Pythagoreans believed in the rotation of the earth, and Philolaus had even imagined the earth to have an orbit around the sun. Aided by suggestions of this sort, Copernicus gradually matured his own system. For many years he withheld from publication the manuscript of his *De orbium cœlestium revolutionibus*, but finally, in 1542, he consented to have it printed. He died before the printing was completed. This saved him from persecution. Others — Giordano Bruno and Galileo — had to suffer for the Copernican system.

Copernicus taught that the earth was spherical, rotated on its axis and revolved around the sun; that the motions of the heavenly bodies are either circular and uniform or compounded of circular and uniform motions. He explained for the first time the variation of the seasons and the cause of the apparent oscillations of the planets. A great defect in his system was his notion that all celestial motions are compounded of circular ones. It cannot be said that the argument made by Copernicus against the Ptolemaic system was conclusive. To overthrow completely the ancient theory required the genius of another man — Kepler.

Johannes Kepler (1571–1630) was at one time in Prague assistant to the Danish astronomer *Tycho Brahe.* Unlike Tycho, Kepler had no talent for observation and experimentation. But he was a great thinker and excelled as a mathematician. He absorbed Copernican ideas, and early grappled with the problem of determining the real paths of the planets. In his first attempts he worked on the dreams of the Pythagoreans concerning figure and number. Intercourse with Tycho led him to reject such mysticism and to study the observations on the planets recorded by his master. He took the planet Mars, and found that no combinations of circles would give a path which could be reconciled with the actual observations. In one case the difference between the observed and his computed values was eight minutes, and he knew that so accurate an observer as Tycho could not make an error so great. He tried an oval orbit for Mars, and rejected it; he tried an ellipse, and it fitted! Thus, after more than four years of assiduous computation, and after trying nineteen imaginary paths and rejecting each because it was more or less inconsistent with observation, Kepler in 1618 discovered the truth. An ellipse! Why did he not think of it before? What a simple matter — after the puzzle is once solved. He worked out what are known as "Kepler's Laws," which accorded with observation but conflicted with the Ptolemaic hypothesis. Thus the old system was logically overthrown. But not until after a bitter struggle between science and theology did the new system find general acceptance.[1]

MECHANICS

The sixteenth century witnessed the revival of statics and the creation of dynamics. The science of statics, which, since the time of Archimedes, had been nearly stationary, was first taken up by *Simon Stevin* (1548-1620) of Bruges in Belgium, a man remarkable for varied attainments in science, independence of thought, and extreme lack of respect for authority. He is the inventor of decimal fractions. In 1605 he published at Leyden a work written in Dutch, which in 1608 was brought out in Latin translation under the title *Hypomnemata mathematica*. Stevin accurately determined the force necessary to sustain a body on an inclined plane and investigated the equilibrium of pulleys. He employed the principle of the parallelogram of forces, but did not expressly formulate it. In fact, he was in possession of a complete doctrine of equi-

---

[1] For an account of this struggle, consult A. D. WHITE, *The Warfare of Science with Theology*, New York, 1896, Vol. I., pp. 114-170.

librium.[1] *Da Vinci*, the famous painter, *Guido Ubaldi*, and Galileo paid some attention to statics.

The creation of the science of dynamics is due to *Galileo Galilei* (1564–1642), a native of Pisa. He studied medicine at the University of Pisa, but in a few years he abandoned it for the more congenial pursuit of mathematics and science. In 1589 he received the appointment, for three years, to the mathematical chair in Pisa. During this time he performed memorable experiments on falling bodies, but his new views met with so much opposition that he was obliged to resign in 1591. From 1592 to 1610 he was professor at Padua. Thereupon he began boldly to preach Copernican doctrines. In consequence he was summoned before the Inquisition at Rome. The theory of the earth's motion was condemned by the Inquisition, and Galileo received an injunction to silence. For some years Galileo remained silent, though always at work. In 1632 he published, contrary to the edict of 1616, a new work, the *Dialogo*, which was a brilliant success as an argument in favour of the Copernican theory. This brought about a second trial. The old man of seventy was subjected to indignity, imprisonment, and threats. On his knees he was forced publicly to "abjure, curse, and detest the error and the heresy of the movement of the earth."[2] At first he was kept in separation from his family and friends, but was allowed

---

[1] For details consult E. Mach, *Science of Mechanics* (ed. McCormack), pp. 24–34.

[2] Quoted by A. D. White, *op. cit.*, Vol. I., p. 142. After the abjuration, as Galileo arose from his kneeling posture, he is said to have murmured the words, "Eppur si muove" ("and yet it moves"). Upon a careful study of documents, G. Berthold comes to the conclusion that this story is legendary. Yet there can be no doubt that the "Eppur si muove" expresses what must have been Galileo's innermost conviction. See Berthold, *Zeitschr. f. Math.* und *Phys.*, Vol. 42, 1897, pp. 5–9; R. Wolf, *Gesch. d. Astronomie*, München, 1877, p. 262.

a little more liberty after he became blind and wasted with disease.[1]

Galileo was among the first to teach that the Holy Scriptures were not intended as a text-book on science — a truth which the world has been slow to recognize.

The first years after 1632 were given to the study of dynamics. In 1638 appeared in Leyden his dialogues on motion, under the title, *Discorsi e dimostrazioni matematiche.* These now are considered his greatest and most substantial achievement.

The first experiments, which Galileo made while he was a young professor at Pisa, were decidedly dramatic. At that time the doctrine that the rate at which a body falls depends upon its weight was generally accepted as true, merely on the authority of Aristotle. It was even held that the acceleration varies as the weight. Prior to Galileo it did not occur to any one actually to try the experiment. The young professor's tests went contrary to the doctrine held for two thousand years. Allowing for the resistance of the air, he found that all bodies fell at the same rate, and that the distance passed over varied as the square of the time. With all the enthusiasm, courage, and imprudence of youth, the experimenter proclaimed that Aristotle, at that time believed by nearly every one to be verbally inspired, was wrong. Galileo met with opposition, but he decided to give his opponents ocular proof. It seems almost as if nature had resorted to an extraordinary freak to furnish Galileo at this critical moment in the history of science, with an unusual convenience for his public demonstration. Yonder tower of Pisa had bent over to facilitate experimentation, from its top, on falling bodies. One morning, before the assembled university, he ascended the leaning

---

[1] A. D. WHITE, *op. cit.,* pp. 142, 143.

tower, and allowed a one pound shot and a one hundred pound shot to drop together. The multitude saw the balls start together, fall together, and heard them strike the ground together. Some were convinced, others returned to their rooms, consulted Aristotle, and, distrusting the evidence of their senses, declared continued allegiance to his doctrine.

The crooked path by which discoveries are sometimes made is curiously illustrated in the assumption at first made by Galileo regarding the nature of uniformly accelerated motion. He takes the velocity to be proportional to the *distance* passed over, and then, by a train of reasoning which we find itself to be fallacious, concludes that this assumption is erroneous. " If the velocity with which a body overcomes four yards is double the velocity with which it passed over the first two yards, then the times necessary for these processes must be equal ; but four yards can be overcome in the same time as two yards only if there is an instantaneous motion. We see, however, that the body takes time in falling and requires, indeed, less time for a fall of two than of four yards. Hence it is not true that the velocity increases proportionally to the distance fallen." [1]

Galileo then proceeds to a second assumption, — velocity is proportional to the time of falling, — and, finding no self-contradiction in it, he goes about to test it experimentally. In a board twelve yards long a trough one inch wide was cut out in a straight line and lined with very smooth parchment. A brass ball, perfectly round and polished, was allowed to run down the inclined plane. About one hundred trials were

[1] Galileo's *Discorsi* of 1638 were in 1890 published in German translation in *Ostwald's Klassiker der exacten Wissenschaften*, Nos. 11, 24, 26. The above quotation is from No. 24, p. 17. A new and complete edition of Galileo's works has been prepared recently for the Italian government by Antonio Favaro, of Padua.

made for different inclinations and lengths of the plane. The distance of descent was found always to vary closely as the squares of the times. It is interesting to notice how Galileo measured the time. Accurate clocks or watches were then not available. He attached a very small spout to the bottom of a water pail and caught in a cup the water escaping through the spout during the time when the body travelled through a given distance. The water was weighed accurately and the times of descent taken proportional to the ascertained weight.[1]

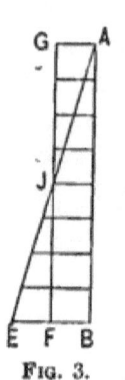

Fig. 3.

To exhibit the relation between velocity and distance, Galileo establishes the theorem that the time in which a body moving from rest with uniformly accelerated velocity travels a given distance is the same as the time it would require to travel the same distance with a uniform velocity equal to half its actual final velocity. This truth he illustrated by Fig. 3.[2] The line EB represents the final velocity, which varies directly as the time represented by AB. The area ABE stands for the distance gone over. This area is evidently equal to that of the rectangle ABFG, where FB stands for the

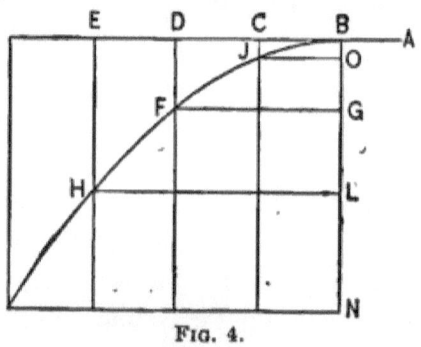

Fig. 4.

average velocity. This geometrical illustration has retained a place in some modern text-books. Still more common is the illustration (Fig. 4) showing the path of a body projected horizontally and acted upon by gravity.[3] In the dialogue on

[1] *Ostwald's Klassiker*, No. 24, p. 25.
[2] *Ibidem*, p. 21.　　　[3] *Ibidem*, p. 84.

this subject Galileo permits Sagredo to remark naïvely, "Truly the conception is new, ingenious, and incisive; it rests on an assumption, namely, that the transverse motion remains constant and that, at the same time, the naturally accelerated motion maintains itself, proportional to the squares of the times, and that such motions mix, indeed, but do not disturb, change, and impede each other, so that finally, by the progressive motion, the path of the projectile is not degenerated — a behaviour hardly comprehensible to me."

Galileo was the first to show that the path of a projectile is a parabola. Previously it was believed by some that a cannon ball moved forward at first in a straight line and then suddenly fell vertically to the ground.

Galileo had an understanding of *centrifugal force* and gave a correct definition of *momentum*. With Stevin and others he also wrote on statics. He formulated the principle of the *parallelogram of forces*, but he did not fully recognize its scope.

Still another subject engaging Galileo's attention was the laws of the pendulum. As in case of falling bodies, so here the first observations were made while he was a young man. In 1583, while he was praying in the cathedral at Pisa, his attention was arrested by the motion of the great lamp which after being lighted had been left swinging. Galileo proceeded to time its oscillations by the only watch in his possession, namely, his own pulse. He found the times, as near as he could tell, to remain the same, even after the motion had greatly diminished. Thus was discovered the isochronism of the pendulum. Galileo was at that time studying medicine, and he applied the pendulum to pulse measurements at the sick-bed. He also proposed its use in astronomical observations. More careful experiments carried out by him later, and described in his *Discorsi*, showed that the time of oscillation was independent of the mass and material of the pendulum and varied as the square root of its length.[1] His last contribution to the art of time measurement was made after he had become blind. In 1641 he dictated to his son Vicenzo and his pupil *Viviani* the description and drawing of a pendulum clock. The original drawing is extant, but a model, said to have been constructed by Viviani in 1649, has been lost. Galileo's invention did not become generally known at that time, and fifteen years later, in 1656, *Christian Huygens* independently invented a pendulum clock, which met with general and rapid appreciation. The honour of this great invention belongs, therefore, to Galileo and Huygens.[2]

Galileo's *Discorsi* of 1638 are masterpieces of popular exposition, which fact alone renders them worthy of perusal. But they contain other points of merit. W. G. Adams well says: "The true method of teaching mechanics is illustrated by the way in which Galileo established the first principles of dynamics, and placed them before his pupils. Due weight should be given both to experimental and to rational mechanics, and the best way of bringing the subject before students is to have parallel but distinct courses of experimental and theoretical lectures attended by students at the same time."[3]

Among his contemporaries it was chiefly the novelties he detected in the skies that made him celebrated, but Lagrange

---

[1] *Ostwald's Klassiker*, No. 11, pp. 75, 84.

[2] The invention of the pendulum clock has been claimed also for the Swiss Joost Bürgi (R. WOLF, *Geschichte der Astronomie*, 1877, p. 369), for Richard Harris of London (*Edinburgh Encyclopædia*, 1830, Vol. 11, p. 117), and for others, but these claims have been rejected by later authorities. On the history of this invention consult E. GERLAND, *Zeitschr. f. Instrumenten Kunde*, Vol. VIII., 1888, p. 77 : W. C. L. v. SCHAÏK in same journal, Vol. VII., pp. 350 and 428; S. GÜNTHER, *Vermischte Untersuchungen*, Leipzig, 1876, pp. 308–344; G. BERTHOLD, *Schlömilch's Zeitschr.*, Vol. 38, 1893, Hist. Lit. Abth., p. 123.

[3] *Nature*, Vol. V., 1871–1872, p. 389.

claims that his astronomical discoveries required only a telescope and perseverance, while, in the case of dynamics, it took an extraordinary genius to discover laws from phenomena which we see constantly and of which the true explanation escaped all earlier philosophers.

LIGHT

The greatest achievement in optics during the Renaissance was the invention of instruments, giving an observer a glimpse of the infinitely distant and of the infinitely small. We refer to the telescope and the microscope.

According to tradition the telescope was invented by accident. The great Huygens in his *Dioptrica* asserts that a man capable of inventing the telescope by mere thinking and application of geometrical principles, without the concurrence of accident, would have been gifted with superhuman genius. To this remarkable statement Mach adds that it does not follow that accident alone is sufficient to produce an invention. The inventor "must *distinguish* the new feature, impress it upon his memory, unite and interweave it with the rest of his thought; in short, he must possess the capacity to *profit by experience.*" [1]

There have been brought forward numerous candidates for the honor of the invention of these marvellous instruments. Four nations, the English, Italian, Dutch, and German, have each endeavoured to secure a decision in favour of one of its own countrymen.

The evidence we possess favours the Dutch. The first telescope was probably constructed in 1608 by *Hans Lippershey*, a native of Wesel, and a manufacturer of spectacles in Mid-

[1] E. MACH, "On the Part Played by Accident in Invention and Discovery," *Monist*, Vol. VI., p. 166.

dleburg.[1]   He prepared his lenses, not of glass, but of rock
crystal. A document found in the archives at the Hague shows
that on October 2, 1608, he applied for a patent.   He was
told to modify his construction and make an instrument enabling the observer to see through it with both eyes.   This he
accomplished the same year.   He did not receive his patent,
but the government of the United Netherlands paid him instead 900 gulden for the instrument and an equal sum for two
other binocular telescopes, completed in 1609.[2]

The invention of the microscope is nearly contemporaneous
with that of the telescope.   It is now usually ascribed to
Zacharias Joannides and his father, though Huygens assigned
it to *Cornelius Drebbel.*[3]   At first the eye-pieces consisted of

[1] DR. H. SERVUS, *Die Geschichte des Fernrohrs*, Berlin, 1886, p. 39.

[2] *Ibidem*, p. 40.   The claim that *Roger Bacon* invented the telescope
is now generally abandoned.   The Italian *Giambattista della Porta*,
known as the inventor of the *camera obscura*, has been named in this
connection on the strength of passages in his *Magia Naturalis* (2d Ed.,
1589) to the effect that by judicious combination of two lenses, one convex and the other concave, objects at a distance as well as objects near at
hand may be magnified to the eye.   But his experiments appear to have
been confined to the preparation of suitable eye-glasses for persons with
abnormal vision ; the invention of the telescope is here out of the question.   In 1571 *Leonard Digges* of Bristol published a book in which the
effect of combining concave and convex lenses is explained, somewhat as
in Porta's book of 1589, but all statements of this sort must be regarded
as having prepared for the invention rather than as having actually constituted it.   Previous to 1831 the best evidence at hand seemed to point
to *Zacharias Joannides* of Middleburg in Netherlands as the inventor
of the telescope, though his countrymen, *Adrian Metius* and *Cornelius
Drebbel*, the Germans *Simon Marius* and *Kepler*, and the Italians *Franciscus Fontana* and *Galileo* have all had their supporters.   All of these,
except Kepler, were actually engaged in the manufacture of telescopes.

[3] G. Govi claims the invention of the microscope for Galileo.   From a
document printed in 1610 he proves that Galileo had modified the telescope
to see very small and very near objects.   Consult G. Govi in *Rendic.
Accad. Napol.*, (2) I., 1887 ; C. R. 107, No. 14, 1888 ; *Poske's Zeitschr.*,

concave lenses. *Franciscus Fontana* of Naples appears to
have been the first to replace the concave eye-lens by a convex one. *Kepler* was the first to suggest a similar change in
the telescope. All the artisans whom we have mentioned in
connection with the microscope are known to have been prominent in the manufacture of telescopes.

The use of the new instruments spread over Europe with
rapidity. In England the mathematician *Thomas Harriot*
had a telescope magnifying fifty times, and he observed the
satellites of Jupiter in 1610, almost as early as did
Galileo.[1]

The news of the invention of the telescope incited *Kepler*,
who had already given much time to the study of optics, to
fresh efforts. In 1611 he published his *Dioptrice*, which is
the earliest work containing an attempt to elaborate the theory
of the telescope. Such an attempt demands a knowledge of
the law of refraction. Kepler arrived at an empirical expression which was merely an approximation. The accurate law
he failed to discover. His approximate result for small angles
$(i < 30°)$ was $i = nr$, where n is a constant, equal to $\frac{3}{2}$ for a ray
passing from air to glass. This was near enough to the truth

Zweiter Jahrgang, 1888, p. 93. Galileo says in his *Sidereus Nuncius*,
which was published at the beginning of the year 1610, that he first heard
of the invention of the telescope "about ten months ago." His microscope was a modified telescope. Hence his microscope must have been
made in 1609 or 1610. Now, if we may trust the testimony contained in
a letter by the Dutch ambassador, Borelius, written in 1655, then Zacharias
Joannides did not construct a telescope until 1610, "long after" (longe
post) he had invented the microscope. See H. Servus, *op. cit.*, pp. 17,
18. According to this Joannides anticipated Galileo.

[1] In 1585 Sir Walter Raleigh sent Harriot to Virginia as surveyor
with Sir Richard Grenville's expedition. Among the mathematical instruments by which the wonder of the Indians was aroused, Harriot mentions "a perspective glass whereby was showed many strange sights."
See *Dic. of Nat. Biography*.

to enable him to give in broad outline the correct theory of the telescope.

The earliest important scientific discoveries with the aid of the telescope were made by *Galileo*. He was led to take up this line of research by rumours which had reached him regarding the invention in Belgium of an instrument through which distant objects could be seen distinctly. He probably heard that this had been effected by the combination of a concave and a convex lens, and he set to work to devise such an instrument himself. Guided by the hints he had received and by his knowledge of dioptrics, he soon succeeded. He made a rough telescope with two glasses fixed at the end of a leaden tube, both having one side flat; the other side of the one lens being concave, and of the other lens convex. It made objects appear three times nearer and nine times larger. Thereupon, sparing neither expense nor labour, he got so far as to construct an instrument which magnified an object nearly a thousand times and brought it more than thirty times nearer.[1]

Galileo went to Venice and showed it to the signoria. Says he: "Many noblemen and senators, although of great age, mounted the steps of the highest church towers at Venice to watch the ships, which were visible through my glass two hours before they were seen entering the harbour."

Galileo's telescopes were much sought after, and he received numerous orders from learned men, princes, and governments — Holland, the birthplace of the telescope, not excepted.[2]

Galileo turned his telescope toward the moon and discovered mountains and craters; he turned it to Jupiter and saw its satellites (January 7, 1610); he pointed it at Saturn and saw

[1] Consult *Sidereus Nuncius* of 1610, reprinted in editions of Galileo's works; also KARL VON GEBLER, *Galileo Galilei and the Roman Curia*, trans. by MRS. GEORGE STURGE, London, 1879, p. 17.

[2] GEBLER, *op. cit.*, p. 18.

the planet threefold — now known to have been due to an imperfect view of the ring; he examined the sun, saw its spots moving, and concluded that the sun rotates. All this was achieved in 1610. His observations seemed to confirm the Copernican theory. The cloud of opposition to Galileo began to gather. Some refused to believe their eyes, and asserted that, while the telescope answered well enough for terrestrial objects, it was false and illusory when pointed at celestial bodies. Others refused to look through it. Among the latter was a university professor. Galileo wrote to Kepler: "Oh, my dear Kepler, how I wish that we could have one hearty laugh together! Here, at Padua, is the principal professor of philosophy, whom I have repeatedly and urgently requested to look at the moon and planets through my glass, which he pertinaciously refuses to do. Why are you not here? What shouts of laughter we should have at this glorious folly! And to hear the professor of philosophy at Pisa labouring before the Grand Duke with logical arguments, as if with magical incantations to charm the new planets out of the sky."[1] The antagonism to Galileo and his hated telescope became stronger. The clergy began to denounce him and his methods. Father Caccini became known as a punster by preaching a sermon from the text, "Ye men of Galilee, why stand ye gazing up into heaven?"[2]

ELECTRICITY AND MAGNETISM

By the side of Galileo, "the originator of modern physics," we may well place Gilbert, "the father of the magnetic philosophy." *William Gilbert* (1540–1603) of Colchester, county of

[1] This translation is taken from O. Lodge, *Pioneers of Science*, 1893, p. 106.

[2] A. D. White, *op. cit.*, Vol. I., p. 133.

Essex, England, studied at St. John's College, Cambridge, then
travelled on the Continent. There, as well as in England, he
"practised as a physician with great success and applause."
He was appointed by Queen Elizabeth her physician-in-
ordinary, and she settled upon him an annual pension for the
purpose of aiding him in the prosecution of his philosophical
studies. His first investigations were in chemistry; but later,
for eighteen years or more, he experimented on electricity and
magnetism. In 1600 he published his great work, the *De
Magnete*. J. F. W. Herschel speaks of this book as "full of
valuable facts and experiments ingeniously reasoned on." It
is the first great work on physical science produced in England.
Galileo pronounced it "great to a degree that is enviable," but
at home it was not appreciated so highly.[1] In subsequent
generations the book was quite forgotten.

Gilbert's contempt for the methods of the schoolmen crops
out everywhere in his book. In fact, his criticisms of worthy
predecessors are at times ungenerous. He withheld his work
from publication for many years. "Why should I," says he
in his preface, "submit this noble and . . . this new and inad-
missible philosophy to the judgment of men who have taken
oath to follow the opinions of others, to the most senseless
corrupters of the arts, to lettered clowns, grammatists, soph-
ists, spouters, and the wrong-headed rabble, to be denounced,
torn to tatters, and heaped with contumely. To you alone,
true philosophers, ingenuous minds, who not only in books but
in things themselves look for knowledge, have I dedicated
these foundations of magnetic science — a new style of philosophizing" (p. xlix.). Modern philosophers "must be made

---

[1] See WILLIAM GILBERT OF COLCHESTER, *On the Loadstone and
Magnetic Bodies, and on the Great Magnet, the Earth*, trans. by P. F.
MOTTELAY, London, 1893, "Biographical Memoir," pp. ix–xxvii. All our
references will be to this edition of the *De Magnete*.

to quit the sort of learning that comes only from books, and that rests only on vain arguments from probability and upon conjectures" (p. 47). "Men of acute intelligence, without actual knowledge of facts, and in the absence of experiment, easily slip and err" (p. 82). Gilbert was the first to use the terms "electric force," "electric attraction," magnetic "pole." Bodies which attract in the same way as amber he called "electrics." Metals and some other bodies he called "non-electrics," because he could not make them attract by friction.

Pupils beginning physics sometimes fail to discriminate between magnetic action and electric attraction or repulsion. History reveals the same error on the part of some early writers. The differentiation between the two was first clearly made by the Milanese mathematician, *Hieronimo Cardano* (1501–1576).[1] Gilbert complains of those who "are ignorant that the causes of the loadstone's movements are very different from those which give to amber its properties" (p. 75). The Italian Baptista Porta had taught that iron rubbed with diamond turns to the north, as if it had been rubbed on a loadstone. To this Gilbert says, "We made the experiment ourselves with seventy-five diamonds in presence of many witnesses, employing a number of iron bars and pieces of wire, manipulating them with the greatest care while they floated in water, supported by corks; but never was it granted me to see the effect mentioned by Porta" (p. 218). Gilbert wages war against Cardan, who "asks why no other metal is drawn by any stone; and his answer is, because no other metal is so cold as iron; as if, forsooth, cold were cause of attraction, or iron were much colder than lead, which neither follows the loadstone nor leans toward it. But this

---

[1] Consult P. BENJAMIN, p. 249.

is sorry trifling, no better than old wives' gossip" (p. 101).
"A needle turns no less rapidly, no less eagerly, to the loadstone though a flame intervenes than if only air stands between" (p. 107). He then makes the interesting observation,
"But were the iron itself red-hot, it certainly would not be
attracted," though it will be "as soon as the temperature has
fallen somewhat" (p. 107). Some modern texts give the elegant experiment performed by Gilbert of magnetizing an iron
bar or wire, while held so as to point north and south, by
being "stretched or hammered or pulled," or by being hammered while cooling from a red heat (pp. 211, 212).

Gilbert's experiments on terrestrial magnetism are epoch
making. To him we owe the "new and till now unheard-of

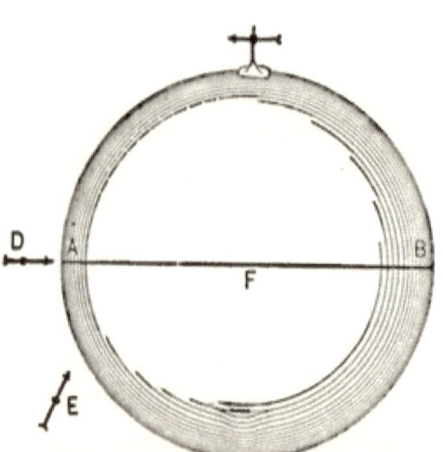

FIG. 5. GILBERT'S TERRELLA.

view of the earth" as a
great magnet (p. 64).[1]
Gilbert followed partly
in the steps of Peregrinus
and used a little load-
stone formed into the
shape of a globe. Plac-
ing pivoted needles near
this magnetic globe, he
observed the directive and
attractive force which it
exerted upon them. In
that small body he found
many properties of the
earth. Hence he called it the "terrella" or "little earth."
"The loadstone possesses the actions peculiar to the globe, of

---

[1] The theory that the earth has a magnetic pole had been advanced in
1546 by *Gerhard Mercator*, but the letter on this subject was not printed
until 1869. It is reprinted in HELLMANN's *Neudrucke*, No. 10, Berlin,
1898.

attraction, polarity, revolution, of taking position in the universe according to the law of the whole" (p. 66). "Toward it, as we see in the case of the earth, magnetic bodies tend from all sides, and adhere to it" (p. 67). "Like the earth it has an equator, . . . [it] has the power of direction and of standing still at north and south" (p. 67).

Since the earth has magnetic poles, it follows from the law of magnetic action that the north-pointing pole of a needle is the *south* pole; "all instrument makers, and navigators, are egregiously mistaken in taking for the north pole of the loadstone the part of the stone that inclines to the north" (p. 27). Gilbert's discovery that the earth is a huge magnet made it easy to explain why the needle points north. Prior to Gilbert all sorts of reasons had been assigned. "The common herd of philosophizers, in search of the causes of magnetic movements, called in causes remote and far away. Martinus Cortesius . . . dreamt of an attractive magnetic point beyond the heavens, acting on iron. Petrus Peregrinus holds that direction has its rise at the celestial poles. Cardan was of the opinion that the rotation of iron is caused by the star in the tail of Ursa Major. The Frenchman Bessard thinks that the magnetic needle turns to the pole of the zodiac. . . . So has ever been the wont of mankind; homely things are vile; things from abroad and things afar are dear to them and the object of longing" (p. 179).

That the needle does not point true north and south was known to the Chinese as early as the eleventh century. That there are variations in declination was clearly recognized by *Columbus* on his memorable voyage of 1492. An atlas issued in 1436 by Andrea Blanco was formerly believed to disclose the knowledge that the declination is not everywhere the same, but Bertelli denies him this knowledge and interprets the indicated corrections for variation in a different manner.[1] Columbus was certainly the first to make known a place of no declination which he found not far from the island of Corvo, one of the Azores. *Baptista Porta* had taught that the declination varied regularly with the longitude, so that terrestrial longitude could be found readily from the observed declination. Gilbert had data on hand to show that this "is false as false can be" (p. 251). However, Gilbert himself falls into error by assuming the declination at any one place to be invariable, and by presuming that the magnetic and geographic equators were identical and that lines of equal dip coincided with the geographic parallels. These are instances showing that the propensity to speculation without checking the results by "sure experiment" sometimes secured control even of Gilbert.

The existence of dip is usually believed to have been discovered in 1576 by *Robert Norman*, a "skilled navigator and ingenious artificer" of Bristol, who announced the new fact in a treatise of 1581, entitled, *The Newe Attractiue*. To Norman's treatise was added a supplement prepared in 1581 by *William Borough*, who dwells more particularly on rules for finding the declination. Hellmann attributes the discovery of dip to *Georg Hartmann* in 1544, but admits that his determination was very inaccurate. Hartmann's letter was not published till 1831.[2]

Gilbert was a strong adherent of the Copernican system. One object of his book was to furnish additional arguments in support of the new doctrine. His experiments exhibit throughout painstaking accuracy, but his application of experimental results to cosmology was inconclusive. Thus, he

[1] BERTELLI, *Sulla Epistola di P. Peregrino*, Rome, 1868, mem. III., 77; BENJAMIN, p. 197.

[2] Hartmann's, Norman's, and Borough's interesting papers are reprinted in HELLMANN'S *Neudrucke*, No. 10.

endeavoured to prove that the earth rotated because of its magnetic quality. No doubt these unfortunate speculations were the cause of the undue neglect from which his book suffered so long. Yet this neglect is no more warranted than would be that of Newton's *Opticks* because of his advocacy of the emission theory. In both cases the ultimate deductions are wrong, but the experimental results are invaluable.

METEOROLOGY

One of the earliest systematic meteorological records is that kept in the years 1582–1597 by the astronomer *Tycho Brahe* at his observatory in Prague.[1] Instruments for weather observations were still few. The wind-vane, first found among the Greeks, was placed in Christian Europe on top of church-steeples, and received the form of a cock, because that bird was the emblem of clerical vigilance.[2]

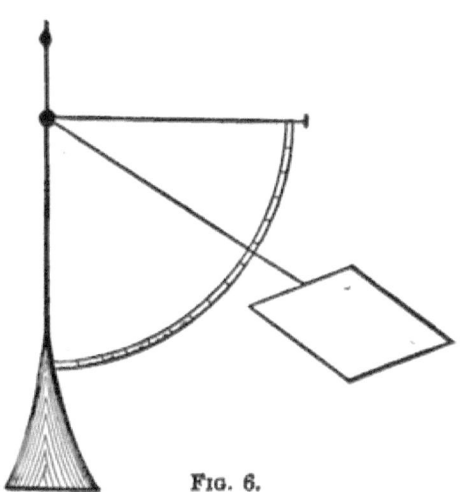

Fig. 6.

About 1570 the astronomer *Egnatio Danti* had erected in Bologna and Florence a number of pendulum anemometers (Fig. 6) for measuring the force of the wind. In modern times this instrument has been used extensively in Europe. Its first invention is often wrongly attributed to Robert Hooke.[3]

[1] G. HELLMANN, *Himmel und Erde*, Vol. II., 1890, p. 113, etc.
[2] *Ibidem*, p. 119.
[3] *Ibidem*, p. 121 ; SPRAT, *Hist. of Royal Soc.*, 1667, p. 173.

The earliest known hygroscope is described in the works of the German cardinal *Nicolaus de Cusa* (1401–1464). He says: "If you suspend from one side of a large balance a large quantity of wool, and from the other side stones, so that they weigh equally in dry air, then you will see that when the air inclines toward dampness, the weight of the wool increases, and when the air tends to dryness, it decreases." The Italians attribute the first hygrometers to Da Vinci. About the middle of the sixteenth century *Mizauld*[1] noticed the effect of moisture on gut-strings. This has since been used repeatedly in the design of hygrometers. About the same time Baptista Porta called attention to the hygroscopic properties of the beards of wild oats. He saw children paste to a beard small pieces of paper, which would bend one way or another, according as the air was dry or moist. In the early part of the seventeenth century wild oats were used extensively as a hygroscopic substance.

THE INDUCTIVE METHOD OF SCIENTIFIC INQUIRY

The necessity of observation and experiment in scientific research was emphasized in the writings of *Francis Bacon*. He was a man of extraordinary literary gifts, and his works on scientific method contain many bright passages, with which popular authors delight to ornament their title-pages and chapter-headings. People unacquainted with the history of scientific progress have even imagined that to Francis Bacon and his *Novum Organum* are principally due the reawakening of the world, the overthrow of Aristotelian physical philosophy, and the introduction into science of the inductive method.

[1] *Ephemerides aëris perpetuae*, Lutetiae, 1554, p. 49; HELLMANN, *op. cit.*, p. 122.

As a matter of fact, Bacon was not a scientific man; he had little practical experience in experimentation; he lacked the scientific instinct to pursue in detail the great truth that nature must be studied directly by observation and experiment. He appears to have rejected the Copernican system, and he treated with contempt the researches of Galileo and Gilbert — the two greatest experimentalists of his day. Bacon undertook to give an infallible rule by which any one could, with perseverance, make scientific discoveries. We "must analyze Nature by proper rejections and exclusions, and then, after a sufficient number of negatives, come to a conclusion on the affirmative instances."[1] He thought nature could be studied by rule, without the aid of hypotheses and scientific imagination. His recipe has met with popular applause, but has never been actually followed by original investigators in physical or chemical laboratories. Says Professor E. Mach: "I do not know whether Swift's academy of schemers in Lagado, in which great discoveries and inventions were made by a sort of verbal game of dice, was intended as a satire on Francis Bacon's method of making discoveries by means of huge synoptic tables constructed by scribes. It certainly would not have been ill-placed."[2]

[1] *Novum Organum*, I., Aphorism CV.

[2] *Monist*, Vol. VI., 1896, p. 174. Consult further O. LODGE, *Pioneers of Science*, pp. 136 *et seq.*; JEVONS, *Principles of Science*, 1892, p. 507; P. DUHEM, *L'Évolution des Théories Physiques*, Louvain, 1896, pp. 8-10; JUSTUS VON LIEBIG, *Reden und Abhandlung*, Leipzig, 1874; DRAPER, *Hist. of the Intell. Develop. of Europe*, 1875, Vol. II., p. 259; WHEWELL, Vol. I., p. 339.

THE SEVENTEENTH CENTURY

The first effects of the Reformation were favourable for the progress of science in Germany. But during and after the Thirty Years' War (1618–1648) civil and religious strife, as well as a political dismemberment into a lax confederation of petty despotisms, ensued. In consequence, science almost died out in Germany.

In France the ascension of Henry IV. to the throne, and the promulgation of the Edict of Nantes (1598), somewhat lessened religious strife; the genius of the French people began to flourish. At the time when the blossoms of science withered away in Germany, they were budding forth in France.

In Italy the fate of Galileo dampened scientific enthusiasm, while in England, where religious contention never fully engrossed the attention of the people, the time of Gilbert was followed by a period of extraordinary scientific achievement.

In the present epoch we shall contemplate the scientific labours of Torricelli in Italy, Guericke in Germany, Huygens in Holland, Pascal, Mariotte, and Descartes in France, Boyle, Hooke, Halley, and Newton in England. It was a period of great experimental as well as theoretical activity.

MECHANICS

As we have seen, Galileo, in his explanation of the path of a projectile in a vacuum, had successfully mastered the first and the second law of motion. Later Descartes wrote on mechanics, but he hardly advanced beyond Galileo. Descartes's statement of the first law of motion (*Principia Philosophiæ*, 1644) was an improvement in form, but his third law is false in substance. The motion of bodies in their direct impact was imperfectly understood by *Galileo*, erroneously given by *Descartes*, and first correctly stated by *Christopher Wren, John Wallis*, and *Christian Huygens*. The laws of motion in their present form were first given by Newton in his *Principia*.

Descartes's achievements in geometry and in philosophy are immeasurably superior to those in physics. He was a meta-physician, and, from a limited amount of experimentation or experience, confidently deduced a large amount of inference, without allowing himself to be disturbed by any possible discrepancy between his final conclusions and the actual facts. He had no appreciation of the slow-going process of Galileo.[1]

Says Descartes: "Without considering the first causes of nature, he (Galileo) sought only for the causes of a few particular effects and thus built without a foundation." "What Galileo says regarding velocity of falling bodies in a vacuum has no foundation; he should have told what gravity is; had he known its nature, then he would have seen that there is none in empty space." "I see nothing in his books which I envy and almost nothing which I would acknowledge as my own."[2] According to his own *a priori* principles, Descartes thought he could easily explain all that Galileo had worked out, while, as a matter of fact, Descartes had no true notion of acceleration, and committed errors avoided by Galileo.

There arose a curious dispute between the Cartesians and the

[1] "Of the mechanical truths which were easily attainable in the beginning of the seventeenth century, Galileo took hold of as many, and Descartes of as few, as was well possible for a man of genius." WHEWELL, Vol. I., p. 338.

[2] DESCARTES, *Lettres*, Vol. II., Paris, 1659, Letter 91, p. 391; DÜHRING, *Krit. Geschichte d. allgem. Princ. d. Mechanik*, Leipzig, 1887, pp. 106–108; KÄSTNER, *Geschichte d. Mathematik*, Vol. IV., pp. 22–26.

Leibnizians on the measure of the efficacy of a moving body. Descartes took the efficacy to be proportional to the *velocity;* Leibniz took it to vary as the *square of the velocity.*[1] The controversy lasted over half a century, until, finally, it was brought to a close by Jean-le-Rond D'Alembert's remarks in the preface to his *Dynamique,* 1743, though before this date Huygens's thought on this subject was perfectly clear. The long dispute was merely one of words; both views were correct. The efficiency of a body in motion varies as its *velocity,* if we consider the *time.* A body thrown vertically upward with double the velocity ascends twice as long a time. The efficiency varies as the *square of the velocity,* if we consider the *distance.* A body thrown vertically upward with double the velocity ascends four times as far. The reference to time leads to what Descartes called the "quantity of motion" (our "momentum"), *mv,* and makes the notion of *force* the primary concept. The reference to the distance leads to the expression *fs,* which makes *work* the primary notion. The former view made $ft = mv$ the fundamental equation; the latter made $fs = \dfrac{mv^2}{2}$ the fundamental equation. With the Cartesians *work* was a derived notion; with the Leibnizians *force* was a derived notion.[2]

---

[1] *Acta Eruditorum,* 1686, "Demonstratio erroris memorabilis cartesii," etc.

[2] For the term *ft* the Frenchman *J. B. Bélanger* proposed in 1847 the name *impulse,* which term is used in the same sense by *J. Clerk Maxwell* in his *Matter and Motion.* Leibniz (1695) called mv^2 the *vis viva* or *living force.* *G. G. Coriolis* preferred to call $\frac{1}{2} mv^2$ the *vis viva,* a term now called *kinetic energy* by the English. Coriolis employed the name *work* for *fs* and was sustained in this usage by *J. V. Poncelet,* who adopted the *kilogramme-metre* as the unit of work. Coriolis and Poncelet were among the first promoters of reform in the teaching of rational mechanics. See MACH, *Science of Mechanics* (Ed. McCormack), pp. 271, 272; MARIE, *Histoire d. Sciences Math. et Phys.,* Vol. XII., 1888, pp. 191, 192.

The Cartesian view, followed by Newton and modern writers of elementary text-books, makes *force, mass, momentum*, the original notions; the Leibnizian view, followed usually by Huygens and by the school of Poncelet, makes *work, mass, vis viva* (energy), the original notions.[1] If certain modern thinkers are correct in affirming the objective reality of kinetic energy and denying the objective reality of force, then the Leibnizian method would seem to be the more philosophical.[2]

The teacher will observe that those parts of mechanics which a beginner usually finds "hard to learn" are the parts which, in the development of the science, were difficult to overcome. Take, for instance, the difference between force and energy, or the concept of mass. Early writers, such as Galileo, Descartes, Leibniz, Huygens, had no clear notion of mass; *weight* and *mass* were taken interchangeably; these terms were one and the same thing. The real distinction between the two became evident when it was discovered that the same body may receive different accelerations by gravity on different parts of the earth's surface. When *Jean Richer* in 1671 went from Paris to Cayenne in French Guiana to make astronomical observations, he found that his pendulum clock, which in Paris kept correct time, fell daily two and a half minutes behind mean solar time. The pendulum was shortened, but after his return to Paris it was found to be too short.[3] The keen-minded Huygens at once discerned the cause, and found a partial explanation in the greater centrifugal tendency of the earth in Cayenne.[4] The distinction between *mass*

---

[1] MACH, *op. cit.*, pp. 148, 250, 270-276 ; H. KLEIN, *Principien der Mechanik*, Leipzig, 1872, pp. 17, 18.

[2] Consult P. G. TAIT, *Recent Advances in Physical Science*, London, 1885, pp. 16, 343–368.

[3] MARIE, *op. cit.*, Vol. V., 1884, p. 102.

[4] Huygens calculated that centrifugal action renders the second's pendulum at the poles $\frac{1}{289}$ shorter than at the equator, and that the cen-

and *weight* was clearly perceived by Newton in his extension of the laws of dynamics to heavenly bodies.[1] On the same spot of the earth, mass and weight are proportional to each other. This is not a self-evident fact; Newton proved it in course of a remarkable series of tests on pendulums. "By experiments made with the greatest accuracy, I have always found the quantity of matter in bodies to be proportional to their weight."[2]

The mathematical theory of the pendulum was first worked out by Huygens in his *De horologio oscillatorio* (Paris, 1673), a work that ranks second only to the *Principia* of Newton. The book opens with a description of pendulum clocks. Of his new theorems, the one on the interchangeability of the point of suspension and centre of oscillation has found its way into elementary text-books.

Before proceeding to Newton's discovery of the law of gravitation, we pass in brief review Descartes's theory of vortices. After the overthrow of the Ptolemaic system and the rejection of the ancient crystalline spheres, the puzzle stared philosophers in the face, what is it that causes the planets to move in their orbits? The answer given in Descartes's theory was eagerly accepted.[3] All space is filled with a fluid, or ether, the parts of which act on each other and cause circular motion. Thus the fluid was formed into a multitude of vortices of different size, velocity, and density. There is an immense vortex

---

trifugal force at the equator is $\frac{1}{289}$ of the absolute weight of a body. See HUYGENS, *Ursache d. Schwere*, trans. by R. MEWES, Berlin, 1896, p. 34.

[1] MACH, *op. cit.*, pp. 161, 251.

[2] *Principia*, Book II., Prop. XXIV., Cor. 7.

[3] It is an interesting fact that, by his theory, Descartes aimed primarily to reconcile the teachings of Copernicus with the doctrine of the immobility of the earth. He taught "that the earth is at rest in its heaven, which does not prevent its being carried along with it, and that it is the same with all the planets."

around the sun, carrying in its whirl the earth and the other planets. The denser bodies, being slower and less subject to centrifugal action, are forced toward the sun, the centre of the vortex. Each planet is in the centre of another vortex by which the ordinary phenomena of gravity are produced. Still smaller vortices produce cohesion between parts of a body. Figure 7 is Descartes's diagram of vortices given in his *Principia.*

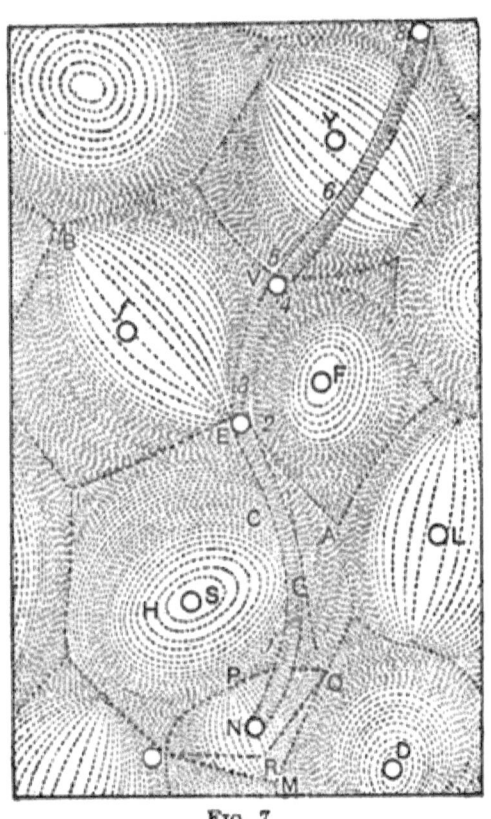

FIG. 7.

This theory is of interest, because it is the faith on which Newton was brought up; it was taught in English and European universities. In 1671 *Jacques Rohault*, a Cartesian, wrote his *Traité de Physique.* This became a classic text in France, and was taught in England and America. *Samuel Clarke's* translation of it (1696) was used as a text at Yale College as late as 1743.[1] Clarke's notes to the original text aimed to expose the fallacies of the Cartesian system, and to advance Newtonian views. In France the Newtonian theory

[1] *Teaching and History of Math. in the U. S.*, Washington, 1890, p. 30.

did not completely dispel the belief in Descartes's vortices until the middle of the eighteenth century.[1]

Descartes's theory of vortices can hardly be ranked among the great scientific theories, such as the Ptolemaic or Copernican system, or the emission theory of light. Descartes made no attempt to reconcile it with Kepler's laws; in fact, it did not explain a single phenomenon satisfactorily. Nor did it lead to the discovery of new truths. However, it referred planetary motions to mechanical causes. Its general features were easily grasped, for a whirlwind or an eddy of water at once suggested a picture to the mind. Then, too, these vortices helped to overthrow the Aristotelian system.[2]

Isaac Newton (1642–1727) was born at Woolsthorpe, in Lincolnshire, the same year in which Galileo died. In his twelfth year his mother sent him to the public school at Grantham, where he began to show decided taste for mechanical inventions. He constructed a water-clock, a windmill, a carriage moved by the person who sat in it, and other toys. He entered Trinity College, Cambridge, in 1660. Cambridge was the birthplace of Newton's genius. Among the physical works read by him while an undergraduate are Kepler's *Optics* and Barrow's *Lectures*. The first ideas of some of his greatest discoveries suggested themselves to him at this time.

---

[1] Voltaire, who visited England in 1727, and afterward became a stanch supporter of Newton's philosophy, says, "A Frenchman who arrives in London finds a great alteration in philosophy, as in other things. He left the world full [*a plenum*], he finds it empty. At Paris you see the universe composed of vortices of subtle matter, in London we see nothing of the kind," WHEWELL, *op. cit.*, Vol. I., p. 431. We cannot blame the Europeans for not believing in "empty" space. In this respect Newton himself was not a Newtonian. See *Correspondence of R. Bentley*, Vol. I., p. 70; *Proc. Roy. Soc. of London*, Vol. 54., 1893, p. 381.

[2] JOHN PLAYFAIR, "Dissertation Fourth" in *Encyclop. Brit.*, 8th ed., Vol. I., pp. 609, 610; O. LODGE, *Pioneers of Science*, pp. 152–156.

In 1664 he made some observations on halos.[1] In 1666, "I began," he says, "to think of gravity extending to the orb of the moon, . . . and thereby compared the force requisite to keep the moon in her orb with the force of gravity at the surface of the earth, and found them answer pretty nearly."[2]

The above thoughts on gravitation occurred to him while he was at his home in Lincolnshire, where he had gone to escape the plague at that time raging in Cambridge. Pemberton gives the following details: "As he sat alone in the garden, he fell into a speculation on the power of gravity; that as this power is not found sensibly diminished at the remotest distance from the centre of the earth to which we can rise, neither at the tops of the loftiest buildings, nor even on the summits of the highest mountains; it appeared to him reasonable to conclude, that this power must extend much farther than was usually thought; why not as high as the moon, said he to himself? And if so, her motion must be influenced by it; perhaps she is retained in her orbit thereby."[3] It was conjectured by Newton, as also by Hooke, Huygens, Halley, Wren, and others, that if Kepler's third law (the square of the time of revolution of each planet is proportional to the cube of its mean distance from the sun) was true, then the attraction between the earth and other members of the solar system varied inversely as the square of the distance. The accuracy of Kepler's third law was doubted at that time. To show that the above conjecture was true required the genius of Newton.

---

[1] NEWTON, *Opticks*, London, 1704, Book II., Part IV., obs. 13, p. 111.

[2] *Portsmouth Collection*, Sect. I., Division XI., No. 41; W. W. R. BALL, *An Essay on Newton's " Principia*," London, 1893, p. 7.

[3] PEMBERTON, *View of Sir Isaac Newton's Philosophy*, London, 1728; W. W. R. BALL, *op. cit.*, p. 9. The well-known anecdote that the idea of universal gravitation was suggested to Newton by the fall of an apple is usually considered legendary, but Ball argues in its favour, and gives the authorities bearing on it, pp. 11, 12.

According to the old account of the discovery, Newton in 1666 based his estimate of the earth's radius on the supposition that there were 60 miles to a degree of latitude. This verified the law of inverse squares only approximately and threw doubt upon Newton's speculations. About 1684 he obtained from Jean Picard's measurement of an arc of the meridian ($69\frac{1}{10}$ miles to a degree) a more accurate value for the earth's radius. Taking this corrected value, the law of inverse squares was verified.

More recent research renders it highly improbable that Newton remained long unacquainted with the fact that the estimate of 60 miles was too small. Norwood's *Seaman's Practice*, 1636, gave the more correct value of $69\frac{1}{2}$ miles to the degree. Snell had given nearly the same result in 1617, and this was referred to in Varenius's *Geography*, an edition of which was prepared in 1672 by Newton himself.[1] Nevertheless, Newton deferred undertaking a recalculation for many years. Why this delay? The astronomer, J. C. Adams, examined a great mass of unpublished letters and manuscripts of Newton forming the *Portsmouth Collection* (which remained private property until 1872, when its owner placed it in the hands of the University of Cambridge), and arrived at the opinion that Newton's difficulties were of a different nature; that the numerical verification was fairly complete in 1666, but that Newton had not been able to determine what the attraction of a spherical body upon an external point would be. His letters to Halley show that he did not suppose the earth to attract as though all its mass were concentrated into a point at the centre. He could not assert, therefore, that the assumed law of gravity was verified by the figures, though for long distances he might have claimed that it yielded close

---

[1] R. T. GLAZEBROOK, article "Newton" in *Dic. Nat. Biog.*

approximations. When Halley visited Newton in 1684, he requested Newton to determine what the orbit of a planet would be if the law of attraction were that of inverse squares. Newton had solved a similar problem for Hooke in 1679, and replied at once that it was an ellipse. After Halley's visit, Newton, with Picard's new value for the earth's radius, reviewed his early calculation, and was able to show that, if the distances between the bodies in the solar system were so great that the bodies might be considered as points, then their motions were in accordance with the assumed law of gravitation. In 1685 he completed his discovery by showing that the sphere whose density at any point depends only on the distance from the centre, attracts an external particle as though its whole mass were concentrated at the centre.[1] It was thus proved that the force of attraction between two spheres is the same as it would be if the mass of each sphere were concentrated at its centre. "No sooner," says Glaisher,

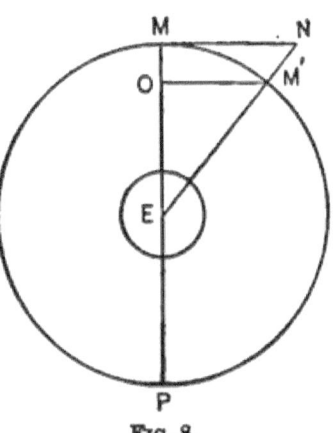

FIG. 8.

"had Newton proved this superb theorem—and we know from his own words that he had no expectation of so beautiful a result till it emerged from his mathematical investi-

---

[1] Consult theorems in *Principia*, Book I., Sec. XII., also Book III., Prop. VIII. For further details on the discovery of the law of gravitation, consult W. W. R. BALL, *op. cit.*; J. W. L. GLAISHER, "Bicentenary Address," *Cambridge Chronicle*, April 20, 1888. We have used also BALL, *Hist. of Math.*, 1888, pp. 295-297. ROSENBERGER's *Isaac Newton und seine Physikalischen Principien* is worthy of reference, even though the author made no use whatever of the information obtained through the *Portsmouth Collection*.

gation — than all the mechanism of the universe at once lay spread before him."

We proceed, with aid of Fig. 8, to explain Newton's calculation. Geodetic measurements gave the circumference of the earth as 123,249,600 Paris feet (*Principia*, Book III., Prop. IV.). The moon's mean distance is about 60 times the earth's radius. Hence, the moon's orbit, assumed to be circular, is 123,249,600 × 60 = 7,394,976,000 feet. The moon revolves around the earth once in 27 d. 7 h. 43 m., or in 39,343 minutes. Hence her orbital velocity is 7,394,976,000 ÷ 39,343 = 187,961.67 ft. per minute. Let the arc MM' represent this velocity, where M is the moon's position in its orbit and E is the earth's centre. Then, evidently, NM', which for a very small angle, MEM', nearly equals MO, represents the distance the moon falls per minute toward the earth. Since

$$\overline{MM'}^2 = MP \cdot MO, \text{ (Book I., Prop. IV., Cor. 9),}$$

we get

$$MO = \overline{MM'}^2 \div MP = 15\tfrac{1}{12} \text{ ft. per minute, nearly.}$$

Since ME equals 60 radii of the earth, the distance a body falls per minute on the earth's surface should be, by the law of inverse squares, $60^2 \times 15\tfrac{1}{12}$ ft. per minute, or $15\tfrac{1}{12}$ ft. per second. More accurately it is "15 ft., 1 inch, and 1 line $\tfrac{4}{9}$." Now, pendulum experiments made by Huygens gave as the distance per second through which a body falls from rest at Paris as "15 ft., 1 inch, 1 line $\tfrac{7}{9}$" (Book III., Prop. IV.). Hence the law of inverse squares is proved to be true.

In the scholium to Prop. IV., Book I., Newton acknowledges his indebtedness to Huygens for the laws of centrifugal force employed in the above calculation.

When Newton presented his *Principia* to the Royal Society, *Robert Hooke* (1635–1703) claimed the law of inverse squares for himself. Newton's reply is contained in a letter to Edmund

Halley.[1] The *Principia* was published in 1687 under the direction and at the expense of Halley.

Though the law expressing the variation in the intensity of gravitational attraction became known over three centuries ago, and though scientific discovery since that time has been more rapid than ever before, we are still unable to explain what causes a stone to fall to the ground. This is indeed a strange fact in the progress of science. That the earth and the moon act upon each other through empty space, without the aid of some medium between them or surrounding them, modern physicists find it difficult to believe. No little interest attaches to the question as to Newton's view on this subject. Did he believe in "action at a distance," or in the idea that matter can act where it is not? In a letter to Bentley he says:

"That gravity should be innate, inherent, and essential to matter, so that one body may act upon another at a distance through a vacuum without the mediation of anything else, by and through which their action and force may be conveyed from one to another, is to me so great an absurdity that I believe no man who has in philosophical matters a competent faculty of thinking can ever fall into."[2]

Yet the opposite belief has sometimes been ascribed to Newton. The doctrine of action at a distance has for its author, not Newton, but *Roger Cotes* (1682–1716), who edited the second edition of the *Principia* in 1713 and asserted the doctrine in his preface. When later the Newtonian philosophy

---

[1] See letter in BALL, *op. cit.*, p. 155.

[2] *Corresp. of R. Bentley*, Vol. I., p. 70 ; *Proc. of Royal Soc. of London*, Vol. 54, 1893, p. 381. For other passages from Newton favouring an ether-hypothesis, see his *Opticks*, Queries 18, 22 ; also *Phil. Trans. Abr.*, Vol. I., p. 145, Nov., 1672 ; BIRCH, *Hist. of Royal Society*, Vol. III., p. 249, 1675.

gained ground in Europe, it was the opinion of Cotes, rather than that of Newton, which prevailed.[1]

Proceeding to the mechanics of liquids and gases, we begin with researches on liquid pressure by *Blaise Pascal* (1623–1662), who is celebrated not only as a precocious mathematician and as the author of the *Provincial Letters*, but also as a physicist. He was born at Clermont in Auvergne. In his brief *Traité de l'équilibre des liqueurs*,[2] written in 1653 and first published in 1663, one year after his death, he enunciates the law, known as "Pascal's Law," that the pressure exerted upon a liquid is transmitted undiminished in all directions and acts with the same force on all equal surfaces in a direction at right angles to them. He shows by experiments identical with those carried out in our modern laboratories with Masson's

---

[1] C. Maxwell, Lecture "On Action at a Distance," *Nature*, Vol. VII., 1872–73, p. 325. Cotes's preface is given in *Sir Isaac Newton's Principia reprinted for Sir William Thomson and Hugh Blackburn*, Glasgow, 1871. Our inability to explain gravity is not due to want of attempts. The first important effort in this line was made by C. Huygens in his *Discours sur la cause de la pésanteur*, part of which was written after the appearance of Newton's *Principia* in 1687. A German translation of the *Discours* has been brought out by Rudolf Mewes, Berlin, 1896. A mechanical gravitation theory was advanced by C. Le Sage, born at Geneva in 1724. See Le Sage, "Lucrèce Newtonien," *Mémoires de l'Académie des Sciences*, Berlin, 1782, pp. 404–432. He teaches that gravity is caused by streams of atoms coming in all directions from space. Later speculations on the cause of gravity were made by *Clerk Maxwell, Lord Kelvin, C. Isenkrahe, Bernhard Riemann, Leonhard Euler, N. v. Dellingshausen, Tolver Preston, Adalbert Rysáneck, Paul du Bois-Reymond, Vaschy, Schramm, Anderson, Möller*, and others. For critical and historical summaries, see C. Isenkrahe, "Ueber die Zurückführung der Schwere auf Absorption" in *Zeitsch. f. Math. and Physik*, 1892, *Suppl.*, pp. 163–204; S. Tolver Preston, "Comparative Review of some Dynamical Theories of Gravitation," *Philosophical Magazine*, (5) Vol. 39, 1895, pp. 145 *et seq.*; W. B. Taylor, "Kinetic Theories of Gravitation," *Smithsonian Report*, 1876, pp. 205–282.

[2] *Œuvres Complètes de Blaise Pascal*, Paris, 1866, Vol. III., pp. 83–98.

apparatus that pressure against a surface, in virtue of the weight of the liquid, depends simply upon its depth. Several vessels of different shapes having movable bottoms of equal areas are suspended, one after the other, from one arm of a balance. The vessels are filled with water to such a height that the pressure is just sufficient to force down the bottom and raise a weight on the other arm of the balance. Pascal also takes two sliding plugs or pistons pressing against a fluid in a closed vessel, the surface of the first being one hundred times greater than the surface of the other; the force of one man acting at the first plug will balance the force of one hundred men at the other. "Hence it follows that a vessel full of water is a new principle of mechanics and a new machine for multiplying forces to any degree we choose."[1]

Except the telescope, no scientific discovery of the seventeenth century excited wonder and curiosity to a greater degree than did the experiments with the barometer and air-pump. Chance expressions that air has weight are already found in Aristotle and Plato, but nothing was *known* till the time of Galileo and Torricelli. A great deal of vague speculation was indulged in regarding the vacuum. Aristotle believed that a vacuum could not exist, and as late a writer as Descartes held the same view. For two thousand years philosophers spoke of the horror that nature has for empty space, — the *horror vacui*, — as if inanimate objects could have *feeling*. Because of this horror, nature was said to prevent the formation of a vacuum by laying hold of anything near by and with it instantly filling up any vacated space. Even Galileo could not quite free himself from this unphilosophical doctrine. He was astonished when told that a suction-pump with a very long suction-pipe, which had just been constructed, would not

[1] *Œuvres Complètes de Blaise Pascal*, Paris, 1866, Vol. III., p. 85.

raise water higher than about thirty-three feet. He remarked
that the *horror vacui* was a force which had its limitations and
could be measured. That air has weight he convinced himself
by the difference in weight of a glass balloon filled with air
under ordinary pressure and then with air under high pressure.[1] He estimated the density of air to be 400 times less
than that of water.

Thus Galileo knew (1) that air has weight; he knew also
(2) what the "resistance to a vacuum" was when measured by
the height of a water column, and also when determined by
the weight against a piston. But the two ideas dwelt separately in his mind.[2] It remained for his pupil Torricelli to
vary the experiments, to unite and interweave the two ideas,
and to place air in the list of pressure-exerting fluids.

Evangelista Torricelli (1608–1647) began his mathematical
studies in a Jesuit school, and continued them under Benedict
Castelli at Rome. He made himself familiar with Galileo's
writings, and published some articles on mechanics. Galileo
was anxious to become acquainted with the author of these
tracts and pressed Torricelli to join him at Florence. He
accepted the invitation, and it is said that his society and
conversation contributed greatly to soothe the last days of the
blind physicist. Galileo died three months later. Galileo's
patron, the Grand Duke of Tuscany, made Torricelli Galileo's
successor as professor of mathematics at the Accademia.

Torricelli devised the scheme of determining the resistance
of a vacuum by a vertical column of mercury, which he expected to be about $\frac{1}{14}$ the length of the corresponding water
column. The "Torricellian experiment" was carried out in
1643 in Florence by *Vincenzo Viviani* (1622–1703), who at

[1] *Ostwald's Klassiker*, No. 11, p. 71. See also MACH, *op. cit.*, pp. 112–
114.

[2] MACH, in *Monist*, Vol. 6, 1896, p. 170.

seventeen had become a pupil of Galileo, and was now studying under the direction of Torricelli.

Torricelli never published an account of his research. He
was at this time too deeply absorbed in mathematical investigations on the cycloid, and he died a few years later. However, he described his experiments in two letters of 1644, to
his friend, M. A. Ricci, in Rome, and these are extant.[1] He
says that the aim of his investigation was " not simply to produce a vacuum, but to make an instrument which shows the
mutations of the air, now heavier and dense, and now lighter
and thin." [2]

In 1644 *Ricci* wrote a letter, describing the Torricellian experiment to *Père Mersenne,* in Paris, who, by his extensive
correspondence, acted as an intermediary between scientific
men. The news created a sensation among French savants.
But the experiment was not repeated in France until the summer of 1646 (by *Pierre Petit,* of Rouen, in conjunction with
Pascal); as no suitable glass tubes were available before that
date.

The account of the Italian experiment which reached Pascal
must have been quite incomplete, for he found it necessary to
reflect on the phenomenon independently. He concludes " that
the vacuum is not impossible in nature, and that she does not
shun it with so great a horror as many imagine." [3]

[1] They were first published in 1663. See a recent reprint by G.
HELLMANN, *Neudrucke*, No. 7.

[2] At the close of the letter, he says, " My principal object is, therefore,
not altogether successful . . . because the level [of the mercury] . . .
changes for another cause which I never thought of, namely, by the heat
and cold, and that very appreciably." Yet only since the time of
Amontons (1704) has it been thought necessary to make corrections for
temperature. See G. HELLMANN, *op. cit.*, pp. 16, (3).

[3] " Nouvelles expériences touchant le vide," *Œuvres Compl. de B.
Pascal*, Paris, 1866, Vol. III., p. 1. See also his *Traité de la pesanteur
de la masse de l'air*, pp. 98–129.

Pascal reasoned that, if the mercury column was held up simply by the pressure of the air, then the column ought to be shorter at a high altitude. He tried it on a church-steeple in Paris, but desiring more decisive results, he wrote to his brother-in-law to try the experiment on the Puy de Dôme, a high mountain in Auvergne. There was a difference of three inches in the height of the mercury, "which ravished us with admiration and astonishment." Pascal repeated the Torricellian experiment, using red wine and a glass tube forty-six feet long. (Evidently glass tubing had become more plentiful.) He experimented with the siphon, and explained its theory. A balloon, half full of air, was found to appear inflated on being taken up on a mountain, and to flatten again, gradually, during the descent.

The doctrine of the *horror vacui* was overthrown through experimental research in Italy and France. A repetition of the process took place in Germany. The early work of the German investigator was carried on independently. *Otto von Guericke* (1602–1686) came of a prominent family in Magdeburg. He studied at German universities, also at Leyden, and then travelled in England and France. In the course of the Thirty Years' War Magdeburg was devastated in 1631, and Guericke and his family barely escaped with their lives. Later he earned a livelihood as engineer in the army of Gustavus Adolphus. In 1646 he became burgomaster of Magdeburg.

The disputations regarding the vacuum made him curious to find out the facts experimentally. Says he, "Oratory, elegance of words, or skill in disputation avails nothing in the field of natural science." In 1663 he completed the manuscript for his work *De vacuo spatio*, but it was not published until 1672.[1]

---

[1] The work consists of seven books, of which the third contains his own experiments and has been recently brought out in German transla-

Guericke first took a tight wine-cask, full of water, and attempted to remove the liquid with a brass pump applied to the cask below. But the bands and iron screws holding the pump to the cask gave way. It was attached more securely, then three strong men pulling at the piston at last succeeded in drawing out the water. Thereupon a noise

FIG. 9.

was heard, as if the residual water within were boiling violently, and this continued until air had replaced the water pumped out.

tion in *Ostwald's Klassiker*, No. 59. The first accounts of Guericke's air-pump and experiments were published by KASPAR SCHOTT in his *Mechanica hydraulico-pneumatica*, 1657, and in his *Technica curiosa*, 1664. Through the publication of 1657 Robert Boyle became acquainted with Guericke's experiments.

The leaky wooden cask was replaced by a copper globe, then water and air were drawn out as before. At first the piston moved easily, but later the strength of two men could hardly move it, when "suddenly with a loud clap and to the terror of all" the sphere collapsed. A more massive and more exactly spherical metallic vessel, Fig. 9, was secured and exhausted. "On opening the stop-cock the air rushed with such force into the copper globe, as if it wanted to drag to itself a person near by. Though you held your face at considerable distance, your breath was taken away; indeed, you could not hold your hand over the stop-cock without danger that it would be violently forced down."

Guericke next invented air-pumps, the first form of which is illustrated in Fig. 10. Its tap with the stop-cock was detachable, so that objects to be experimented upon might be placed in the receiver. As an extra precaution against leakage, the stop-cock was made to stand under water which was poured into the conical vessel. Numerous experiments were made with this pump. A clock in a vacuum cannot be heard to strike; a flame dies out in it; a bird opens its bill wide, struggles for air, and dies; fishes perish; grapes can be preserved six months *in vacuo*. A long tube, connected with an exhausted globe above and dipping in water below, was his water barometer. He explains the rise of the water in the tube by the pressure of the air. He observes fluctuations in the height of the water column and uses the instrument for weather predictions. A miniature man of wood, floating on the water, moved up and down inside the tube and by his finger indicated the pressure of the air at any moment. Guericke's experiment of weighing a receiver, first when full of air and again when exhausted, has held its place in elementary books. The same is true of his "Magdeburg hemispheres." He constructed such hemispheres, about 1.2 ft. in diameter, and made a test in 1654 at Regensburg before the Reichstag and Emperor Ferdinand III. According to his

ICONISMUS 6   Cap. 4 Lib. 3

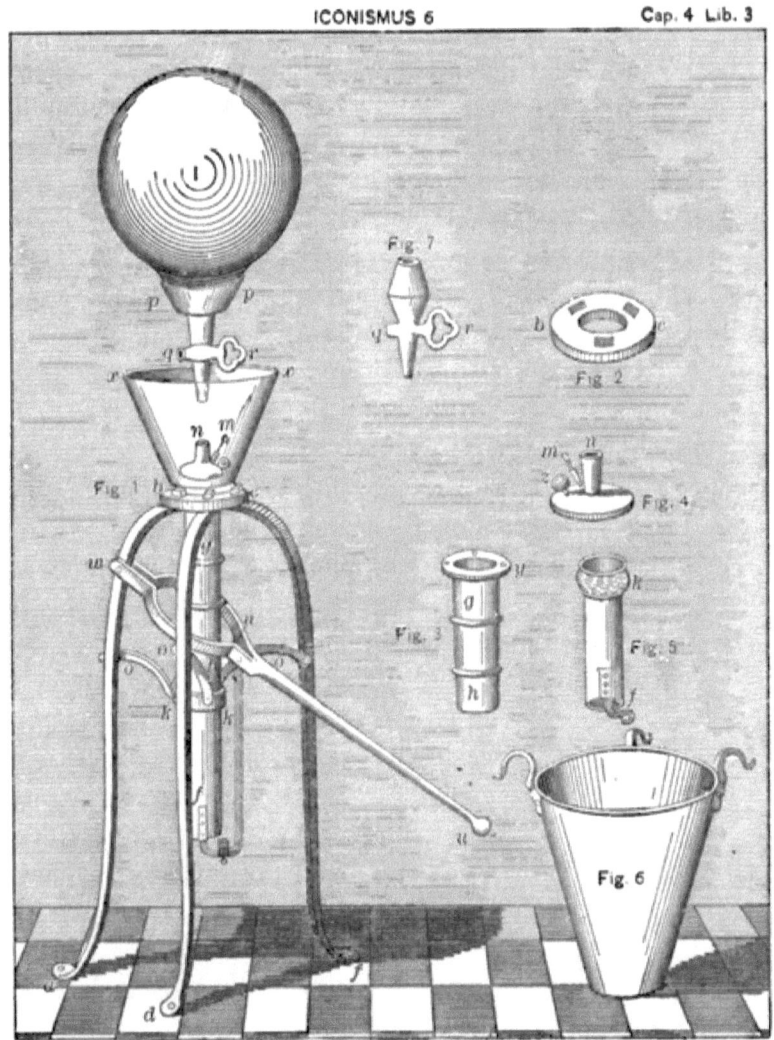

Fig. 10.

calculations, a force of 2686 pounds was needed to overcome the atmospheric pressure holding the hemispheres together.

They were pulled apart only after applying sixteen horses, four pairs on each hemisphere. His book contains a large engraving, naïvely illustrating how the experiment was made.

On that occasion Guericke made other experiments, and he happened to assert that if you were to blow your breath into a large exhausted receiver, you would that moment breathe your last. The truth of this being doubted, he illustrated the power of "suction" by a new experiment. A cylinder of a large pump had a rope attached to its piston, which led over a pulley and was divided into branches on which twenty or thirty men could pull. As soon as the cylinder was connected with an exhausted receiver, the piston was suddenly pushed down by the atmospheric pressure and the men at the ropes were thrown forward.

It was on this occasion that Guericke heard for the first time of the Torricellian experiments made eleven years earlier.[1]

In England the mechanics of the air was first studied by *Robert Boyle* (1627–1691). He was born at Lismore Castle in Ireland. In his autobiography he speaks of "his acquaintance with some children of his own age, whose stuttering habitude he so long counterfeited that at last he contracted it;" diverse cures "were tried with as much successlessness as diligence."[2] After spending nearly four years at Eton College, he left in 1638 for the Continent. At Geneva, one night, a terrific thunder-storm made him fear that the day of judg-

---

[1] A pair of Guericke's "Magdeburg hemispheres" were on exhibition at the Columbian Exposition. As to the fate of Guericke's original air-pump, consult G. BERTHOLD in *Wiedem. Annalen*, Neue Folge, 54, 1895, pp. 724–726. Guericke is said to have spent 20,000 thaler for apparatus.

[2] *The Works of the Honourable Robert Boyle*, in five volumes, to which is prefixed the Life of the Author, edited by THOMAS BIRCH, London, 1743, Vol. I., p. 6 (of biography).

ment was at hand. At this time he became converted to religion, and many of his later writings are on theology. On his return home, in 1644, a youth of eighteen, he found the country in great confusion; nevertheless he received a strong impetus for scientific research from the meetings in London, in 1645, of a philosophical society, — the *Invisible College*, as he called it, — which after the Restoration was incorporated as the Royal Society. In 1654 he settled at Oxford, where he erected a laboratory, kept several operators at work, and engaged Robert Hooke as his chemical assistant.[1] After reading of Guericke's air-pump, he let Hooke make a less clumsy pump, which was completed in 1659. As early as 1660 Boyle published his *New Experiments . . . touching the Spring of the Air.*

He left Oxford for London in 1668. For forty years he was in feeble health. His memory was so treacherous that he was often tempted to abandon study, yet he was a voluminous writer, and possessed an immense reputation both at home and abroad. Before 1657 he purposely refrained from "seriously and orderly" reading the works of Gassendi, Descartes, or Francis Bacon, "that I might not be prepossessed with any theory or principles till I spent some time in trying what things themselves would incline me to think."[2]

Boyle placed the barometer in the receiver of the air-pump and observed the ebullition of heated liquids and the freezing of water on exhaustion.

Except for an absurd criticism by a would-be physicist, Boyle would probably never have discovered the law bearing his name. *Franciscus Linus*, professor at Lüttich in the Netherlands, had read Boyle's *New Experiments*, and declared that

---

[1] See article "Boyle, Robert," in *Dic. of Nat. Biog.*

[2] *Works*, Vol. I., p. 194.

the air is very insufficient to perform such great matters as
the counterpoising of a mercurial cylinder of 29 inches; he
claimed to have found that the mercury hangs by invisible
threads (*funiculi*) from the upper end of the tube, and to have
felt them when he closed the upper end of the tube with
his finger. This criticism incited Boyle to renewed research.
"We shall now endeavour to manifest by experiments purposely made, that the spring of the air is capable of doing far
more than it is necessary for us to ascribe to it, to solve the
phænomena of the Torricellian experiment."[1] "We took then
a long glass tube, which by a dexterous hand and the help of a
lamp was in such a manner crooked at the bottom, that the
part turned up was almost parallel to the rest of the tube and,
the orifice of this shorter leg . . . being hermetically sealed,
the length of it was divided into inches (each of which was
divided into eight parts) by a straight list of paper, which
containing those divisions, was carefully pasted all along it."
A similar strip of paper was pasted on the longer leg. Then
"as much quicksilver as served to fill the arch or bended part
of the siphon" was poured in so as to be at the same height
in both legs. "This done, we began pouring quicksilver into
the longer leg . . . till the air in the shorter leg was by condensation reduced to take up but half the space it possessed
. . . we cast our eyes upon the longer leg of the glass . . .
and we observed, not without delight and satisfaction, that
the quicksilver in that longer part of the tube was 29 inches
higher than the other." This tube was broken by accident,
and a new one, about eight feet long, was prepared. It was
too long to be used in his chamber, so he took it on "a pair
of stairs" and suspended it by strings so "that it did scarce
touch the box" placed underneath. Pressures less than one

---

[1] See "Defence against Linus," 1662, *Works*, Vol. I., p. 100.

atmosphere were also obtained. Altogether he subjected the enclosed air to pressures varying from $1\frac{3}{8}$ inches of mercury to $117\frac{9}{16}$ inches, passing from one extreme to the other in about forty steps, and every time comparing the observed pressures with what they should be "according to the hypothesis that supposes the pressures and expansions to be in reciprocal proportion." The observed and theoretical values agree fairly well.

In 1666 Boyle published his *Hydrostatical Paradoxes*, in which he takes pains to refute the old doctrine that a light liquid can exert no pressure against a heavier liquid. That such refutations seemed necessary at so late a date indicates the slow assimilation of correct ideas on fluid pressure.

"Boyle's Law" was rediscovered independently, fourteen years after Boyle's publication of it, by the prominent French physicist, *Edme Mariotte* (1620–1684). In France it is always called "Mariotte's Law."[1] Mariotte published it in his treatise, *Sur la nature de l'air*, 1676. He says, "We employed a tube of 40 inches, which I filled with mercury up to $27\frac{1}{2}$ inches, $12\frac{1}{2}$ inches of air being left, which, being plunged 1 inch into a vessel of mercury, leaving 39 inches above, contained 14 inches of mercury and 25 inches of air expanded to double its volume." By repeated experimentation "it became sufficiently evident that one may take it as a certain rule or law of nature that air condenses in proportion to the weight by which it is loaded." He had a clearer realization of the importance of this law than had Boyle.

---

[1] MARIE, in his large *Histoire des Sciences Math. et Physi.*, Vol. IV., 1884, pp. 239–242, gives an account of Boyle without mentioning the law in that connection. Mariotte is represented as the sole discoverer (p. 176). The same course is followed by A. LIBES in his *Histoire Philosophique des Progrès de la Physique*, Paris, 1810, Vol. II., pp. 134–140, 195.

To Mariotte is attributed the instauration of experimental physics in France. As Boyle was prominent in the organization of the Royal Society of London, so Mariotte was one of the first and leading members of the Académie des Sciences, founded in 1666. By carefully measuring the height of the mercury column in a deep cellar, and then at the newly built astronomical observatory, located on high ground in Paris, he obtained an approximate formula for estimating height by the barometer. He wrote an important article on percussion.

In 1674 *Denis Papin* described an air-pump in which the flask-like receptacle with a stop-cock, such as had been employed by Guericke and Boyle, was replaced by a plate and bell glass. The credit for this improvement is usually given to Papin, but he himself ascribes it to Huygens, who is now known to have made this desirable innovation in 1661.[1] Papin was a pupil and assistant to Huygens.

In the study of falling bodies and the motions of projectiles the resistance of the air has always complicated the phenomena, has usually perplexed the investigators, and has often supplied critics with all sorts of objections. *Galileo* made allowances for the resistance of the air. About 1670 *Mariotte* concluded from experiments at the Paris observatory that the resistance to falling bodies is proportional to the square of the time. *Newton* inclined to the same conclusion, while *La Hire* favoured the cube of the time.

In 1679 Newton remarked "that a falling body ought by reason of the earth's diurnall motion to advance eastward and not fall to the west as the vulgar opinion is." We may here state, parenthetically, that in France *Mersenne* and *Petit* fired bullets vertically upward, expecting them to strike the ground

---

[1] E. GERLAND, *Wiedemann's Annalen*, Vol. II., 1878, p. 666.

far to the westward.[1] But the bullets could not be found!
Descartes, the French oracle of the time, was consulted, and
he seriously replied that the bullets had received such intense
velocity that they lost their weight and flew away from the earth.

Newton's prediction applied, not to a body rising and then
falling, but to one falling from rest. The experiment was
tried by his contemporary, *Robert Hooke*, who reported to the
Royal Society that he "had found the ball in every one of the
said experiments fall to the southeast of the perpendicular
point found by the same ball hanging perpendicular." The
experiments were made in the open air, and the results were
somewhat discordant. "But," says Hooke, "within doors it
succeeded also."[2] The strange southerly component of the
deviation was probably ascribed to errors of observation, but
careful experiments made by *G. B. Guglielmini* in 1791 from a
tower at Bologna, by *J. F. Benzenberg* in 1802 from St.
Michael's tower in Hamburg, and by *F. Reich* in 1831 down
a mine shaft at Freiberg in Saxony, all showed, in addition to
the predicted easterly deviation, also a small southerly displacement. For this no satisfactory explanation has yet been
given.[3]

In projectiles the actual path, as represented by the ballistic
curve, deviates considerably from Galileo's parabolas. It is
mathematically almost unmanageable. The path appears in
the northern hemisphere to be slightly bent to the right, owing

[1] If disturbances due to the atmosphere are negligible, then the bullets
should fall a small distance to the west. See W. FERREL, *A Popular
Treatise on the Winds*, New York, 1889, p. 88.

[2] BIRCH, *History of the Royal Society*, London, 1757, Vol. III., p. 519,
Vol. IV., p. 5. See also BALL, *An Essay on Newton's " Principia,"* pp.
146, 149, 150.

[3] ROSENBERGER, Part III., pp. 96, 97, 432–437. J. F. W. GRONAU, *His-
torische Entwicklung der Lehre vom Luftwiderstande*, Danzig, 1868, pp.
1–28.

to the rotation of the earth. That the resistance of the air complicates the path of a rotating sphere is known to every base-ball or tennis player.[1]

LIGHT

The law of refraction was discovered by *Willebrord Snell* (1591-1626), professor of mechanics at Leyden. He never published his discovery, but both Huygens and Isaak Voss claim to have examined Snell's manuscript. He stated the law in inconvenient form as follows: For the same media the ratio of the cosecants of the angle of incidence and of refraction retains always the same value. As the cosecants vary inversely as the sines, the equivalence of this to the modern form becomes evident. As far as known, Snell did not attempt a theoretical deduction of the law, but he verified it experimentally. The law of sines, as found in modern books, was given by *Descartes* in his *La Dioptrique*, 1637. He does not mention Snell, and probably discovered the law independently.[2] Descartes made no experiments, but deduced the law theoretically from the following assumptions: (1) the velocity of light is greater in a denser medium (now known to be wrong);

[1] For the effect of the earth's rotation, consult FERREL, *op. cit.*, p. 86 ; POISSON, *Journ. École Polytechnique*, XXVI., 1838. In *ibidem*, XXVII., 1839, POISSON considers the effect of their rotation in the air. See also MAGNUS, *Poggendorff Annalen*, LXXXVIII., 1853, p. 1.

[2] Various opinions have been held on this point. HELLER, Vol. II., pp. 65, 78, argues in favour of the independent discovery ; POGGENDORFF, p. 312, and ROSENBERGER, Part II., p. 113, incline to the opinion that Descartes plagiarized from Snell. Arago, on the other hand, declared Descartes the sole discoverer. See "Fresnel" in ARAGO's *Biographies*, 2d series, Boston, 1859, pp. 187, 188. The question is minutely discussed by P. KRAMER, *Zeitsch. f. Math. u. Phys.*, Vol. 27, 1882, Supplement, p. 235, and, after the discovery of some new documents, again by D. J. KORTEWEG, *Revue de Métaphysique et de Morale*, July, 1896, pp. 489-501.

(2) for the same media these velocities have the same ratio for all angles of incidence; (3) the velocity component parallel to the refracting surface remains unchanged during refraction (now known to be wrong). The improbability of the correctness of these assumptions brought about attacks upon the demonstration from the mathematician Fermat and others. Fermat deduced the law from the assumption that light travels from a point in one medium to a point in another medium in the least time, and that the velocity is less in the denser medium.[1]

A great achievement of the seventeenth century was the discovery of the gradual propagation of light. Previously its speed was usually supposed to be infinite. The first attempt to measure the velocity was made by *Galileo*.[2] He ascertained the time required for a person A to signal with a lantern to B and receive back a signal from B. This was tried in night-time, when the two observers were stationed close together, and also when they were nearly a mile apart. If a difference in time could be detected, then light would travel with finite velocity. Galileo was not able to settle the question from his experiments. But he made a suggestion on a wholly different problem which accidentally led another investigator to success. He remarked that the frequent disappearance of Jupiter's satellites behind the planet might be made to serve in longitude determinations. About 1642 the Italian astronomer, *Giovanni Domenico Cassini*, one of a number of great scientists called to Paris by Louis XIV., undertook a prolonged study of the Jovian system. About thirty years later a young Dane, *Olaf Römer* (1644–1710), was induced to settle in Paris. He was a native of Aarhus and had studied at Copenhagen. At Paris he

---

[1] ROSENBERGER, Part II., p. 114.
[2] *Ostwald's Klassiker*, No. 11, pp. 39, 40.

observed, together with *Jean Picard*, the eclipses of Jupiter's moons. It was noticed that the times of revolution of these moons in their orbits were not the same at all periods of the year, and were greater than the average when the apparent size of Jupiter was diminishing. Considering it in the highest degree improbable that the actual motions should be affected with any inequality of this sort, Römer became convinced that the observed irregularities must be explained on the supposition that the velocity of light is finite. In September, 1676, Römer stated to the French Academy of Sciences that in November next the eclipses of the first satellite would be about ten minutes later than the time gotten from computations based on the observations of the preceding August, and that the discrepancy could be explained by assuming that it took time for light to come from Jupiter to the earth. On November 9 an eclipse took place at 5 h. 35 m. 45 s., while by computation it should have been at 5 h. 25 m. 45 s. On November 22 he explained his theory to the Academy more fully, and said that it required light 22 minutes to cross the earth's orbit. (The more correct value is now known to be 16 minutes and 36 seconds.) The Academy did not at once accept Römer's theory. Picard favoured it, but Cassini did not. Römer had based his computation on the first satellite, and he frankly stated that similar calculations from observations on the three other moons would not have led to success. In Cassini's mind this fact operated strongly against the acceptance of Römer's explanation. Regarding the behaviour of these three bodies, Römer could only say that "they have irregularities not yet determined." In 1680 Cassini published improved ephemerides of Jupiter's moons, but made no mention of Römer's hypothesis.

The young Dane's fame increased to such an extent that he was made tutor to the Dauphin, and in 1681 Christian V.

called him to Denmark as astronomer-royal. After Römer's return to his native country confidence in his theory waned at Paris. It is not known how much more he worked on the problem, and whether he removed the objection arising in connection with the other moons. He left behind many astronomical observations, nearly all of which were destroyed by the fire which devastated the town of Copenhagen in 1728.[1]

In England Römer's theory was enthusiastically supported by Edmund Halley and verified in an unexpected manner by *James Bradley* (1693–1762), then Savilian Professor of Astronomy at Oxford. While endeavouring to determine the parallax of a star, he was surprised to find that its displacement was not at all as he expected it to be. He had almost despaired of being able to explain this, when an unexpected light fell upon him. "Accompanying a pleasure party in a sail on the Thames one day about September, 1728, he noticed that the wind seemed to shift each time that the boat put about, and a question put to the boatman brought the (to him) significant reply that the changes in direction of the vane at the top of the mast were merely due to changes in the boat's course, the wind remaining steady throughout. This was the clue he needed. He divined at once that the progressive transmission of light, combined with the advance of the earth in its orbit, must cause an annual shifting of the direction in which the heavenly bodies are seen by an amount depending upon the ratio of the two velocities."[2] From the value of this "aberration of light" Bradley estimated that solar rays reach the earth in 8 m. 13 s. This value was more nearly correct than Römer's 11 m., determined half a century earlier.

---

[1] We have used an article on Olaf Römer by ALEX. WERNICKE, *Zeitsch. f. Math. u. Physik*, Vol. 25, 1880, Hist. Abtheil., pp. 1–6 ; also W. DOBERCK, in *Nature*, Vol. 17, 1877, p. 105.

[2] "Bradley, James," in *Dic. Nat. Biog.*

Thus Bradley verified Römer's theory, and the gradual propagation of light came to be accepted as an established fact.

At a meeting of the French Academy of Sciences, in 1678, in the presence of Römer, Cassini, and others, a remarkable paper on the theory of light was presented by *Christian Huygens* (1629-1695). He was a native of The Hague, and had studied at the university in Leyden. The perusal of some of his earliest mathematical theorems led Descartes to predict his future greatness. He was induced by Louis XIV. to settle in Paris, where he remained from 1666 to 1681. Like his great contemporaries, Newton and Leibniz, Huygens never married.

Huygens's *Traité de la lumière*, of 1678, referred to above, was printed in 1690.[1] It is the earliest important attempt at

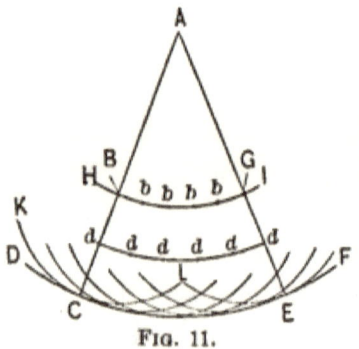

Fig. 11.

an exposition of the wave theory of light. Before Huygens, a rough outline of such a theory had been given in 1665, by Robert Hooke. Huygens develops the important principle, known by his name, relating to the propagation of waves. Around each particle of a vibrating medium as a centre, a wave is formed. Thus, if, in Fig. 11, *DCF* is a spherical wave which starts from *A* as centre, then a particle *B* within this sphere will be the centre of a special wave *KCL*, touching *DCF* at C. In the same way every other particle inside the sphere *DCL* forms a wave of its own. All these innumerable feeble wavelets are spheres, each touching *DCL* at one point, and contributing to its formation. Huygens assumes the

---

[1] Reprinted in German translation in *Ostwald's Klassiker*, No. 20. Consult also *Œuvres Complètes de Christiaän Huygens, publicées par la Société Hollandaise des Sciences*, La Haye, 1888-1895.

existence of an all-pervading ether, and explains reflection and refraction of light by the wave theory in the manner current in modern texts. Atmospheric refraction, and the marvels of double refraction in the Iceland spar, are dwelt upon. This division of a ray was first observed in Iceland spar in 1669, by *Erasmus Bartholinus*, of Copenhagen. Huygens gave the method of constructing the path of the ordinary and extraordinary ray, and observed that these rays were polarized. He assumed the vibrations in the ether to be longitudinal, as in sound, and was, therefore, not able to explain the strange phenomenon of polarization. Nor could he, by his theory, explain the origin of colours. He endeavoured to deduce from the wave theory the fact that light travels rectilinearly in a homogeneous medium. His argument was not conclusive. The main reason why Newton rejected the undulatory theory was its apparent inability to explain satisfactorily why light travels in straight lines. Newton threw the weight of his great authority on the side of the emission theory, and for over a century Huygens's ideas were laid aside and neglected.

Notwithstanding Newton's advocacy of a theory now known to be erroneous, his researches on light are of the greatest importance, and give evidence of extraordinary powers. Newton's first observations are on coronas, and date back to his student days in 1664. Later come his experiments on dispersion. "In the year 1666 (at which time I applied myself to the grinding of optick glasses of other figures than spherical) I procured me a triangular glass prism to try therewith the celebrated phenomena of colours."

The formation of colours from white light had been observed long ago. *Seneca* (2–66 A.D.) spoke of the identity of rainbow colours and those formed by the edges of a piece of glass. The breaking up or condensation of white light into colours was discussed by *Marcus Marci*, professor of medicine at Prague

(1648), by *Grimaldi*, *Descartes*, *Hooke*, and others.[1] *Isaac Barrow*, Newton's teacher at Cambridge, held a theory resembling one of Marcus Marci, that red was strongly condensed light, that violet was strongly rarefied light. It remained for Newton to remove the cobwebs and point out the cause of dispersion.

In a darkened room he made a small circular opening in the shutter and placed the prism inside, near the hole, so that the light was refracted to the opposite wall. "Comparing the length of this coloured spectrum with its breadth, I found it about five times greater — a disproportion so extravagant, that it excited me to a more than ordinary curiosity of examining from whence it might proceed."[2]

Before reaching the right explanation he advanced several hypotheses, only to find that each was disproved by the facts. One of these guesses is of particular interest to the college students of to-day, as it shows that Newton's profound mind had dwelt upon a subject prominent in modern athletics, namely, the subject of "curved pitching." Surely the modern student would find it hard to guess what possible relation there might be supposed to exist between the performance of a twirler on the diamond and optical theories. Here is what Newton said: "Then I began to suspect, whether the rays, after their trajection through the prism, did not move in curve lines and according to their more or less curvity tend to divers parts of the wall. And it increased my suspicion, when I

---

[1] Pater Trigautius, in the description of his mission to China, narrates that prisms were highly valued for their colour effects, and were usually owned only by persons in high authority, and that a single piece sold for 500 pieces of gold. PRIESTLEY, *Gesch. d. Optik*, trans. by *G. S. Klügel*, Leipzig, 1776, p. 132.

[2] *Phil. Trans.*, Abr., Vol. I., p. 128. Newton sent this article to the Royal Society in 1672.

remembered that I had often seen a tennis ball struck with an oblique racket, describe such a curve line. For, a circular as well as a progressive motion being communicated to it by that stroke, its parts on that side, where the motions conspire, must press and beat the contiguous air more violently than on the other, and there excite a reluctancy and reaction of the air proportionably greater. And for the same reason, if the rays of light should possibly be globular bodies, and by their oblique passage out of one medium into another, acquire a circulating motion, they ought to feel the greater resistance from the ambient æther, on that side, where the motions conspire, and thence be continually bowed to the other. But notwithstanding this plausible ground of suspicion, when I came to examine it, I could observe no such curvity in them. And besides (which was enough for my purpose) I observed, that the difference betwixt the length of the image, and the diameter of the hole, through which the light was transmitted, was proportionable to their distance.

"The gradual removal of these suspicions at length led me to the *experimentum crucis*, which was this: I took two boards, and placed one of them close *behind the prism at the window*, so that the light might pass through a small hole, made in it for the purpose, and fall on the other board, which I placed at about twelve feet distance, having first made a small hole in it also, for some of that incident light to pass through. Then, I placed another prism behind the second board." On turning the first prism about its axis, the image which fell on the second board was made to move up and down upon that board, so that all its parts could successively pass through the hole in that board, and fall upon the prism behind it. The places where the light fell against the wall were noted. It was seen that the blue light, which was most refracted in the first prism, was also most refracted in the second prism, the red being least refracted in both prisms. "And so the true cause of the length of that image was detected to be no other than that light is not similar or homogeneal, but consists of *difform rays, some of which are more refrangible than others.*"[1] (See Fig. 12.)

When Newton made these experiments, he was interested in the improvement of the refracting telescope. The deficiencies noticed in that instrument had always been attributed to spherical aberration and the attempt was being made so to

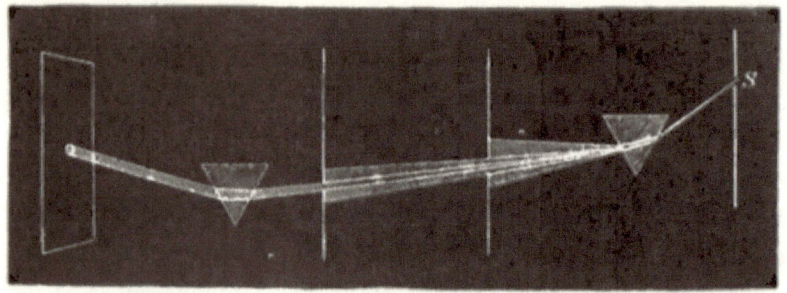

alter the spherical form of lenses as to give clear images. Newton satisfied himself that, besides spherical aberration, there was another source of trouble, namely, chromatic aberration. "The confused vision of objects seen through refracting bodies by heterogeneal light arises from the different refrangibility of several sorts of rays." (*Opticks*, Book I., Prop. V.) Could this evil be removed? Probably, if different substances possessed different dispersive powers. So Newton contrived an experiment. In a prismatic vessel filled with water (probably it was impregnated with *saccharum saturni* — sugar of lead),[2] he placed a glass prism and examined rays passing through. From his tests he thought he could conclude that re-

---

[1] *Phil. Trans.*, Abr., Vol. I., p. 130. These experiments are also described in Newton's *Opticks*, Book I., Props. I.-V.

[2] *Opticks*, p. 51; "Newton, Isaac," in *Dic. Nat. Biog.*

fraction must always be accompanied by dispersion. Achromatic lenses seemed to him an impossibility. Evidently, here Newton did not exercise his usual caution. He happened to have used a prism of glass and one of water of equal dispersive powers. Other liquids than his impregnated water would have given different results. From very limited experimental evidence he drew a broad inference, to which he adhered with marvellous tenacity, but which later experimenters have found to be erroneous.

Despairing of the possibility of producing achromatic refractors, he entered upon the design of reflectors. At that time, the reflecting telescope had been the subject of considerable attention. *Niccolò Zucchi* (1586–1670), a Jesuit in Rome, is considered the inventor of it. Another Jesuit, *Marin Mersenne*, in France, suggested a different type of reflector, as did also the Scotch mathematician and astronomer, *James Gregory* (1638–1675). But they did not carry out their designs. Newton constructed his first reflecting telescope in 1668. It was six inches long, had a diameter of one inch, and magnified 30 to 40 times. Later he made a larger instrument, which he presented to the Royal Society in 1672, with the inscription, "Invented by Sir Isaac Newton and made with his own hands, 1671." It was shown to the king and was examined by Robert Hooke, Christopher Wren, and others. It was greatly admired, and a description of it was sent to Huygens in Paris.[1] The telescope is preserved in the library of the Royal Society.

Newton's discoveries were well received by the Royal Society, but as soon as they were published in the *Philosophical Transactions* he was opposed by several critics, —

[1] H. SERVUS, *Gesch. d. Fernrohrs*, 1886, pp. 121–132 ; D. BREWSTER, *Life of Sir Isaac Newton*, New York, 1831, p. 40.

Linus, Lucas, Pardies, Hooke, Huygens. Newton was over sensitive to criticism, and in December 9, 1675, wrote to Leibniz, "I was so persecuted with discussions arising from the publication of my theory of light, that I blamed my own imprudence for parting with so substantial a blessing as my quiet, to run after a shadow."

Hooke upheld the undulatory theory of light as against Newton's corpuscular theory. Newton's reply to Hooke, as well as other papers communicated between 1672 and 1676, show that he had carefully weighed the arguments for and against each hypothesis. We can readily imagine how the young scientist pondered over the two rival theories; and when he hesitatingly rejected the wave theory, he little dreamed that his views would ever command such great authority, and bias the minds of physicists to such an extent as to delay for a whole century the acceptance of the true theory. Newton had experimented on colours formed by thin plates.[1] He saw plainly how the phenomena might be explained by the undulatory theory. "Since the vibrations which make blue and violet are supposed shorter than those which make red and yellow, they must be reflected at a less thickness of the plate; which is sufficient to explicate all the ordinary phenomena of those plates or bubbles, and also of all natural bodies, whose parts are like so many fragments of such plates. These seem to be the most plain, genuine, and necessary conditions of this hypothesis; and they agree so justly with my theory, that, if the animadversor think fit to apply them, he need not, on that account, apprehend a

---

[1] "Newton's Rings" are explained in NEWTON's *Opticks*, published in 1704, Book II., Obs. I. *et seq.* The colours of thin plates had been observed by Boyle and Hooke. The latter gave correct accounts of the leading phenomena as exhibited in the coloured rings in soap-bubbles and between plates of glass compressed together.

divorce from it; but yet, how he will defend it from other difficulties I know not."[1]   In Newton's mind the insuperable barrier to the acceptance of the wave theory, as it was developed at that time, was its inability to explain the rectilinear path of rays.   He says: "To me the fundamental supposition itself seems impossible, namely, that the waves or vibrations of any fluid can, like the rays of light, be propagated in straight lines, without a continual and very extravagant spreading and bending every way into the quiescent medium, where they are terminated by it.   I mistake if there be not both experiment and demonstration to the contrary."[2]   If light consisted of vibrations, it would, like sound, "bend into the shadow."

The emission theory, on the other hand, offered an easy explanation.   A luminous body emits streams of minute particles moving in straight lines, which cause vision by their impact on the retina.   Refraction was explained by assuming that the flying particle begins to be attracted towards the refracting surface when it comes very near, so that the component of its velocity along the normal is increased.   When the particle passes from a denser to a rarer medium, this component is decreased, while the component velocity perpendicular to the normal remains unaltered in both cases.   Thus the bending of the ray is explained.   As a consequence, the velocity of the particle is greater through the denser medium.[3]   The fact that, in a transparent substance, there exists both reflection and refraction was very difficult to explain on the emission theory.   How can a surface at one time refract and at

---

[1] *Phil. Trans.*, Abr., Vol. I., p. 145; quoted in G. PEACOCK, *Miscellaneous Works of the Late Thomas Young*, Vol. I., pp. 145, 146.

[2] *Phil. Trans.*, Abr., Vol. I., p. 146; *Miscellaneous Works of Thomas Young*, Vol. I., p. 152.

[3] NEWTON'S *Opticks*, 1704, Book II., Part III., Prop. X.

another time reflect an impinging particle? To account for this, Newton advanced the theory of "fits" of easy reflection and easy transmission, communicated to the particles by the all-pervading ether.[1] Observe that Newton's emission theory postulates the existence, not only of the flying particles constituting light, but also of an ether — all the mechanism needed for the wave theory, and more.

Newton gave an explanation of the rainbow, the correct outline of which had been given previously by Archbishop Antonius de Domini in a book published in 1611, as also by Descartes and Huygens.

Newton experimented also on diffraction ("inflection") of light. The discovery of this phenomenon was made by *Francesco Maria Grimaldi* (1618–1663), professor of mathematics at the Jesuit College in Bologna. It was described in his work, *Physico-mathesis de lumine*, 1666. Through a small hole Grimaldi introduced a pencil of light into a dark room. The shadow cast by a rod held in the cone of light was allowed to fall upon a white surface. To his surprise he found the shadow wider than the computed geometrical shadow; moreover, it was bordered by one, two, and sometimes three coloured bands. When the light was very strong, he saw, in addition, coloured bands inside the shadow itself. On replacing the rod by an opaque plate with a small hole in it, the illuminated circle was found larger than it should have been, on the supposition that the rays travelled past the edges of the hole in exactly straight lines. This and other experiments established the fact that light bends very slightly around a corner. He called the new phenomenon "diffraction."[2]

---

[1] *Opticks*, Book II., Part III., Prop. XIII. ; see also T. Preston, *The Theory of Light*, 2d ed., 1895, p. 19. Preston gives a good résumé of the emission theory.

[2] Rosenberger, Part II., pp. 131, 132.

Grimaldi's experiments were ably conducted, but he was unable to contribute anything substantial to their theory. Newton repeated Grimaldi's experiments in modified form and endeavoured to explain them by the emission theory.[1]

It is remarkable that Newton should have experimented so much with the solar spectrum and have failed to observe the Fraunhofer lines. We cannot attribute this failure to his introduction of light through a circular opening, for in some cases (Book I., Prop. IV., p. 49) he employed a narrow slit. It cannot be ascribed to his placing the prism close to the opening so as to receive upon it very divergent light, since in the case just referred to the prism was at a distance of 10 or 12 feet from the slit. The fact that he received the spectrum on paper would not necessarily debar him from seeing dark lines; at any rate, he sometimes "looked through the prism upon the hole" (Book I., Prop. II., Exp. 4, p. 22). In the experiment (p. 49), the conditions were about the same as those under which Wollaston later saw a few of the lines. Unfortunately, during the very experiments in which the discovery of the lines would have been easiest, Newton was obliged to rely on the observations of an assistant with "more critical" eyes than his own,[2] but who was probably less alert for unexpected phenomena.

HEAT

During the seventeenth century we witness the early development of the thermometer, a physical instrument which has enjoyed wider application than almost any other. Modern historical research concurs in ascribing its invention to

[1] See *Opticks*, Book III., pp. 113–137.

[2] Book I., Part II., Exp. 7, p. 92; see also an article on "Newton, Wollaston, and Fraunhofer Lines," by ALEXANDER JOHNSON in *Nature*, Vol. 26, 1882, p. 572.

Galileo.[1]   A glass bulb of the size of a hen's egg, with a long
stem of the thickness of a straw, and dipping into water, which
was made to rise part way up the tube by previous warming
of the bulb, constituted Galileo's first thermometer.   It was
affected, of course, by fluctuations of atmospheric pressure as
well as of temperature, and was really a thermo-baroscope.
Galileo's pupil, *Viviani*, gives 1593 as the date of the invention; *Castelli*, another pupil, says that in 1603 he saw Galileo
use it in experimental lectures.   All the early thermometers
contained air, and the stem was arbitrarily graduated.   Being
affected by changes in atmospheric pressure, Galileo's air
thermometer was very imperfect.

The first improvement was introduced by the French physician, *Jean Rey*,[2] who simply *inverted* Galileo's instrument, filling the bulb with water and the stem with air.   Thus, water
was made the thermometric substance.   On January 1, 1632,
he communicated this method to the great intermediary among
scientists, Pater Mersenne.   As Rey could not bring himself
to close the upper end of the stem, there was constant danger
of errors from evaporation of the water.   Schwenter says that
before 1636 artisans had succeeded in so choosing the relative
dimensions of bulb and stem, that the liquid rose and fell the
whole length of the stem in course of one year.

---

[1] E. Wohlwill, "Zur Geschichte der Erfindung und Verbreitung
des Thermometers," *Poggendorff's Annalen*, Vol. 124, 1865, pp. 163-
178; F. Burckhardt, *Die Erfindung des Thermometers und seine
Gestaltung im 17. Jahrhundert*.   Basel, 1867; E. Gerland, *Das Thermometer*, Berlin, 1885.   Of Gerland's publication we have made extensive
use.   The invention of the thermometer has been variously ascribed to
the famous mechanic, *Cornelius Drebbel* of Holland, to the anatomist,
Sanctorius of Padua, to *Father Paul* of Cracow, to the London physician,
Robert Fludd, to the German, *Otto von Guericke*.

[2] G. Hellmann in *Himmel und Erde*, Vol. II., p. 172; E. Gerland,
op. cit., p. 10.

To some minds the rise and fall of the thermometer presented an example of perpetual motion, and one writer actually called the instrument a *"perpetuum mobile* showing degrees of heat and cold."[1]

A quarter of a century after Rey's innovation, the idea of sealing the tube was carried out by the Florentine academicians, probably on the suggestion of Grand Duke Ferdinand II. of Tuscany. The tube was filled with spirit of wine and a graduated scale was attached to the stem.

These academicians, not more numerous than the muses, were pupils of Galileo, and made the *Accademia del Cimento* (academy of experiment) famous. In this small organization the spirit of Galileo revived for a time in Italy; but the society lasted only ten years, 1657–1667. What was the cause of this early dissolution? According to some writers,[2] *Leopold de' Medici*, the brother of the Grand Duke, and with him founder and patron of the organization, was given the cardinal's hat only on condition that the Academy be broken up. According to others[3] there arose dissensions among the members themselves.

Before the organization of this academy, the Italians had already done much for meteorology. Besides the invention of the thermometer and barometer, they invented the rain-gauge, first used by *Benedetto Castelli* in 1639.[4] The problem of selecting two fixed temperatures for the thermometer and of subdividing the interval into a suitable number of degrees was taken up by the *Accademia del Cimento*. Following the example of the philosophers and physicians, they chose as

[1] See E. Wohlwill, *op. cit.*, p. 169.

[2] Poggendorff, p. 351 ; Rosenberger, Part II., p. 162.

[3] Gerland, *op. cit.*, p. 45 ; also his article in *Wiedemann's Annalen,* Vol. IV., p. 604.

[4] G. Hellmann, *op. cit.*, p. 176.

fixed points the cold of winter and the heat of summer, dividing the intervening space into 80 or 40 equal spaces. To determine more accurately the position of these points, they defined the one to be the temperature of snow or ice in the severest frost, and the other to be the temperature in the bodies of cows and deer. The melting-point of ice was found by them to be invariable, and, in their medical scale, to be at $13\frac{1}{2}°$. In 1829 some of the Florentine thermometers were discovered among old glass-ware, and Libri actually found them to read $13\frac{1}{2}°$ in melting ice. They had been used in Florence sixteen years in meteorological observations, and by reducing the average temperature to one of the modern scales, and comparing with modern observations, Libri thought he could draw the inference that the climate of Florence had remained unaltered during the two hundred years.[1]

The fixed points chosen by the Florentine Academy did not prove satisfactory, and all sorts of improvements were suggested. *Dalencé* in 1688 adopted (1) the temperature of air during freezing, and (2) that of melting butter. The final adoption of the temperatures of melting ice and boiling water was not reached until the eighteenth century, though *Huygens* had recommended these as early as 1665.[2]

The Florentine thermometers became famous. They were introduced into England by Boyle. They reached France by way of Poland. An envoy of the Queen of Poland was presented in 1657 by the Grand Duke with thermometers and other instruments. Her secretary forwarded one of the thermometers to the astronomer *Ismaël Boulliau* in Paris and stated that "the Grand Duke always carries one in his pocket."[3] The

[1] Libri, *Poggendorff's Annalen*, Vol. 21, p. 325; see also Gerland, *Das Thermometer*, p. 45.

[2] E. Gerland, *Zeitschr. f. Instrk.*, Vol. 13, 1893, p. 390.

[3] Maze, *Comptes Rendus*, Vol. 121, 1895, p. 230.

thermometer was about one decimeter long and contained alcohol. Boulliau himself constructed in 1659 a thermometer in which mercury was used for the first time (so far as known) as a thermometric substance. Recently a record of temperature observations by Boulliau, extending from May, 1658, to September, 1660, has been found. Next to the Florentine record, begun in 1655, it is the oldest in existence.[1]

We are surprised to find that Newton's immediate predecessors had anticipated our modern theory of heat. *Heat a Mode of Motion* is the title of Tyndall's well-known work (1862), yet *Descartes, Amontons, Boyle, Francis Bacon, Hooke,* and *Newton* already looked upon heat as a mode of motion. Of course, in the seventeenth century, this theory rested upon somewhat slender experimental evidence, else the doctrine could hardly have been cast to the winds by the eighteenth-century philosophers. Boyle experimented on the mechanical production of heat and illustrated the heating due to arrested motion by such examples as the hammer driving a nail.

Boyle observed also the effects of atmospheric pressure on ebullition and experimented with freezing mixtures. Newton, in 1701, made a statement in the *Philosophical Transactions* which involves the hypothesis that the rate of cooling of a body is proportional to its excess of temperature over the surrounding medium.[2] This surmise has since been tested experimentally by *Dulong* and *Petit,* and has been shown to be true only within a small range of temperature.[3]

---

[1] MAZE, *Comptes Rendus*, Vol. 120, 1895, p. 732.
[2] MACH, *Princ. d. Wärmelehre*, p. 132.
[3] *Ann. de chim. et de Phys.* 2ᵉ, Vol. VII., 1817, pp. 225, 237.

ELECTRICITY AND MAGNETISM

The correction of Gilbert's error in asserting that magnetic declination "is constant at a given place," and the discovery of the "secular variation of the declination," is usually attributed to *Henry Gellibrand* (1597–1637), professor at Gresham College. He pointed out that in 1580, "*Mr. Burrows* (a man of unquestionable abilities in the mathematiques)" found the declination near London to be 11° 15' E.; that in 1622 *Edmund Gunter* found it to be at the same place 6° 13'; that in 1634 he himself found it to be not much more than 4° E.[1] This subject received the careful attention of *Edmund Halley* (1656–1742), who was professor at Oxford and later astronomer-royal. He endeavoured to explain magnetic variation by assuming four fixed magnetic poles. As this did not account for the facts, he supposed that the earth consisted of two concentric magnetic shells with poles differently placed and not coincident with the geographic poles, the inner shell rotating slowly. In 1698, William III. was induced to send Halley upon a long voyage on the Atlantic and Pacific oceans for the purpose of testing his hypothesis.[2] He came back, not with the desired proof, but with useful observations on "variation." About the beginning of the eighteenth century he constructed charts of equal variation (declination), which became famous. One of his original isogonic maps has been found recently in the British Museum. It seems that he published two totally distinct charts.[3]

---

[1] Consult HENRY GELLIBRAND, *A Discourse Mathematical on the Variation of the Magneticall Needle*, London, 1635. Reprinted in G. HELLMANN'S *Neudrucke*, No. 9, Berlin, 1897.

[2] BENJAMIN, p. 448.

[3] L. A. BAUER, "Halley's Earliest Equal variation Chart," *Terrestrial Magnetism*, Vol. I., 1896, p. 29; L. A. BAUER, *Nature*, May 23, 1895.

Some interesting observations were recorded in the *Philosophical Transactions* of 1676 and 1684 regarding the magnetic effects of lightning. Thus in 1681, a ship bound for Boston was struck by lightning. Observations of the stars showed that "the compasses were changed;" "the north point was turn'd clear south." The ship was steered to Boston with the compass reversed.[1]

Phenomena due to electric attraction and repulsion continued to interest and amuse investigators. Thus, *Boyle* observed that dry hair is easily electrified by friction. "That false locks of hair, brought to a certain degree of dryness, will be attracted by the flesh of some persons, I had proof in two beautiful ladies who wore them; for, at some times, I observed that they could not keep them from flying to their cheeks, and from striking there, tho' neither of them had occasion for or did use paint." One of the ladies "gave me leave to satisfy myself farther; and desiring her to hold her warm hand at a convenient distance from one of those locks taken off and placed in the free air, as soon as she did this, the lower end of the lock, which was free, applied itself presently to her hand."[2]

Again, Newton astonished the Royal Society by the description of an experiment with a round piece of glass set in a brass ring and supported by it about one-eighth of an inch from the table. "Rubbing a pretty while the glass briskly with some rough and raking stuff, till some very little fragments of very thin paper, laid on the table under the glass, began to be attracted and move nimbly to and fro . . . leaping up to the

---

It is worthy of remark that Halley constructed in 1686, and published in the *Philosophical Transactions*, 1688, No. 183, the earliest *wind map*. It is reprinted in HELLMANN's *Neudrucke*, No. 8, Berlin, 1897.

[1] E. HOPPE, *Entw. d. Lehre v. d. Elektricität bis auf Hauksbee*, Hamburg, 1887, p. 18.

[2] *Boyle's Works*, by PETER SHAW, 2d ed., London, 1738, Vol. I., p. 506 *et seq.*; E. HOPPE, *op. cit.*, p. 17.

glass and resting there awhile; then leaping down and resting there; then leaping up and perhaps down and up again."[1]

Otto von Guericke of Magdeburg generated electricity by holding his hands against a rotating sphere of sulphur. This once famous contrivance is the forerunner of the friction electric machine. He discovered electric induction and made a number of other interesting observations, but his speculations on electricity — his "mundane virtues" — were as unfortunate as were Gilbert's cosmological magnetic theories.

Boyle made an important experiment showing that electric attraction takes place through a vacuum. In 1676 *Picard*, while carrying one evening a mercury barometer from the observatory in Paris to the Porte Saint Michel, saw that each motion of the mercury caused a glow in the Torricellian vacuum. The cause of this light was attributed to a substance called mercurial phosphorus. This name was suggested by the new glow phenomena (phosphorescence) of phosphorus, which were then astonishing the scientific world. The origin of Picard's light was studied in England by *Francis Hauksbee*. He let air rush from above into a vacuum through a tube dipping into a basin of mercury under the bell-jar, and watched the air blowing the mercury up "with violence against the sides of the glass that held it, appearing all round as a body of fire, made up of abundance of glowing globules descending again into itself."[2] From this and other tests with mercury Hauksbee concluded that no light could be obtained without motion and without a partial vacuum. He observed that attraction accompanied the phenomena and concluded that the light is due to electricity. He was the first to show that an electric charge resides only on the surface of a body, and that metals may become electrified by friction.

[1] T. Birch, *Hist. of Royal Society*, Vol. III., London, 1757, p. 250; E. Hoppe, *op. cit.*, p. 14.

[2] *Phil. Trans.*, 1705, No. 303, p. 2129; Hoppe, *op. cit.*, p. 21.

SOUND

Vibratory strings were made the subject of investigation by *Galileo* and *Marin Mersenne.* Galileo pointed out the dependence of pitch upon the number of vibrations perceived in unit of time. Mersenne noticed that a string gives, besides its fundamental, two overtones. At Oxford, *William Noble* and *Thomas Pigott* showed by paper riders put at different places on a vibrating string that it vibrates not only as a whole, but also in halves, thirds, etc.[1] Mersenne determined the velocity of sound in air by the difference in time between the flash and the report of fire-arms at known distances. He got 1380 feet per second. *Pierre Gassendi* (1592–1655) used cannon as well as pistols, and disproved the peripatetic tenet that the velocity depends upon its source and its pitch. His test gave 1473 Paris feet. The illustrious members of the Paris Academy, D. Cassini, Picard, Römer, Huygens, found the value 1172 Paris feet per second.

Newton published in his *Principia* (Book II., Props. XLVIII., XLIX., L.) a theoretical deduction for the velocity of sound. He concluded that this velocity varied directly as the square root of the "elastic force," and inversely as the square root of the "density of the medium"; the velocity is "equal to that which heavy bodies acquire by falling with an equally accelerated motion, and in their fall describing half the altitude A," where A is the height of a homogeneous atmosphere, taken as 29,725 feet. This gave 979 feet as the velocity, while experiment indicated about 1142 English feet. Newton threw out conjectures as to the cause of the discrepancy between the experimental and theoretical values, but the true explanation was given over a century later by *Pierre Simon Laplace* (1749–1827). Newton failed to take into account the

---

[1] *Phil. Trans.*, 1677 ; HELLER, Vol. II., p. 339.

changes of elasticity due to the heat of compression and the
cold of rarefaction.   His expression amounts to $v = \sqrt{\dfrac{p}{d}}$;
Laplace's correction makes it $v = \sqrt{\dfrac{1.41\,p}{d}}$, where p is the
pressure of the air and d its density.

THE EIGHTEENTH CENTURY

THE progress of physics during the first eighty years of the seventeenth century was truly extraordinary. Nothing like it is seen during the earlier epochs of human history; nothing like it is exhibited during the eighteenth century. The names of Galileo, Guericke, Boyle, and Newton adorn the period when experiment assumed a place of supreme authority. In the eighteenth century there comes a reaction. On the whole, speculation is less effectively restrained and guided by experiment.

Another important cause makes the period less brilliant. It brought forth few great experimental physicists — none of such transcendent genius as Galileo, Huygens, Newton. Mathematics and mathematical astronomy were enriched during the eighteenth century by the remarkable researches of the Bernoullis, Euler, Clairaut, D'Alembert, Lagrange, Laplace, but physics proper was cultivated by men of more limited powers.

MECHANICS

The mechanical principles, as stated by Newton, suffice to explain any practical problem, whether in statics or dynamics. Nevertheless, it has been found convenient to deduce particular laws by which certain groups of problems may be treated by routine. As examples, we cite "D'Alembert's Principle" and the laws of the "Conservation of Momentum," "Conservation of the Centre of Gravity," "Conservation of Areas."

The eighteenth century has contributed much toward the development of these principles, enabling mechanical phenomena to be viewed from new standpoints. But their subjects, together with the analytical development of mechanics, lie outside the scope of this work.[1]

It only remains for us to mention the new contrivance, invented by *George Atwood* (1746–1807), for the study of the laws of falling bodies. Galileo had retarded the velocity of falling bodies by means of the inclined gutter, and thereby facilitated experimentation. Atwood accomplished this end by suspending two weights by a thread over an easily running pulley.

Atwood was a fellow and tutor of Trinity College, Cambridge, where his public lectures in experimental philosophy were remarkable both for the fluent ease of delivery and for the ingenuity of their experimental illustrations. His influence on the scientific studies of the university was great. As a writer he was less gifted than as a lecturer.[2] In 1784 he published a treatise *On the Rectilinear Motion and Rotation of Bodies*. The description of Atwood's machine, given therein, is not the earliest account of it made public. Atwood invented the machine several years previously, and a full account of it was given by *J. H. de Magellan*, a "gentil-homme Portugais" residing in England, in a letter addressed in French to A. Volta, professor at the University of Pavia, who had ordered a machine to be sent to him from England. The letter was printed in London in 1780.

---

[1] The reader may consult E. Mach, *The Science of Mechanics*, trans. by T. J. McCormack, Chicago, 1893; E. Dühring, *Krit. Gesch. d. allgem. Princ. d. Mechanik*, Leipzig, 1887.

[2] *Dic. Nat. Biog.* See also T. Young's *Misc. Works*, Vol. II., pp. 617–623.

LIGHT

During the seventeenth century we have witnessed a conflict between two theories of light. We have seen how Newton, from the facts then known, balanced the arguments for and against each theory and hesitatingly decided in favour of the emission theory, while on the continent his great contemporary, Huygens, advocated the wave theory. Says S. P. Langley, "These two great men, then, each looked around in the darkness as far as his light carried him. All beyond that was chance to each; and fate willed that Newton, whose light shone farther than his rival's, found it extend just far enough to show the entrance to the wrong way. He reaches the conclusion that we all know; one not only wrong in regard to light, but which bears pernicious results on the whole theory of heat, since light, being conceded to be material, radiant heat, if affiliated to light, must be regarded as material too; and Newton's influence is so permanent, that we shall see this strange conclusion drawn by the contemporaries of Herschel from his experiments made a hundred years later. It would seem then that the result of this unhappy corpuscular theory was more far-reaching than we commonly suppose." [1]

The history of physics affords two capital instances of the danger to science of placing excessive confidence in authority, no matter how great. The unscientific physical speculations of Aristotle held the world bound within their grasp for two thousand years; the unfortunate corpuscular theory of Newton controlled scientific thought for over a century. The philosophy of the eighteenth century was actually farther from the truth than that of Newton's predecessors. Newton's repute seemed to act like a spell. "The adoption of phlo-

[1] S. P. LANGLEY, *The History of a Doctrine*, 1888, p. 4, delivered at the Cleveland meeting of the A. A. A. S.

giston was, as we may reasonably infer, facilitated by it, and remotely Newton is perhaps also responsible in part for the doctrine of caloric a hundred years later.　After him, at any rate, there is a great backward movement."[1]

The only prominent writer of the eighteenth century who advocated the undulatory theory was *Leonhard Euler* (1707–1783).[2]　He advanced only theoretical considerations in its favour, and convinced no one.　In 1750 he published his *Lettres à une Princesse d'Allemagne sur quelques sujets de physique.* The German translator of this work thought it necessary to interpolate explanations, lest some innocent reader might be led to believe in a theory which was not held now (1792) " by a single physicist of prominence."[3]　Euler explained diversity in colours by the difference in duration of vibrations.　He made the conjecture that the different media of the eye had the property of preventing the dispersion of colours, and suggested that lenses be prepared out of two different substances, with the view of removing chromatic defects.　He had a theory as to how this might be done, but was not able actually to produce a lens free from colour.　This failure he attributed to the difficulty of accurate construction.　The only good which resulted from his efforts was this: he excited the curiosity of *Samuel Klingenstierna*, professor at Upsala, who began to repeat Newton's experiments on achromatism and arrived at results at variance with Newton's.　At this stage, *John Dollond*, a London optician, began a series of tests.　They, too, went contrary to Newton's.　Dollond then tested different kinds of glass, and in 1757 wrote a letter to Klingenstierna, in which he points out that the ratio of the sine of incidence to the sine of the

---

[1] S. P. LANGLEY, *The History of a Doctrine*, 1888, p. 5.

[2] Papers thereon appear in *Memoiren der Berliner Akademie*, 1746, 1752.

[3] ROSENBERGER, *I. Newton u. s. Physik. Princ.*, 1895, p. 332.

mean angle of refraction is 1.53 for crown glass and 1.583 for flint glass.[1] Hence he concluded that achromatism must be possible in lenses. The practical realization of this idea proved to be difficult and required (to use his own words) "a resolute perseverance."[2] In 1758 he at last succeeded, and presented an achromatic telescope to the Royal Society. It created a sensation throughout Europe. Dollond's success seemed to disprove Euler's theory of dispersion and caused him much embarrassment. "If my theory is right," Euler says, "then it follows that Mr. Dollond's object-lenses are not free from dispersion of colours, to which, however. Mr. Short explicitly testifies. It is as difficult for me to call in question so solemn a testimony, as it is to give up a theory which seems to be so well founded."[3] For some time he persisted in the belief that experiments with Dollond's objectives, made in the dark, would show colour effects.

After Dollond's death, in 1761, his son, *Peter Dollond*, manufactured (in partnership with the mechanic Ramsden) refractors of great merit. After repeated failures, achromatic lenses came to be applied successfully also to microscopes.

The achromatic telescope greatly facilitated the growth of modern astronomy. How great an advantage was secured becomes the more apparent when we remember that Huygens's method of removing colour effects by the use of lenses of great focal length led to the construction by him of very long tubeless refractors (the objectives being mounted on high poles), which were exceedingly clumsy and at the same time yielded inferior optical results. One object lens presented by him to the Royal Society had a focal length of 123 feet.

When Dollond's telescopes had become famous, the claims

---

[1] H. Servus, *Geschichte des Fernrohrs*, 1886, p. 83.
[2] Consult *Phil. Trans.*, Vol. 50, 1758, p. 733.
[3] *Mem. d. Berliner Akademie*, 1762, p. 260 ; Servus, *op. cit.*, p. 85,

of another man were laid before the public. As early as 1729 *Chester More Hall*, of More Hall in Essex, while studying the mechanism of the human eye, was led to the design of lenses without colour. He employed several working opticians to grind his lenses, and several object-glasses were completed. But he never published any account of his labours. Perhaps he kept them secret, hoping to perfect his instruments still further. At any rate the invention was *lost*, and Dollond's work was independent of Hall's.[1]

Contemporaneous with the early development of the achromatic telescope is the construction of large reflecting telescopes. Again England displayed superior skill. In 1723, about half a century after Newton made his reflectors, *John Hadley* presented to the Royal Society an instrument six feet long. It equalled in performance the Huygenian refractor 123 feet in length! Further progress in the design of concave mirrors was made by *James Short* of Edinburgh, and especially by *William Herschel* (1738–1822). To improve the "space-penetrating power" Herschel increased the light-gathering power by the use of larger mirrors. He experimented in the shaping and polishing of concave mirrors with an enthusiasm and skill never surpassed. Mirrors of 10, 20, 30 feet, and finally one of 40 feet focal length, left his hands. The last, completed in 1789, was four feet in diameter and weighed 2500 pounds. The telescope led to Herschel's discovery of the two Saturnian satellites nearest to the ring. Only two reflectors larger than this have ever been constructed. In 1745 was completed by *Lord Rosse* at Parsonstown in Ireland a gigantic reflector, with a mirror six feet across and a tube

[1] D. BREWSTER, *Life of Sir I. Newton,* New York, 1831, pp. 64–67. For further details on Hall and achromatism, consult the article "Telescope" in the *Encyclopædia Britannica,* 9th ed., and the article "Optics" in the *Edinburgh Encyclopædia,* p. 607, note.

58 feet long and seven feet in diameter. So large was this tube that Dean Peacock walked through it once with uplifted umbrella.[1] This "light-grasper" displayed celestial objects with extraordinary splendour. "Never in my life," exclaims Sir James South, "did I see such glorious siderial pictures!" The second large reflector, with a mirror over 61 inches in diameter, is now being finished for the University of America in Washington.

There are two objections to reflecting telescopes which have not yet been successfully overcome. The great weight of a large speculum mirror makes it liable to distortion. The delicate lustre of its surface cannot be preserved permanently, and must be restored by the difficult operation of repolishing.[2]

HEAT

Guillaume Amontons (1663–1705) effected in 1702 an improvement of Galileo's air thermometer. In his youth Amontons became deaf; but this was not regarded by him as an affliction, since it permitted scientific pursuits with less molestation from the outer world. He held a government position in Paris. His air thermometer was of constant volume and consisted of a U-shaped tube with the shorter arm ending in a bulb and the longer measuring 45 inches. Degrees of temperature were

[1] A. M. CLERKE, *A Popular History of Astronomy*, New York, 1893, pp. 145, 147.

[2] Consult further the history of the telescope by C. S. HASTINGS in *Smithsonian Report*, 1892 ; also GEORGE E. HALE, "On the Comparative Value of Refracting and Reflecting Telescopes for Astrophysical Investigations," *Astrophysical Journal*, Vol. V., 1897, pp. 119–131. Students interested in the history of *anamorphosis* during the sixteenth and seventeenth centuries may consult H. RTOSS, "Geschichte der optischen und katoptrischen anamorphosen," *Zeitsch. d. Math. u. Phys.*, Vol. 39, 1894, Hist. Lit. Abth., p. 1.

indicated by the height (in inches) of the mercury column in the longer arm necessary to keep the volume constant. The instrument was intended as a standard, by which a mercury thermometer in Paris, say, could be compared with one in St. Petersburg without the necessity of transmitting thermometers from one place to the other. But the invention met with little favour. He chose the boiling-point of water as a fixed point, but, being unaware of the dependence of the boiling-point upon air pressure, he could not attain extreme accuracy.[1] It is an interesting fact that Amontons's researches amount to an experimental proof of the law of gases now named after Charles and Gay-Lussac, and that he first arrived at the notion of absolute temperature. "It appears," says he, "that the extreme cold of this thermometer is that which would reduce the air by its spring to sustain no load at all, which would be a degree of cold much more considerable than what is esteemed very cold." From Amontons's data the absolute zero in our centigrade scale is found to be $-239.5°$. Lambert, who repeated Amontons's experiments with greater accuracy,[2] obtained data yielding $-270.3°$. The value now accepted is $-272.8°$. Lambert uses this language: "Now a degree of heat equal to zero is really what may be called absolute cold. Hence at absolute cold the volume of the air is zero, or as good as zero. That is to say, at absolute cold the air falls together so compactly that its parts absolutely touch, that it becomes, so to speak, water-proof."

Stimulated by Amontons's researches *Gabriel Daniel Fahren-*

---

[1] E. GERLAND, "Ueber Amontons' und Lambert's Verdienste um die Thermometrie," *Zeitsch. f. Instrumentenkunde*, Vol. VIII., 1888, pp. 319–322. Abstract given in POSKE's *Zeitschrift*, Vol. II., 1889, pp. 142, 143.

[2] LAMBERT, *Pyrometrie*, Berlin, 1779, p. 29; E. GERLAND, *Instrumentenkunde*, Vol. VIII., p. 322.

heit (1686–1736) began to study the accurate construction of thermometers. He was a native of Danzig, but went to Amsterdam to secure a business education; he became interested in physics, and travelled in England, Denmark, and Sweden. He was a manufacturer of meteorological instruments. That he attained considerable celebrity is evident from his election to the Royal Society of London in 1724. The same year he contributed to the *Philosophical Transactions* five short papers in Latin. Therein he revealed for the first time his process of making thermometers.[1] Fahrenheit was in communication with Olaf Römer, whom he probably visited in Copenhagen. During the cold winter of 1709 both are said to have taken records of temperatures.

Fahrenheit was greatly interested in Amontons's observations of the constancy of the boiling-point (previously observed by Huygens, Newton, and Halley). Curious to know how other liquids would behave, he made a series of tests, and found that, like water, each had a fixed boiling-point.[2] Later he noticed that the boiling-point varied with a change in atmospheric pressure.[3] Attention to this fact contributed vastly towards exact thermometry. Fahrenheit deserves great credit for first bringing about the general use of mercury in thermometers. (The earliest mercury-in-glass thermometer, it will be remembered, is due to Ismaël Boulliau, 1659.) The success of Fahrenheit's mercury thermometers was largely due to a method which he invented for cleaning the mercury.

Fahrenheit made two kinds of thermometers, — the one filled

---

[1] The five papers, together with articles on thermometry by Réaumur and Celsius, are brought out in German translation in *Ostwald's Klassiker*, No. 57, Leipzig, 1894.

[2] *Phil. Trans.*, Vol. 30, 1724, pp. 1–3 ; *Ostwald's Klass.*, No. 57, p. 3.

[3] *Phil. Trans.*, Vol. 33, pp. 179, 180 ; *Ostwald's Klass.*, No. 57, p. 17.

with spirit of wine, the other with mercury. Various lengths were chosen for the stem. In 1724 he wrote as follows: "The scale of those thermometers which are used only in meteorological observations begins with 0 and ends with 96. This scale depends upon the determination of three fixed points, which are obtained as follows: the first, the lowest, ... is found by a mixture of ice, water, and sal-ammoniac or sea salt; if the thermometer is dipped in this mixture, then the liquid falls to the point marked 0. This experiment succeeds better in winter than in summer. The second point is obtained, if water and ice are mixed without the salts just mentioned; if the thermometer is dipped in this mixture, it will stand at 32° ...; the third point is at the 96th degree, and the alcohol expands to that point if the thermometer be held in the mouth or armpit of a healthy person." [1]

His earliest thermometers were constructed differently. Taking only two fixed points, the first and last points mentioned above, he divided the interval in 180 equal parts, but he placed 0 half-way between, so that there were 90° to the upper and 90° to the lower fixed point. After about 1714 he divided the interval into 24 equal parts. According to his contemporary, Boerhave, this change was made on Römer's suggestion. The 0 was placed this time at the lower fixed point. The degrees, being found too large, were subdivided into four parts. Thereby the fixed points came to be designated 0 and 96, respectively. It is not unlikely that he used the melting temperature of ice as a "check," to see whether his alcohol thermometers gave consistent readings for intervening points. This would explain how it happened that, unlike every one else, he had three fixed points. Later, when he began to use mercury, he took, in place of the temperature

---

[1] *Ostwald's Klassiker*, No. 57, pp. 6, 7.

of the human body, the boiling-point of water. On his scale
this *happened to be at* 212°.[1]

While the Fahrenheit thermometers were adopted by the
Dutch and English, other nations were slow to appreciate
their value. In France Réaumur designed thermometers.
*René Antoine Ferchault, Seigneur Réaumur, des Angles et de la
Bermodière* (1683–1757), was born at Rochelle and died at
Bermodière. He is known for his researches in zoölogy,
botany, and physics. He was not familiar with Fahrenheit's
achievements. Dissatisfied with Amontons's air thermometer
(the only thermometer which he considered at all fit for use)
and strongly opposed to the use of mercury on account of
its small coefficient of expansion, he endeavoured to construct
instruments with spirit of wine which should be convenient
and yet reach the desired degree of accuracy. His experiments accidentally led to the beautiful observation of the contraction in volume which may result on the mixing of liquids.[2]
He found that spirit of wine (mixed with ¼ water) expanded
between the freezing and the boiling temperatures of water
from 1000 to 1080 volumes; so he divided the intervening
distance on the stem into 80 parts. But Réaumur's thermometers did not turn out well. All sorts of incredible
readings were reported, and different instruments did not
agree. *Jean Antoine Nollet* endeavoured to improve Réaumur's
thermometers, but more was achieved by *Jean André Deluc*
(1727–1817) of Geneva. He returned to the use of mercury,
and emphasized its advantages by arguments so powerful, that

---

[1] E. GERLAND, *Das Thermometer*, Berlin, 1885, pp. 14, 15. For further
details on Fahrenheit's career, see ALBERT MOMBER in *Altpreussische
Monatsschrift*, Vol. 24 (*Provinzialblätter*, Vol. 89), Königsberg, 1887,
pp. 138–156.

[2] *Ostwald's Klassiker*, No. 57, pp. 100–116, 127. Réaumur's three
articles on thermometers appear in German translation on pages 19–116.

a physicist enthusiastically exclaimed, "Surely nature has given us this mineral for the making of thermometers."[1]

On the other hand *Micheli du Crest*, another scientist of Geneva, had no use for mercury, except to *calibrate* capillary tubes. He and *De l'Isle* in St. Petersburg introduced this process about the same time.[2] In 1757 Du Crest raised the boiling-point of alcohol by subjecting it to the pressure of air enclosed in the upper enlarged end. He anticipated Celsius in the design of a centesimal scale. Rejecting the temperature of freezing water as a fixed point, he chose the temperature of the earth as determined in the cellar at the Paris Observatory, 84 feet deep. This was not a new idea with him. Boyle referred to the constancy of temperature in deep cellars. For thermometric purposes this temperature was first used by Dalencé. Du Crest divided the interval between this and the boiling-point into 100 steps, and thereby obtained degrees agreeing closely with Réaumur's. Part of his physical researches was carried on during his twenty years of political imprisonment.

Centigrade scales were adopted after Du Crest by Celsius and Strömer. *Andreas Celsius* (1701–1744) was professor of astronomy at Upsala. His researches are mainly astronomical. A publication of 1742[3] contains the description of his thermometer, with 100 divisions between the freezing- and the boiling-point of water. The latter point was marked 0°, the former 100°. The inversion of the scale, making the freezing-point 0° and the boiling-point 100°, was effected eight years

---

[1] DELUC, *Recherches sur les Modifications de l'Atmosphère*, Genève, 1772, p. 330. E. GERLAND, *op. cit.*, p. 20.

[2] J. H. GRAF, *Das Leben und Wirken des Physikers und Geodäten Jacques Barthélemy Micheli du Crest*, Bern, 1890, p. 114.

[3] *Abhandl. d. schwedisch. Akademie*, Vol. IV., pp. 197-205; trans. in *Ostwald's Klass.*, No. 57, pp. 117-124.

later by *Mārten Strömer,* a colleague of Celsius. The final form of our modern centigrade scale is, therefore, not that of Celsius, but that of Strömer.[1] The number of different thermometric scales in actual use in the eighteenth century increased greatly. *George Martine* in 1740 mentions 13 of them; *J. H. Lambert* in 1779 enumerates 19.[2] All but three of them have passed into oblivion. Would that the centigrade scale were the sole survivor! In England and America the Fahrenheit scale predominates; in Germany the Réaumur; in France the Celsius. Among scientific men the last has found almost universal acceptance.

The earliest thermometer depending on the expansion and contraction of metallic rods was invented about 1747 by *Pieter van Musschenbroek* of Leyden. It was improved by *Jean Théophile Desaguliers.* About thirty-five years later came the pyrometer of *Josiah Wedgwood,*[3] by which the high temperatures of a furnace were measured by the diminution in bulk of a block prepared from a pure fire-clay according to certain directions.[4]

In 1705 there was invented the first important device for the practical application of steam power. For over 1000 years after Heron's eolipile no progress had been made. During the

---

[1] Unless indeed the credit of inversion be given also to *Christin,* a professor in Lyons. See *Poggendorff's Annalen,* Vol. 157, 1876, p. 352. Celsius and Strömer may have been prompted to make their improvements in thermometry by the botanist *Linné,* who once wrote in a letter, " I was the first who planned to make our thermometers in which 0 is the freezing-point and 100 the degree of boiling water." *Comptes Rendus,* Vol. 18, p. 1063. It will be remembered that the earliest suggestion of the use of these temperatures as fixed points was made by Huygens.

[2] MARTINE, *Essays medical and philosophical,* London, 1740; LAMBERT, *Pyrometrie,* Berlin, 1779.

[3] *Phil. Trans.,* Vol. 72, 1782; Vol. 74, 1784.

[4] G. T. HALLOWAY, "The Evolution of the Thermometer," *Science Progress,* Vol. IV., 1895–1896, p. 417.

seventeenth century steam-fountains were designed, but they were merely modifications of Heron's engine, and were probably applied only for ornamental purposes.[1] Some effort was also made by Morland, Papin, and Savery to construct practical machines for the raising of water or driving of mill-works. The first successful attempt to combine the principles and forms of mechanism then known into an economical and convenient machine was made by *Thomas Newcomen*, a blacksmith of Dartmouth, England. It is probable that he knew of Savery's engine; Savery lived only fifteen miles from the residence of Newcomen. Assisted by John Calley, Newcomen constructed an engine — an "atmospheric steam-engine." A patent was secured in 1705. In 1711 such a machine was set up at Wolverhampton for the raising of water. Steam passing from the boiler into the cylinder held the piston up against the external atmospheric pressure until the passage between the cylinder and boiler was closed by a cock. Then the steam in the cylinder was condensed by a jet of water. A partial vacuum was formed and the air above pressed the piston down. This piston was suspended from one end of an overhead beam, the other end of the beam carrying the pump-rod. Desaguliers tells the story that a boy, Humphrey Potter, who was charged with the duty of opening and closing the stop-cock between the boiler and cylinder for every stroke, contrived by catches and strings an automatic motion of the cock.[2] The fly-wheel was introduced in 1736 by Jonathan Hulls. The next great improvements were introduced in Scotland by *James Watt* (1736–1819). He was educated as a mathematical instrument maker. In 1760 he opened a shop in Glasgow. Becoming interested in the steam-engine and its history, he began to

[1] R. H. Thurston, *A History of the Growth of the Steam-engine*, New York, 1893, p. 20.

[2] Thurston, *op. cit.*, p. 61.

experiment in a scientific manner. He took up chemistry and was assisted in his studies by Dr. Black, the discoverer of "latent heat."[1] Observing the great loss of heat in the New-comen engine due to the cooling of the cylinder by the jet of water at every stroke, he began to think of means to keep the cylinder "always as hot as the steam that entered it." He has told us how, finally, the happy thought securing this end occurred to him: "I had gone to take a walk on a fine Sabbath afternoon. I had entered the Green by the gate at the foot of Charlotte Street, and had passed the old washing-house. I was thinking upon the engine at the time, and had gone as far as the herd's house, when the idea came into my mind that, as steam was an elastic body, it would rush into a vacuum, and, if a communication were made between the cylinder and an exhausted vessel, it would rush into it, and might be there condensed without cooling the cylinder."[2] The piston was now moved by the expansion of steam, not by air pressure, as in Newcomen's engine. Watt introduced a separate con-denser, a steam-jacket, and other improvements. He de-servedly commands a preëminent place among those who took part in the development of the steam-engine.

During the previous century the leading scientists saw more or less clearly that heat was due to molecular motion. But this correct view was finally abandoned in the eighteenth century in favour of a materialistic theory. We have here a good illustration of the fact that the path of science is not always in a forward direction — not always like the march of an army toward some definite end. Says Langley, "I believe this comparison of the progress of science to that of an army, which obeys an impulse from one head, has more error than

---

[1] THURSTON, op. cit., p. 83. Then, and for a long time after, the study of heat was taken up in chemistry, not in physics.

[2] THURSTON, op. cit., p. 87.

truth in it; and, though all similes are more or less mislead-ing, I would prefer to ask you to think rather of a moving crowd, where the direction of the whole comes somehow from the independent impulses of its individual members; not wholly unlike a pack of hounds, which, in the long run, per-haps, catches its game, but where, nevertheless, when at fault, each individual goes his own way, by scent, not by sight, some running back and some forward; where the louder-voiced bring many to follow them, nearly as often in the wrong path as in the right one; where the entire pack even has been known to move off bodily on a false scent." [1]

The earliest traces of the theory that heat is matter are found in ancient Greece among Democritus and Epicurus. In modern times it was advocated by *Pierre Gassendi* (1592–1655), who was at one time professor of mathematics at the *Collège Royal* in Paris. He was a man of ability, but in physics his efforts were speculative rather than experimental.[2] The acceptance of the theory that heat is a material agent was facilitated through the previous introduction by *Georg Ernst Stahl* (1660–1734), professor at the University of Halle, of the erroneous theory of combustion, according to which a burning body gave off a substance called "phlogiston." One such agent paved the way for the other. In 1738 the French Academy of Sciences offered a prize question on the nature of heat. The winners of the prize (Euler was one of the three) favoured the materialistic theory.[3] At first the only properties postu-lated for this material agent, called heat, were that it was highly elastic and that its particles repelled each other. By this repulsion the fact that hot bodies give off heat could be

---

[1] S. P. LANGLEY, *op. cit.*, p. 2.

[2] G. BERTHOLD, *Rumford und d. Mech. Wärmetheorie*, Heidelberg, 1875, pp. 2–5.

[3] BERTHOLD, *op. cit.*, p. 6.

explained. Later it was assumed that the heat particles attracted ordinary matter, and that this heat was distributed
among bodies in quantities proportional to their mutual attractions (or their capacities for heat). By the close of the
eighteenth century this theory met with almost universal
acceptance. Marat, afterwards famous as a leader in the
French Revolution, gave in 1780 an exposition of this theory
by starting from Newton's corpuscular theory of light. It
was first vigorously attacked by an American, Count Rumford,
but as late as 1856 it received preference over the dynamic
theory in the article "Heat" in the *Encyclopædia Britannica*
(8th edition).

In spite of erroneous theories some new facts were found
out regarding heat. Black discovered what he termed "latent
heat" and "capacity for heat" (specific heat). *Joseph Black*
(1728–1799) was born at Bordeaux, where his father, a native
of Belfast, was settled as a wine merchant. He was professor
at Glasgow, and at Edinburgh after 1766. He is well known
as the founder of pneumatic chemistry.

In 1756 he began to meditate over the perplexing slowness
with which ice melts and water is dissipated in boiling. He
finally concluded that a large quantity of heat is consumed
simply in bringing about these changes of state, without even
the least alteration in temperature, and that the cause of this
disappearance is a quasi-chemical combination between the
particles of the substance and the subtle fluid called heat.
According to his view this heat was "latent"; according to
the modern view there is no "latent heat," but a transformation of energy takes place, the energy in form of heat becoming potential energy conferred on the material particles.[1]
Modern students need not feel disheartened over their failure

---

[1] *Dic. of Nat. Biog.*

to obtain at once accurate values for the heat of vaporization of water. The famous Black and his pupil, Irvine, obtained 417, later 450; the true value (at standard atmospheric pressure) being 536. For the heat of fusion he obtained by the method of mixtures 77.8, the more accurate value being 80.03 (Bunsen).

During Black's lifetime his great discoveries on heat remained unpublished, but after 1761 he explained them in his lectures, dwelling with sedate eloquence on the beneficent effects of the arrangement in checking and regulating the processes of nature.[1] His discoveries not only formed the basis of calorimetry, but they gave the first impulse to Watt's improvements in the steam-engine.

Disliking the publicity of authorship, Black did not vindicate his claims to priority. As might be expected, the same ideas were worked out by others. *Jean André Deluc* in Paris and *Johann Karl Wilke* in Sweden worked along the same lines.

The great chemist, *Antoine Laurent Lavoisier* (1743–1794), guillotined during the French Revolution, may be regarded as a disciple of Black. In conjunction with *Pierre Simon Laplace* (1749–1827), Lavoisier determined, about 1783, the specific heats of a number of substances. They designed the instrument now known as Laplace's ice calorimeter, but Black and Wilke had employed the method of the ice calorimeter before them.[2]

---

[1] *Dic. Nat. Biog.*

[2] Lavoisier and Laplace's joint papers appear in *Mémoires de l'Académie*, 1780, p. 355 (actually printed three or four years after this date). They are reprinted in German translation in *Ostwald's Klassiker*, No. 40. The reference to Wilke is on p. 22 of this reprint.

ELECTRICITY AND MAGNETISM

No branch of physics was cultivated during the eighteenth century so successfully as electricity. Research was confined to electro-statics until about 1790, when the study of current electricity began.

Stephen Gray (?-1736), a pensioner at the Charterhouse, England, discovered that the difference in electric conductivity depends, not upon the colour of objects or some similar quality, but on the material of which bodies are composed. Thus, metal wire conducts; silk does not. He demonstrated that the human body is a conductor, and was the first to electrify a human being (1730). A boy was suspended in the air by silken strings. Later Gray observed that conductors can be insulated by placing them on cakes of resin.

In France, Gray's experiments attracted the attention of *Charles François de Cisternay du Fay* (1698-1739), who had been educated as a soldier but devoted his maturer years to scientific pursuits. Experimentation led him to the unexpected conclusion that all bodies admit of being electrified; in other words, that all bodies possess the property which for ages was supposed to be peculiar to amber. Hence the classification of bodies (introduced by Gilbert) into "electrics" (capable of being electrified by friction) and "non-electrics" (not possessing this property) was found to have no foundation in fact. Du Fay noticed the discharging power of flames. Suspending himself by silk cords, in the manner taught by Gray, he observed that when he was electrified and another person came near, there issued from his body pricking shoots, making a crackling noise. In the dark these shoots were so many sparks of fire. "The Abbé Nollet says he shall never forget the surprise which the first electrical spark which was ever drawn from the human body excited, both in Mr. Du Fay and in himself." [1]

Du Fay discovered that there are two kinds of electricity, which he named the *vitreous* and the *resinous*. Later the same observation was made independently by *Ebenezer Kinnersley* of Philadelphia. To explain electric attraction and repulsion Du Fay postulated the existence of two fluids which are separated by friction and which neutralize each other when they combine. This is the earliest important attempt at a theory of electric phenomena. It was elaborated more fully as a rival of Franklin's one-fluid theory by the Englishman *Robert Symmer*.

Considerable attention was paid at this time to the perfection of the electric friction machine. It assumed a supreme importance in laboratories, until finally it was supplanted by the influence machines of Holtz and Töpler. For Hauksbee's glass globe, *Andrew Gordon* in Erfurt substituted a glass cylinder. *Martin Planta* of Grison, Switzerland, and later the optician *Jesse Ramsden*, of London, introduced circular glass plates. In place of the dry palm of the hand, held against the rotating glass, *Johann Heinrich Winkler* of Leipzig prepared a leather cushion rubber, which was pressed against the glass by a spring. *John Canton*, in 1762, secured still better results by applying tin amalgam to the rubber. [2]

About 1745 electric experimentation became so popular that in Holland and Germany public exhibitions were given. Many persons experimented for their own amusement. Among these was *Ewald Georg von Kleist* (died 1748), dean of the cathedral in Camin, Pomerania. Once, in 1745, he endeavoured to charge a bottle by conduction. He observed that, when he held in

---

[1] PRIESTLEY, *Hist. of Elect.*, London, 1775, p. 47.

[2] For drawings of various machines, see G. ALBRECHT, *Gesch. d. Electricität*, 1885, pp. 20–30; PRIESTLEY, *Hist. of Elect.*, Plates IV.–VIII.

his hand a small phial with a nail in it and electrified the nail by contact with the conductor of a machine, the nail became so strongly electrified that by touching it with the other hand he received a shock which stunned his arms and shoulders. The same discovery was made in 1746 in a similar manner at Leyden, Holland. *Pieter van Musschenbroek* (1692–1761), in his day a renowned physicist, attempted to electrify water in a bottle. At a trial, *Cunaeus*, one of his friends, held the bottle in one hand, and after a while proceeded with the other hand to remove the wire connecting the water to the prime conductor. He was surprised by a sudden shock in his arms and breast. Thus was discovered what we now call the " Leyden jar."[1] Musschenbroek repeated the experiment and then wrote to Réaumur "that he would not take another shock for the kingdom of France." More heroic sentiments were expressed by Professor Bose of Wittenberg. He wished he might die by the electric shock, that the account of his death might furnish an article for the memoirs of the French Academy of Sciences.[2]

The invention of the Leyden jar gave still greater *éclat* to electricity. In almost every country of Europe numbers of persons gained a livelihood by going about and showing the experiments. Winkler of Leipzig proved that Von Kleist was wrong in supposing that the human body played an essential part in the discharge of the jar. He pointed out that any conductor connecting the inside coating to the outside fully answered the purpose.

Musschenbroek's letter to Réaumur did not deter French philosophers from experimentation. *Abbé Nollet,* who in

---

[1] According to another account, Cunaeus made this discovery at his home, while endeavouring to repeat some experiments he had seen Musschenbroek perform.

[2] PRIESTLEY, *op. cit.,* p. 86.

France was even more celebrated than was Musschenbroek in
Holland, repeated the Leyden jar experiments on himself.
He then, in the King's presence, passed the discharge through
180 guards. Later the Carthusian monks at the convent in
Paris were formed into a line 900 feet long, by means of iron
wires between every two persons, and the whole company,
upon the discharge of the jar, gave a sudden spring at the
same instant. This behaviour of the austere monks must have
been ludicrous in the extreme. Experimenters in France and
elsewhere killed birds and other animals by the discharge of
the Leyden jar; they passed the discharge long distances
through water across rivers and lakes; they magnetized
needles by it and melted thin wire. The discovery of the
Leyden jar was hailed as a great advance in science. No
doubt its importance was at the time overestimated.

Some of the boldest researches and profoundest theories of
the eighteenth century were soon to be advanced in far-off
America by *Benjamin Franklin* (1706–1790). Although in his
youth only a printer's apprentice, he developed into a man of
unusual powers, not only in the fields of politics and diplo-
macy, but also in physical research. At the age of forty he
happened to see Dr. Spence from Scotland perform some
electrical experiments at Boston. The subject was new to
him. After returning to Philadelphia the Library Company
in that city received from *Peter Collinson*, a London merchant
and member of the Royal Society, a glass tube, with instruc-
tions how to use it in electrical experiments. Franklin's
curiosity having been excited, he began to read Watson's experiments, and also to experiment for himself.[1] In his first

---

[1] *Works of Benjamin Franklin*, edited by JARED SPARKS, Boston, 1837,
Vol. V., pp. 173–180. This volume contains Franklin's famous letters on
electricity ; also an appendix containing letters by various scientific men
respecting Franklin's discoveries.

letter to Collinson, March 28, 1747, he expresses thanks for the "electric tube," and says: "I never was before engaged in any study that so totally engaged my attention and my time as this has lately done."[1] His home came to be frequented by curiosity seekers. There was formed a small group of investigators, consisting of *Franklin, Ebenezer Kinnersley, Thomas Hopkinson,* and *Philip Sing.* In the next letter to Collinson, July 11, 1747, Franklin describes the "wonderful effect of pointed bodies, both in drawing off and throwing off the electrical fire." This action of points had been observed by others, but Franklin was the first fully to realize its importance and to put it to use.

This same letter contains Franklin's theory of electricity, which explained phenomena more satisfactorily than any other proposed up to that time. He supposed that "electric fire is a common element," existing in all bodies. If a body acquired more than its normal share, it was called "plus"; if less, it was designated "minus." Thus, instead of Du Fay's two-fluid theory, Franklin advocated a one-fluid theory. To him we owe the terms "plus" and "minus," or "positive" and "negative" electricity. This material theory held its own until the times of Faraday and Maxwell. Since then we have become quite convinced that electricity is not matter. Franklin explained the charged Leyden jar as containing on one coating an excess of the fluid, "a plenum of electrical fire," and on the other a "vacuum of the same fire," but really containing no more electricity than before charging.[2] He showed experimentally that "the whole force of the bottle and power of giving a shock is in the glass itself" (p. 201).

In 1748 Franklin sold his printing house, newspaper, and almanac, with the view of retiring from business and devoting

---

[1] *Works*, Vol. V., p. 181.   [2] *Ibidem*, p. 191.

all his time to electrical experiments. He equipped himself
with new apparatus. His friend Kinnersley proved that the
Leyden phial can be as easily electrified by sparks passing to
the outside as to the inside (p. 197). In 1749 Franklin states
in a letter to Collinson that "hot weather is coming on, when
electrical experiments are not so agreeable," and he proposed
to end the season with an electric party. "A turkey is to be
killed for our dinner by the electrical shock, and roasted by the
electrical jack, before a fire kindled by the electrified bottle"
(p. 211). But before the summer of 1749 he entered upon
more serious reflections. At this time Franklin first suggested
the idea of explaining lightning on electrical principles. The
conjecture that the nature of lightning was the same as that of
the electric spark had been made before. Gray, Wall, Nollet,
Freke, Winkler, had all expressed this thought.[1] Franklin
probably did not know of these conjectures. Though contrary
to the then prevalent theory of lightning, they certainly warranted some one in making an experimental test. Thunder
and lightning were generally believed to be due to exploding
gases, though opinions differed as to the nature of the gases.
In 1737 Franklin believed lightning to be due to "the inflammable breath of the Pyrites, which is a subtle sulphur, and
takes fire of itself." As already stated, in the early summer
of 1749, he advanced the electrical theory, and conceived bold
plans for experimentation. The heat of summer did not deter
him and Kinnersley from experimentation. Under the date of
November 7, 1749, the following passage is found in his note-
book: "Electrical fluid agrees with lightning in these particulars: (1) Giving light; (2) colour of the light; (3) crooked
direction; (4) swift motion; (5) being conducted by metals;
(6) crack or noise in exploding; (7) subsisting in water or

[1] BENJAMIN, p. 575.

ice; (8) rending bodies it passes through; (9) destroying animals; (10) melting metals; (11) firing inflammable substances; (12) sulphurous smell." Will lightning be attracted and drawn off by points like the electric fluid in his jars? "Since they agree in all the particulars wherein we can already compare them, is it not probable that they agree likewise in this? Let the experiment be made." By the action of points he proposed to draw down the lightning. "On the top of some high tower or steeple, place a kind of sentry-box (as in Fig. 13), big enough to contain a man and an electrical stand. From the middle of the stand let an iron rod rise and pass, bending out of the door, and then upright twenty or thirty feet, pointed very sharp at the end. If the electrical stand be kept clean and dry, a man standing on it, when such clouds are passing low, might be electrified and afford sparks, the rod drawing fire to him from a cloud." "If these things are so, may not the knowledge of this power of points be of use to mankind in preserv-

FIG. 13.

ing houses, churches, ships, etc., from the stroke of lightning? . . ."[1]

Such are the thoughts communicated in a letter to Collinson in July, 1750, and submitted by him to the Royal Society. That body at first received the new ideas with derision. The plans seemed visionary.[2] As the Royal Society failed to publish anything but a brief notice of Franklin's researches, Col-

---

[1] *Works*, Vol. V., pp. 236, 237.

[2] Three years later (1753), after Franklin's researches had met with enthusiastic appreciation on the part of French scientists and the French king, the Royal Society awarded him the Copley medal. The president's address on the occasion of the award is given in Franklin's *Works*, Vol. V., pp. 499–504. In 1756 Franklin was elected member of the Royal Society.

linson determined to bring out the letters without its imprint.
By the additional letters that arrived later, they swelled to a
quarto volume which passed through five editions.   Seventeen
years after the first publication, Priestley wrote: "Nothing
was ever written upon the subject of electricity which was
more generally read and admired in all parts of Europe than
these letters.   There is hardly any European language into
which they have not been translated; and, as if this were
not sufficient to make them properly known, a translation of
them has lately been made in Latin." [1]

In America popular curiosity ran high.   Kinnersley started
on a lecturing tour, showing electric experiments and winning
applause.   In New York, Newport, and Boston these lectures
produced a genuine sensation.   "Faneuil Hall resounded with
the cracks and snaps of his jars and globes, long before they
echoed the impassioned eloquence of the orators of the Revolution." [2]

Franklin was of the opinion that no building in Philadelphia
or hill near by was high enough to enable him to perform the
experiment with the sentry-box.   While he was endeavouring
to raise money by means of a lottery for the erection of a spire
of sufficient height, news came that the experiment had been
tried successfully at Marly-la-Ville, near Paris, by *Dalibard*,
under the auspices of the French king.   How was it done?
Simply by a rod 13 metres (40 feet) high, insulated at its
base, and resting upon a small table within a small cabin.
Dalibard instructed an old dragoon to watch for clouds.   A
brass wire mounted in a glass bottle was gotten ready for the
purpose of drawing off sparks from the rod.   After several
days' waiting, a thunder-cloud appeared on May 10, 1752.   The
dragoon approached the wire to the rod, and there was a lively

[1] PRIESTLEY, *Hist. of Elect.*, p. 154.   [2] BENJAMIN, p. 585.

crackling of sparks. The flame and sulphurous odour were evidently infernal. The terrified dragoon dropped the wire and shouted to his neighbours to send for the village priest. The latter was braver than the dragoon. He began to experiment for himself and drew sparks from the rod. He communicated the results to Dalibard.[1] "Franklin's idea ceases to be a conjecture," writes Dalibard; "here it has become a reality." A week later *Delor* in Paris repeated the experiment with a rod 32 metres (99 feet) high.

Franklin himself did not regard the tests in Paris conclusive. He was not fully convinced that the Frenchmen's rods had become electrified by lightning. The rods did not reach up into the clouds. A new idea flashed into his mind. Why not send a kite up into the very interior of the cloud, and conduct the lightning down on its cord? He prepared a kite. "Make a small cross," he writes afterwards to Collinson, "of two light strips of cedar, the arms so long as to reach to the four corners of a large thin silk handkerchief when extended; tie the corners of the handkerchief to the extremities of the cross, so you have the body of a kite; . . . to the top of the upright stick of the cross is to be fixed a very sharp-pointed wire, rising a foot or more above the wood. To the end of the twine next the hand is to be tied a silk ribbon, and where the silk and twine join, a key may be fastened."[2] With this apparatus he went out on the common, accompanied only by his son. He placed himself under a shed to avoid the rain, and raised the kite. A thunder-cloud passed, but as yet there was no sign of electricity. He almost despaired of success, when suddenly he observed the loose fibres of the string erect

[1] The priest's letter, as also Dalibard's communication to the French Academy, are given in Franklin's *Works*, Vol. V., pp. 288–293. See also BENJAMIN, p. 588.

[2] FRANKLIN'S *Works*, Vol. V., p. 295.

themselves. He now presented a knuckle to the key, and received a strong spark.[1] What exquisite pleasure that spark must have given him! More sparks were obtained; a Leyden jar was charged, a shock given, etc. He had demonstrated that lightning is an electric phenomenon.

"In September, 1752," says Franklin, "I erected an iron rod to draw the lightning down into my house, in order to make some experiments on it, with two bells to give notice when the rod should be electrified."[2] He then concluded from a number of experiments "that the clouds of thunder-gust are most commonly in a negative state of electricity, but sometimes in a positive state" (p. 304).[3] Hence, "for the most part, in thunder-strokes it is the earth that strikes into the clouds, and not the clouds that strike into the earth" (p. 305).

Franklin's experiments on atmospheric electricity were repeated everywhere. The French physician, *Louis Guillaume Lemonnier,* found that the atmosphere is always electric, even when no clouds are in sight. *Georg Wilhelm Richmann,* of St. Petersburg, was struck dead while experimenting with lightning in 1753. Detailed reports of the effect on the various organs of his body were published by scientific societies. Says Priestley,[4] "It is not given to every electrician to die in so glorious a manner as the justly envied Richmann."

Franklin's suggestion to protect buildings by lightning-rods was first carried out in 1754 by *Procopius Divisch,* a clergyman at Prenditz, in Mähren. In 1760 Franklin erected one on a building in Philadelphia. *William Watson* erected the first lightning-rod in England in 1762. In 1782 there were about

---

[1] FRANKLIN's *Works,* Vol. V., p. 175.

[2] *Ibidem,* p. 301.

[3] That atmospheric electricity may vary in sign had been noticed before this by John Canton.

[4] *Hist. of Elect.,* p. 86.

400 rods in Philadelphia. At first some opposition to their erection was made by certain theologians. It was argued that as thunder and lightning were tokens of divine wrath, it was impious to interfere with their power of destruction.[1] To this argument *John Winthrop*, the first professor of physics at Harvard College, gave the common-sense reply: "It is as much our duty to secure ourselves against the effects of lightning as against those of rain, snow, and wind, by the means God has put into our hands."[2]

Experience soon proved that rods were not an absolute protection against lightning. Failure to protect was then and long afterwards attributed either to bad earth connection or to dull points. Various improvements in construction were suggested.[3] But the real difficulty was not recognized until nearly a century later. Franklin's theory of the action of the rod was incomplete. We now begin to see that the failure of carefully erected rods to protect is due to the fact that the discharge may be oscillatory.[4]

[1] A. D. WHITE, *Warfare of Science with Theology*, 1896, Vol. I., p. 366.

[2] For an account of *John Winthrop*, see W. J. YOUMANS, *Pioneers of Science in America*, New York, 1896.

[3] See, for instance, a paper by ROBERT PATTERSON of Philadelphia in *Trans. Am. Philos. Society*, Vol. III., 1793, pp. 122, 321.

[4] Franklin supplied Harvard College with electrical apparatus. In a letter of 1753 he speaks of the shipment of Leyden jars. Before this time the instruction in electricity at Harvard must have been quite meagre. Among manuscript notes of excellent lectures on astronomy, and a few on light and electricity, prepared by John Winthrop in 1750, there is only one lecture on electricity and magnetism. Trowbridge gives part of these notes as follows: "If a flaxen string be extended and supported, and at one end an excited tube be applied, light bodies will be attracted, and that at the distance of 1200 feet at the other end. This electricity since the year 1743 has made a considerable noise in the world, upon which it is supposed several of the (at present) hidden phenomena of nature depend. . . . Men have been so electrized as to have considerable light

In 1703 Dutch travellers brought tourmaline from Ceylon. They observed that it was capable of attracting the light ashes on glowing peat. Its properties were examined by *Franz Ulrich Theodor Æpinus* and *Johann Karl Wilke*, who concluded that it became electrified by heating, its ends carrying charges of opposite sign. *Torbern Olof Bergman* showed in 1766 that it was not so much the heat that produced electricity as it was the difference in temperature between its parts; that on cooling the charge at each end is reversed. *Benjamin Wilson* and *John Canton* found that the electric property of tourmaline was shared by other crystals.

During the latter part of the eighteenth century the first important steps were taken in the way of exact measurements in static electricity. In this field of research we meet two great names, Cavendish and Coulomb. *Henry Cavendish*[1] (1731–1810) attended Peterhouse College, Cambridge, and afterward lived chiefly in London. The great obscurity hanging over his private history has rendered it impossible to ascertain what influences induced him to devote himself to experimental science. He experimented in chemistry, heat, electricity, but he took little pains to publish his results and to secure priority of discovery. He lived a strangely retired life. Being of frugal habits, he allowed his large income to accumulate. "He received no stranger at his residence; he ordered his dinner daily by a note left on the hall table, and from his morbid

round their heads and bodies, not unlike the light represented around the heads of saints by painters." Trowbridge adds that "the entire apparatus to illustrate the subject of electricity and magnetism in Harvard University until 1820 consisted merely of two Franklin electrical machines, a collection of Leyden jars, and small apparatus to illustrate the effects of electrical attractions and repulsions shown by electrified pith balls or similar light objects." See JOHN TROWBRIDGE, *What is Electricity?* 1897, p. 26.

[1] *Dic. Nat. Biog.*

shyness he objected to any communication with his female domestics."[1] "He probably uttered fewer words in the course of his life than any man who ever lived to fourscore years, not at all excepting the monks of La Trappe."[2] Cavendish's whole existence was in his laboratory and his library.[3] His experiments on electrostatics were completed before the end of the year 1773, but remained unpublished. He printed only two electric papers, and these contained matter of secondary importance. About a century later, in 1879, James Clerk Maxwell published a book under the title, *Electrical Researches of the Honourable Henry Cavendish*, written between 1771 and 1781. "These papers," says Maxwell, "prove that Cavendish had anticipated nearly all those great facts in electricity which at a later period were made known to the scientific world through the writings of Coulomb and the French philosophers." Cavendish made the capacity of condensers a subject of investigation, and constructed for himself a complete set of condensers of known capacity, by which he measured the capacity of various pieces of apparatus. A battery of 49 jars was found to contain 321,000 "inches of electricity" (about $\frac{1}{3}$ micro-farad). His "inches of electricity" express the diameter of the sphere of equivalent capacity. Our modern electrostatic measurements of capacity differ from this simply in the use

---

[1] *Dic. Nat. Biog.*

[2] LORD BROUGHAM, *Lives of Philosophers*, London, 1855, p. 106.

[3] Henry Cavendish happened once at a dinner to sit next to William Herschel, who had been constructing telescopes of such unheard-of magnitude and accuracy of figure that a star could be seen without "rays." Cavendish slowly addressed the astronomer with, "Is it true, Dr. Herschel, that you see the stars round?" "Round as a button," exclaimed the doctor, when the conversation dropped, till at the close of dinner, Cavendish repeated interrogatively, "Round as a button?" "Round as a button," briskly rejoined the doctor, and no more was said. From article "Herschel, Sir William," in *Dic. Nat. Biog.*

of "centimeters" and "radius" in place of "inches" and
"diameter." Cavendish anticipated Faraday in the discovery
of specific inductive capacity of different substances, and measured this quantity for several substances. For paraffin he
found the values 1.81 to 2.47, while more recently Boltzmann
has given 2.32, Wüllner 1.96, Gordon 1.994.[1] The preceding
ideas presuppose the notion of potential. This was introduced by Cavendish under the name "degree of electrifica-
tion." He proved that static charges reside on the surfaces
of conductors and that the electric force varies inversely as
the square of the distance, or at least cannot differ from that
ratio by more than $\frac{1}{50}$ part. In 1781 he completed an inquiry
which amounts to an anticipation of Ohm's Law.[2]

It is a matter of regret that Cavendish did not give scientists
of his day the benefit of his far-reaching results. It is remarkable that, while Cavendish originated new concepts, and
engaged largely in electric measurements, he was no inventor
of new apparatus. Coulomb invented the torsion electrometer;
Abraham Bennet, in 1786, brought forth the gold-leaf electroscope; but Cavendish designed no similar instruments. He
used the pith-ball electrometer.

Charles Augustin Coulomb (1736–1806) was born at Angou-
lême, studied in Paris, and at an early age entered the army.
After several years' service in the West Indies, he returned to
Paris and served as engineer. He engaged at the same time
in scientific research. When a project of navigable canals in
Bretagne was under consideration, Coulomb was appointed by
the minister of marine to examine the ground. His report was
unfavourable. This displeased some influential persons, and
under the pretext that he had no orders from the minister of

---

[1] MAXWELL, *Elect. Researches of the Hon. H. Cavendish*, p. liii.

[2] *Ibidem*, pp. lix., §§ 574, 575, 629, 686. The law is not worked out
by him as carefully and systematically as by Ohm over forty years later.

war, they placed him in confinement. Later the government of Bretagne saw its error, and offered Coulomb a large recompense, but he accepted only a seconds watch, which he afterwards used in experimentation. Says Thomas Young: "His moral character is said to have been as correct as his mathematical investigations."[1]

Coulomb entered upon researches on the torsional elasticity of hairs and wires. This led in 1777 to the torsion balance, or "balance de torsion." Some similar device had been previously suggested in England by John Michell.[2] The torsion balance has held its place in texts on electricity for a century, though now the instrument is no longer used in the laboratory. Coulomb experimented with great ingenuity and accuracy, and proved with it that Newton's law of inverse squares holds also in electric and in magnetic attraction and repulsion.[3] He proved that the action varies as the product of the quantities of electricity; he showed also that electric charges exist on the surfaces of conductors and compared the surface charges on various parts of a conductor. Coulomb was an advocate of the two-fluid theory and believed that attraction and repulsion take place by an "actio in distans," without an intervening medium. His electrical memoirs, which appeared between 1785 and 1789, furnished the data on which Poisson later founded his mathematical theory of electricity.[4]

From very early times it was known that certain species of water-animals are capable of giving shocks. After the inven-

[1] *Misc. Works*, Vol. II., p. 540.

[2] HELLER, Vol. II., p. 499.

[3] That magnetic action follows the law of inverse squares was shown before this (about 1760) by Tobias Mayer of Göttingen. See ALBRECHT, *Gesch. d' Elect.*, p. 75.

[4] Coulomb's seven papers appeared originally in the *Mémoirs de l'Académie royale des sciences*, 1785 and 1786. The first four are printed in German translation in *Ostwald's Klassiker*, No. 13.

tion of the Leyden jar, men began to ponder over the similarity in the physiological effect of its discharge to that of shocks given by these animals. *John Walsh* made the first thorough investigation of this subject at La Rochelle and proved that the shocks imparted by the fishes are electrical. Connecting the back and under side of the fish with a conductor, a discharge took place.[1]

Among those interested in animal electricity was *Aloisio Galvani* (1737–1798), a physician and professor of anatomy in Bologna. By accident he was led to the great discovery of current electricity or "galvanism." The story goes that his wife was in poor health and was ordered to eat frogs' legs. Galvani prepared them himself. When he had taken off their skins, he laid them on a table near the conductor of a charged electric machine and left the room. His wife chanced to hold the scalpel near the machine while at the same time the scalpel's point touched the exposed crural nerve of a frog's leg. A spark passed and the leg convulsed violently. She acquainted her husband of this, and he repeated the experiment. This occurred on November 6, 1780. Galvani's own account is more prosaic.[2] His wife plays no rôle in the discovery; only one frog is dissected; an assistant first notices the twitching.

Galvani set about to discover the cause. It seemed necessary to touch a nerve and to have a spark. The effect was the same when the legs were placed in a vacuum. The question arose, will atmospheric electricity serve as well as that from the machine? He suspended frogs' legs by iron hooks from an iron trellis in the garden. The legs exhibited motion. It was

---

[1] His papers appeared in the *Phil. Trans.* for 1773 and 1774.

[2] See *Ostwald's Klassiker*, No. 52, p. 4. This number is a German translation of *Galvani's* article, "De viribus electricitatis in moto musculari commentarius," in *Comment. Acad. scient. Bonon.*, 1791.

violent when storm-clouds passed, but could be seen at times during a clear sky. At first he attributed the twitching to changes in atmospheric electricity. He abandoned this view after he succeeded in producing the same effects indoors by placing the frogs' legs on a metallic plate and allowing the wire piercing the crural nerve to touch the plate. The cause must lie in the leg, the plate, or the wire. Galvani placed the leg on glass and touched the crural nerve and a muscle of the foot, both at the same time, with the ends of a bent rod. If the rod was of glass, no effect was seen; if it was of copper and iron, or copper and silver, then prolonged convulsions followed. The fact that a rod of iron alone produced motion, though it was not so continuous and pronounced as when it consisted of two metals, led Galvani to the conclusion that the rod served merely as a conductor. Further tests seemed to him to locate the source of electricity in the nerve.

Galvani's observations were of startling novelty and astonished scientific men everywhere. More profound than his own was the reasoning on this subject by his countryman, *Alessandro Volta* (1745–1827), who occupied the chair of physics for five years at the gymnasium of his native town, Como, and after 1779, for twenty-five years, the chair of physics at the university of Pavia. He had been a diligent experimenter in electricity and in 1775 had invented the electrophorus. He found that the electric discharge through a nerve could produce other effects than motion. If a bent rod of two metals touched the eye above, while the other end was held in his mouth, a sensation of light followed at the moment of making contact. A silver and a gold coin held against the tongue produced a bitter taste as soon as the coins were connected by a wire.[1] Thus, the electricity was able not only to produce

---

[1] This bitter taste had been observed previously in Germany by Johann Georg Sulzer. See EDM. HOPPE, *Gesch. d. Elect.*, Leipzig, 1884, p. 128.

motion, but to affect the nerves of vision and taste. Volta conjectured that the essential thing in all these experiments was the contact of different metals. After 1794 he set about to prove this hypothesis. If Galvani was right in placing the seat of electricity in the frog's leg and in attributing to the metal rod merely the function of discharger, as in the Leyden jar, then one metal should produce twitching as easily as two. If the ends of a wire of one metal are at different temperatures, then vigorous convulsions follow; they disappear almost entirely on equalization of temperature. Hence Volta concluded that slight effects due to a wire of a single metal are due to slight difference in its condition. This new electricity, declared Volta, might as well be called "metallic" as "animal." The strongest proof of his contact theory was given by means of his condensing electroscope. This was a gold-leaf electroscope combined with a small condenser. A feeble source, like that in a compound bar of two dissimilar metals, could supply considerable electricity to the condenser without materially raising its potential. But when the upper plate of the condenser was removed, the potential rose and the leaves diverged. This experiment seemed to prove that electricity was generated at the contact of the two different metals, one metal becoming positively charged, the other negatively.

On March 20, 1800, Volta wrote a letter to Joseph Banks, then president of the Royal Society of London, in which he describes the voltaic pile, called by him "organe électrique artificiel" in distinction to the "organe électrique naturel" of the torpedo.[1] Two dissimilar plates, say zinc and copper, were placed in contact. Over this went a piece of flannel or blotting paper moistened with water or brine. Then followed

---

[1] *Phil. Trans.*, 1800, p. 405.

another pair of zinc and copper plates, and so on, each pair of plates being separated by a moist conductor. Such a pile, consisting of a dozen or more pairs of plates, multiplied the effect of a single pair. In the same letter Volta explains the "couronne de tasses" or "crown of cups." It consisted of cups containing brine or dilute acid, into which dipped strips half zinc and half copper. The zinc end of one strip dipped into one cup, the copper end into another. This is the first voltaic cell.

Six weeks after Volta had written that memorable letter, the first pile was constructed in England by *William Nicholson* and *Sir Anthony Carlisle*, and on May 2, the decomposition of water by it was observed. This experiment was the foundation of electro-chemistry. It was described in *Nicholson's Journal* for July, 1800, and appeared before Volta's own account of the voltaic pile was printed in the *Philosophical Transactions*.[1] Volta's researches met with immediate appreciation. As early as 1791 he was elected member of the Royal Society of London. In 1801 Napoleon called him to Paris to perform before the Institute his experiments on the pile. The French awarded him a gold medal.

The controversy between Volta and Galvani divided electricians into two hostile parties. The most prominent of Galvani's supporters was Alexander von Humboldt in Germany; the most prominent of Volta's were Coulomb and other French physicists. The contact theory was applied to the explanation of the voltaic cell. This theory has been a bone of contention from that time to the present. Only in very recent years has it finally succumbed to a modern chemical theory.

---

[1] The electric decomposition of water was accomplished at an earlier date by Dr. Ash at Oxford, Fabbroni in Florence, Crève in Mainz, but Nicholson and Carlisle were the first to systematically study the phenomenon and to prove that the separated gases actually were hydrogen and oxygen. See HOPPE, *op. cit.*, pp. 132–139.

SOUND

Joseph Sauveur (1653–1716) carried on important researches in acoustics. He was born at La Flêche. At the age of seventeen he travelled on foot to Paris to seek his fortune. In 1686 he became professor of mathematics at the Collège Royal. He was a stammerer and had such a poor ear for music that he could compare pitches only with the assistance of musicians.[1] Yet his papers on acoustics, published in the Memoirs of the Academy, 1700–1703, are very important. Independently of Noble and Pigott, he discovered overtones in strings. He used paper riders to locate nodes and anti-nodes. He observed sympathetic vibrations and gave a correct explanation of beats. He tuned two organ pipes in the ratio 24 : 25, and observed four beats per second. From this he concluded that the pipe of higher pitch made 100 vibrations per second. He determined rates of vibration with considerable precision.[2] *Vittorio Francesco Stancari* of Bologna made such measurements by the use of toothed wheels.[3]

The early development of the siren took place in England. The experiments of Robert Hooke were continued between 1793 and 1801 by John Robinson, professor of physics at the University of Edinburgh. A wheel was made to strike in rapid succession the teeth of a pinion, so as to force out a portion of air from between them; or a pipe through which air was passing was alternately opened and shut by the revolution of a stopcock or valve.[4]

[1] ROSENBERGER. Part II., p. 269.

[2] Consult further E. MACH on Joseph Sauveur in *Mittheil. d. deutsch. math. Ges. zu Prag*, 1892 ; abstracted in *Poske's Zeitschr.*, Vol. VI., pp. 39–41.

[3] ERNST ROBEL, *Die Sirenen, Ein Beitrag zur Entwickelungsgeschichte der Akustik*, Berlin, 1891, Theil I., p. 5.

[4] *Ibidem*, pp. 7–10. Consult also ROBINSON, "Temperament of the Scale of Music" in third edition of the *Encyclopædia Britannica;* THOMAS YOUNG, *Lectures on Nat. Phil.*, London, 1807, Vol. I., p. 378.

THE NINETEENTH CENTURY

In physical speculation the nineteenth century has overthrown the leading theories of the previous one hundred years, and has largely built anew on the older foundations laid during the seventeenth century. The emission theory of light gave way to the wave theory; the substance called " caloric " was set aside, and the fact was established that heat is due to molecular motion. The imponderables, assumed to exist by the advocates of the one-fluid and the two-fluid theories of electricity, were discarded in favour of the view that the phenomena of electricity and magnetism are to be explained, in some way, by the existence of pulsations and strains in the luminiferous ether. The effluvia of a magnet, capable of passing through glass without resistance, are of interest now only to the historian. The chemical substance phlogiston is no more. Of the half dozen imponderables which filled space during the eighteenth century, only one remains; and this one, apparently, has proved its right of existence. By it, the two great branches of light and electromagnetism are becoming practically one. Notwithstanding the enormous multiplication of observed phenomena, we are simplifying our interpretation of them by bringing into consistent and comprehensive order that which formerly seemed to be capricious and isolated. The very fact that intimate relations are perceived to exist between wide realms of physics, once thought to be perfectly distinct, seems to show that we are moving in the right direction. Radiant energy has developed into a subject of central importance.

Stimulated and aided by the progress of its sister science

chemistry, physics has made marvellous progress during the past one hundred years. At the beginning of the century the chemist with his balance had established the law of the Conservation of Mass. Then came the physicist and set forth in bold relief the all-embracing principle of the Conservation of Energy.

No epoch has seen such a vast army of scientific workers, or beheld the acquisition of such extensive experimental knowledge on all physical subjects. Theory and practice have gone hand in hand. Steam and electricity have been made to minister to the needs and comfort of mankind.

Nevertheless it takes no fine acumen to perceive that much remains to be done. It is left for the twentieth or some later century to reveal fully the mysteries of the structure of matter and the ether. Are not both of them dynamical systems, subject to the laws of motion, of momentum, and energy? Present indications suggest this view.

To this scientific advance all leading European nations have contributed. In Great Britain the new period of productiveness was ushered in when the doting attitude of Englishmen toward Newton was changed, and the truth was perceived that no human mind, however great, can be infallible on all points. Among the earlier scientists of this time are the Herschels, Thomas Young, Sir Humphry Davy, and Sir David Brewster.

Germany, impoverished, devastated, and politically shattered by religious struggles, began after the Napoleonic wars to recover and to put forth extraordinary scientific effort. The attitude of German physicists of the early part of this century toward philosophers and mathematicians was grotesque. The obscure and undemonstrated assertions of the philosophers Hegel and Schelling worked injuriously upon science.[1] But

[1] HELMHOLTZ in *Wiedemann's Annalen,* Neue Folge, Vol. 54, 1895, pp. 2 *et seq.* Helmholtz says in his lecture, "On the relation of natural

a reaction set in. There arose in Berlin an empirical school of scientists, comprising Poggendorff, Riess, Dove, H. G. Magnus. They looked with contempt upon metaphysical obscurantism. Magnus, the leader of this school, did much toward the evolution of the modern physical laboratory.

Strange to say, Magnus would have nothing to do with mathematics. This one-sided and ill-founded conception of the use of mathematics in physical research was not shared by his great pupils Krönig, Clausius, and Helmholtz. Nor did all German contemporaries of Magnus shun mathematical physics. This branch was cultivated at Göttingen by Gauss and Wilhelm Weber, and at Königsberg by Ernst Franz Neumann. The first movement toward unity of action among physical experimentalists and mathematicians took place in the organization at Berlin in 1844 of the Physical Society, which grew out of a physical "colloquium" held by Magnus.[1]

France, at the beginning of the nineteenth century, possessed an array of scientific men of unsurpassed brilliancy. We need mention only Lagrange, Laplace, Fresnel, Arago, Biot, Carnot, Fourier. Not till the middle of this century did some of the other countries equal her in scientific productiveness.

In the United States comparatively little was achieved before the last quarter of the century, and that little failed, at the time, to catch the eye of the scientific public abroad.

science to general science," *Popular Lectures*, transl. by E. ATKINSON, London, 1873, p. 7: "Hegel . . . launched out, with unusual vehemence and acrimony, against the natural philosophers and especially against Sir Isaac Newton, as the first and greatest representative of physical investigation. The philosophers accused the scientific men of narrowness; the scientific men retorted that the philosophers were crazy." Consult also RUDOLPH VIRCHOW, "Transition from the Philosophic to the Scientific Age," *Smithsonian Report*, 1894, pp. 681-695.

[1] G. WIEDEMANN in *Wied. Annal.*, Vol. 39, 1890, "Vorwort."

LIGHT

We are indebted to *Thomas Young* (1773–1829), a native of Milverton, Somersetshire, for the revival of the undulatory theory of light after a century of neglect. This great scientist had an extraordinary childhood. He could read with considerable fluency at the age of two. When four years old he had read the Bible twice through; when six he could repeat the whole of Goldsmith's Deserted Village. He devoured books, whether classical, literary, or scientific, in rapid succession; and, strange to say, he grew up with unimpaired physical and intellectual powers. At about sixteen he abstained from the use of sugar on account of his opposition to the slave-trade. At nineteen he entered upon a medical education, which was pursued first in London, then in Edinburgh, Göttingen, and finally at Cambridge. In 1800 he began medical practice in London. The year following he accepted the office of Professor of Natural Philosophy in the Royal Institution, the metropolitan school of science established in the year preceding by Count Rumford. He held this position two years. From January to May, 1802, he delivered there a series of lectures. These and a later series were published in 1807 under the title, *Lectures on Natural Philosophy and the Mechanical Arts*, a treatise still worthy of perusal. In 1802 he was appointed Foreign Secretary of the Royal Society. This office he held for the remainder of his life.

Young's earliest researches were on the anatomical and optical properties of the eye. Then followed the first epoch of optical discovery, 1801–1804. His theory was laughed at, and he proceeded to other studies. The twelve succeeding years were given to medical practice and to the study of philology, especially the decipherment of hieroglyphic writing. But when Fresnel, in France, began to experiment on light and to bring into prominence the theory of Young, then the latter resumed his early studies, and entered upon his second epoch of optical investigation.

In 1801 Young read before the Royal Society a paper on the colour of thin plates, in which he expressed himself strongly in favour of the undulatory theory of light. The great step taken in this article is the introduction of the *principle of interference.* "When two undulations, from different origins, coincide either perfectly or very nearly in direction, their joint effect is a combination of the motions belonging to each."[1] Imperfect hints of this principle occur in Robert Hooke's *Micrographia,* but Young was unaware of these until after he had arrived at the notion independently. Young was the first to make a thorough application of it to sound and light. By this principle he explained the colours of thin plates and the diffraction colours of scratched or "striated surfaces."[2] Young's observations were made with great exactness, but the mode of exposition in these, as in most of his memoirs, was condensed and somewhat obscure. His papers, containing the great principle of interference, constituted by far the most important publication on physical optics issued since the time of Newton. Yet they made no impression upon the scientific public. They were attacked violently by Lord Brougham in Nos. II. and IX. of the *Edinburgh Review.* Young's articles were declared to contain "nothing which deserves the name either of experiment or discovery," to be "destitute of every species of merit." "We wish to raise our feeble voice," says Brougham,

---

[1] *Miscellaneous Works of the Late Thomas Young,* edited by GEORGE PEACOCK, London, 1855, Vol. I., p. 157. See also p. 170.

[2] The colours of scratches on polished surfaces were observed first by Robert Boyle. Later, examples of lines drawn on glass were produced by Mr. Barton, which, when transferred to steel — as in the case of the buttons which are known by his name — produce a very brilliant effect of coloration. GEORGE PEACOCK'S *Life of Dr. Young,* 1855, p. 149.

"against innovations that can have no other effect than to check the progress of science." After exposing the law of interference as "absurd" and "illogical," the reviewer says, "We now dismiss, for the present, the feeble lucubrations of this author, in which we have searched without success for some traces of learning, acuteness, and ingenuity, that might compensate his evident deficiency in the powers of solid thinking, calm and patient investigation, and successful development of the laws of nature, by steady and modest observation of her operations."[1] Young issued an able reply, published in the form of a pamphlet, which failed to turn public opinion in favour of his theory, because, as he said, "one copy only was sold."[2] Says Tyndall,[3] "For twenty years this man of genius was quenched — hidden from the appreciative intellect of his countrymen — deemed in fact a dreamer, through the vigorous sarcasm of a writer who had then possession of the public ear. . . . To the celebrated Frenchmen, Fresnel and Arago, he was first indebted for the restitution of his rights."

Augustin Jean Fresnel (1788–1827) was born at Broglie in Normandy. He advanced very slowly in his studies, being at eight years of age scarcely able to read.[4] The state of his health was always delicate. Unlike Thomas Young, he gave no promise of becoming a great savant. At the age of thirteen he went to the central school at Caen, at sixteen to the Polytechnic School in Paris, then to the *École des ponts et chaussées*. Then he served as government engineer for about eight years. He was a strong Royalist, and joined the army organized to oppose the return of Napoleon from Elba. As a result he was

---

[1] *Edinburgh Review*, No. IX., 6th ed., Vol. V., p. 103 ; *Young's Works*, I., p. 193.

[2] *Ibidem*, I., 215.

[3] *Six Lectures on Light*, 2d ed., New York, 1877, p. 51.

[4] F. Arago, *Biographies*, 2d Series, Boston, 1859, p. 176.

deprived of his office. On the reinstatement of Louis XVIII. Fresnel obtained a new position as engineer. He entered upon his experimental researches in 1815. A letter of December, 1814, contains the following: "I do not know what is meant by polarization of light." Within a year he transmitted to the Academy an important memoir on diffraction (October, 1815). Other memoirs followed in rapid succession.[1] By placing a wire in a beam of light diverging from a point, the distances of the resulting fringes from the axis of the beam were accurately measured. He noticed, as Young had done earlier, the disappearance of the bands within the shadow, when the light which passed on one side of the wire was cut off before it reached the screen. Fresnel was led to the discovery of the principle of interference, without being aware that Young had achieved this more than thirteen years before. Many physicists were not inclined to admit that the phenomena were due to interference. Diffraction fringes had been known since the time of Grimaldi, and had been explained on the emission-theory by means of hypothetical laws of attraction and repulsion between the light corpuscles and the edges of the object causing diffraction. To remove these objections Fresnel designed the memorable experiment which yielded two small sources of light, without resorting to apertures or edges of opaque obstacles. By the use of two plane metallic mirrors, forming with each other an angle of nearly 180°, he avoided diffraction, and yet with the reflected beams produced interference.

Arago and *Poinsot* were commissioned to report on Fresnel's first memoir. Arago entered upon the subject with zeal and became the first convert in France to the undulatory theory.

---

[1] Consult *Œuvres complètes d'Augustin Fresnel*, Paris, 1866, in three volumes, with introduction by ÉMILE VERDET.

Some of Fresnel's mathematical assumptions were not satisfactory; hence *Laplace, Poisson,* and others belonging to the
strictly mathematical school at first disdained to consider the
theory. By their opposition Fresnel was spurred to greater
exertion. Young had not verified his explanations by extensive numerical calculations. Fresnel applied mathematical analysis to a much greater extent, and the undulatory
theory began to carry conviction to many minds. He gave a
complete answer to the old objection against the wave theory,
that the latter could not explain the existence of shadows or
the approximate rectilinear propagation of light.

Unlike Young, Fresnel made extensive use of Huygens's
principle of secondary waves, stated by Fresnel as follows:
"The vibrations of a luminous wave at any one of its points
may be considered as the sum of the elementary movements
conveyed to it at the same moment, from the separate action
of all the portions of the unobstructed wave considered in any
one of its anterior positions."[1]

It was Arago who first drew Fresnel's attention to Young's
researches, and who sent to the English physician the first
memoir of the French savant. It is a pleasure to note the
absence of bitter contests of priority. Fresnel writes Young
in 1816: "But if anything could console me for not having
the advantage of priority, it was for me to have met a savant
who has enriched physics with so great a number of important discoveries, and has at the same time contributed greatly
to strengthen my confidence in the theory that I have
adopted."[2] Young writes to Fresnel, October 16, 1819: "I return a thousand thanks, Monsieur, for the gift of your admirable memoir, which surely merits a very high rank amongst

---

[1] G. Peacock, *Life of Thomas Young,* London, 1855, p. 167.
[2] *Young's Works,* Vol. I., p. 378.

the papers which have contributed most to the progress of optics." [1]

Let us proceed to double refraction and the polarization of light. Double refraction had been observed in Iceland spar by Erasmus Bartholinus. Polarization had been studied by Huygens and Newton. Huygens had stated the true law of extraordinary refraction in uniaxal crystals. The property of "two-sidedness" or "polarization" was known to them as an isolated fact observed only in connection with double refraction. A century elapsed and then Malus observed that polarization may accompany reflection. Thus light may be polarized in other ways than by the action of crystallized bodies.

Étienne Louis Malus (1775–1812) was born in Paris. He was educated as a military engineer and served in the French army in Germany and Egypt. Later, during his superintendence of the work then in progress at Antwerp and at Strassburg, he found time to undertake the investigation of a prize question proposed by the French Institute, calling for a mathematical theory of double refraction. By accident he was led to the discovery alluded to above. He looked through a piece of crystal at the image of the sun reflected from the windows of the Luxembourg Palace, to the house in the Rue d'Enfer, where he lived, and was much surprised to find one of the double images disappear for a certain position of the crystal.[2] He tried to explain the singular phenomenon by some modification of the light undergone in traversing the atmosphere. But when night came, he found that the light of a taper, falling upon the surface of water at an angle of 36°, acted similarly and, in fact, was polarized. Moreover, if the two rays from calc-spar fell simultaneously on the surface of water at an angle of 36°, and if the ordinary ray was partly reflected, then the extraordinary ray was not reflected at all, and *vice versa.* Thus, in one evening, Malus created a new branch of modern physics.

At this time no explanation of polarization had been given by the wave theory, which was in great danger of being over-thrown by the new mass of evidence furnished by Malus. Thomas Young wrote in 1811 to Malus (who was a pronounced partisan of the emission theory): "Your experiments demon-strate the *insufficiency* of a theory (that of interferences), which I had adopted, but they do not prove its *falsity.*"[1] As Whewell says,[2] this was without doubt "the darkest time of the history of the theory." Young did not conceal the difficulty; nor did he despair of reconciling a seeming contradiction. Six years passed, then light began to dawn. On January 12, 1817, Young wrote to Arago, "It is a principle in this theory, that all undu-lations are simply propagated through homogeneous mediums in concentric spherical surfaces like the undulations of sound, consisting simply in the direct and retrograde motions of the particles in the direction of the radius, with their concomitant condensations and rarefactions. And yet it is possible to explain in this theory a transverse vibration, propagated also in the direction of the radius, and with equal velocity, the motions of the particles being in a certain constant direction with respect to that radius; and this is a *polarization.*"[3] This was a happy suggestion which made it possible to see how a ray could exhibit two-sidedness. Later, instead of the "con-stant direction" spoken of by Young, the particular direction *transverse to the ray* was fixed upon. Fresnel arrived at this mode of explanation independently, but its publication ap-

[1] ARAGO's *Biographies*, 2d Series, 1859, p. 159.
[2] *Inductive Sciences*, New York, 1858, Vol. II., p. 100.
[3] *Young's Works*, Vol. I., p. 383.

peared after Young's. Some idea of the difficulty encountered in grasping the notion of transverse vibrations is obtained from Arago's narration to Whewell, "that when he [Arago] and Fresnel had obtained their joint experimental results of the non-interference of oppositely polarized pencils, and when Fresnel pointed out that transverse vibrations were the only possible translation of this fact into the undulatory theory, he himself protested that he had not courage to publish such a conception; and, accordingly, the second part of the Memoir was published in Fresnel's name alone."[1] Fresnel advanced the whole subject of polarized light. The rich colours produced by polarized light passing through certain crystals were discovered by Arago in 1811. Partisans of the two rival optical theories hastened to find explanations of this phenomenon of depolarization. On the undulatory theory explanations were given first by Young, then more fully by Arago and Fresnel. On the corpuscular theory, the facts were accounted for by Biot in a complicated research of great mathematical elegance. This was received favourably by Laplace and other mathematicians, who found the speculations of Biot more congenial to their habits of thought than those of Fresnel. Arago entered the lists against Biot, and the discussion was carried on with such bitterness that the two physicists, once intimately associated, became wholly estranged.[2] About 1816 Biot discovered that plates of tourmaline show double refraction, but absorb the ordinary ray. This led him to the construction of the well-known tourmaline tongs for the study of polarization phenomena. He gave also the important laws of rotary polarization and their application to the analysis of various substances.

[1] *Inductive Sciences*, Vol. II., p. 101.
[2] *Proceedings of the American Academy of Arts and Sciences*, Vol. VI., 1862–1865, p. 16 *et seq.*, "Jean Baptiste Biot."

The phenomena of polarized light in crystals were ex.
amined with great success by *Sir David Brewster* (1781–1868).
Although educated for the Church, he never engaged in its
active duties. In 1799 he was induced by his fellow-student,
Brougham, to repeat and study Newton's experiments on
diffraction. From that time on Brewster was engaged almost
continually in original research. He became professor of
physics at St. Andrews, and later, principal of the University
of Edinburgh. In 1819 he established, in connection with
Jameson, the *Edinburgh Philosophical Journal.* He was the
leading organizer of the British Association for the Advancement of Science, which held its first meeting at York in 1831.
He became famous as the inventor of the kaleidoscope, for
which the demand in both England and America was greater,
for a time, than could be met. Brewster, like Biot, was never
friendly to the undulatory theory. "The discoverer of the
law of polarization of biaxal crystals, of optical mineralogy,
and of double refraction by compression" was in a frame of
mind to assert, even after the maturer researches of Young,
Fresnel, and Arago had been given to the world, that "his
chief objection to the undulatory theory of light was that he
could not think the Creator guilty of so clumsy a contrivance
as the filling of space with ether in order to produce light." [1]

After 1825 the emission theory, though still supported by
several scientists of prominence, was abandoned by the majority
of physicists, especially by the younger men. Nevertheless,
the *crucial test*, which destroyed once for all the validity of the
emission theory, was not performed until the middle of the
century. According to the emission theory the velocity of
light is greater in an optically denser medium, while, according to the undulatory theory, it is smaller. Wheatstone, who

---

[1] TYNDALL, *Six Lectures on Light*, 2d ed., New York, 1877, p. 49.

as early as 1834 had been determining the duration of the
electric spark by aid of rotating mirrors, suggested that the
same method might be used to ascertain the velocity of light
and to find out whether the speed was greater in the more
refracting medium. The idea was taken up by Arago, but as
his eyesight was poor, the undertaking was left to younger
men. The mechanical difficulties were great; a mirror must
be made to rotate at a speed of over one thousand revolu-
tions per second. By some, Arago's project was considered
chimerical, because it was thought impossible for the eye to
seize the instantaneous image of a flash reflected from a mirror
rotating with such enormous speed. Bertrand remarked that
"an attentive and assiduous observer may, according to computations of M. Babinet, hope to catch the ray once in three
years."[1] The experiment was undertaken by Foucault. He
adopted the combination of apparatus now described in almost
every general treatise on physics, by which the difficulty
mentioned above was removed.[2] The success of his experiments was announced to the Academy of Sciences, May 6,
1850. He found the velocity of light in water to be less than
in air; from that moment Newton's emission theory was dead.

Jean Léon Foucault (1819–1868) was born in Paris. He
studied medicine, but between the years 1845 and 1849 entered
upon physical researches. At this time he worked in conjunction with Fizeau. After their separation, each made determinations of the velocity of light. Foucault's research on the
velocity in air relative to that in water, mentioned above, was
carried on at his pavilion in the Rue d'Assas, and was submitted by him in 1853 as a thesis for the degree of Doctor of

[1] PH. GILBERT, Léon Foucault, sa vie et son œuvre scientifique.
Bruxelles, 1879, p. 32.
[2] For details, see DELAUNAY, "Essay on the Velocity of Light,"
Smithsonian Report, 1864, pp. 135–165.

Science.[1] In 1851 Foucault presented a memoir giving his famous demonstration of the rotation of the earth by means of the pendulum.[2] The following year he invented that marvellous piece of mechanism, the gyroscope. In 1854 Napoleon III. secured a place for him at the Paris Observatory as physicist. Much was contributed by Foucault toward greater perfection of astronomical instruments.[3]

Foucault's early co-worker, *Hippolyte Louis Fizeau* (1819–

---

[1] Ph. Gilbert, *op. cit.*, p. 32.

[2] The experiment was made in four places. The first one was a cellar two metres deep at his pavilion in the Rue d'Assas. A brass ball weighing five kilogrammes was suspended by a steel wire. The ball was drawn aside, held in that position by a thread until it was at complete rest, then set free by burning the thread. The pendulum began oscillating in a *fixed* vertical plane, making thereby the fact of the earth's rotation experimentally evident. To the eye the plane of oscillation seemed to rotate and the earth to be at rest. Theory indicated that the angle of this apparent motion in a given time was equal to the angle through which the earth rotated in the same time, multiplied by the sine of the angle of latitude of the place where the experiment was made. An accurate verification of this law required more favourable conditions. Arago offered Foucault the use of the observatory building, where a pendulum eleven metres long enabled him to demonstrate the law with exactitude. Through the favour of Napoleon III., the Pantheon was chosen for the third test. A ball of twenty-eight kilogrammes was suspended there by a wire sixty-seven metres long and 1.4 millimetres thick. The Pantheon was thronged with visitors. The fourth exhibition was made at the Universal Exposition of 1855. These pendulum experiments became very famous. The only previous record of similar observations dates from the time of the *Accademia del Cimento*. Viviani is credited with the statement, " We have observed that all pendulums suspended by a single thread deviate from their primitive vertical plane and do so always in the same direction." See Ph. Gilbert, *op. cit.*, p. 55. But there is nothing to show that the Italian had divined the cause.

[3] Foucault possessed a poorly developed body. Says Lissajous : "It seemed as if nature had undertaken to establish a striking contrast between Foucault's physique and his intellectual powers. Who could have divined the man of genius under this frail appearance ?" *Ibidem*, 13.

1896)[1], was born in Paris. Being in possession of a fortune which left him free to follow his own inclinations, he devoted himself to physics. The means for his researches were largely supplied from his own private resources. In 1849 he made the earliest experimental determination of the absolute velocity of light. Römer's and Bradley's measurements had been based on astronomical observation. Fizeau rotated a toothed wheel, which intercepted light at regular intervals. The intermittent flashes were reflected from a distant fixed mirror. The research was carried on in the suburbs of Paris, between Suresnes and Montmartre, a distance of 8633 metres.[2] His article in the *Comptes Rendus* (Vol. 29, p. 90) appeared in 1849, the year before Foucault's paper on the relative velocity of light in air and water (Vol. 30, p. 551). In the year 1862 Foucault applied his method to the determination of the absolute velocity, and found values surpassing in accuracy all previous measurements.[3]

Fizeau made interesting experiments on the relative motion of ether and matter, showing that the ether within a transparent medium is carried forward by the moving medium, but with a velocity less than that of the medium. These results have been confirmed by Michelson and Morley.[4]

Fizeau's method of finding the velocity of light was adopted with some modifications by *Alfred Cornu* in Paris and by *James Young* and *George Forbes* in England. In Cornu's experiments of 1874 the fixed mirror was at a distance of 23 kilometres.[5] Young and Forbes's measurements, published

---

[1] *Nature*, Vol. 54, 1896, p. 523; P. Larousse, *Grand Dictionnaire Universel*.

[2] Ph. Gilbert, *op. cit.*, p. 36.

[3] *Comptes Rendus*, Vol. 55, 1862, pp. 501, 792.

[4] *Am. Jour. of Sci.* (3), Vol. 31, p. 377, 1886.

[5] *Annales de l'Observatoire de Paris* (*Mémoires*, Vol. 13, 1876).

in 1882,[1] seemed to show that the blue rays travel about 1.8 per cent faster than the red. The correctness of this result has been doubted. If true, stars should appear coloured just before and after an eclipse; moreover, Michelson, by Foucault's method, should have seen a spectral drawing out of the image of the slit, yielding a coloured image ten millimetres in width.[2]

The best determinations of light-velocity have been made in the United States. In 1867 *Simon Newcomb* (born 1835), then of the Naval Observatory, recommended the repetition of Foucault's experiment that closer values for the solar parallax might be obtained. A preliminary test was made in 1878 by *Albert A. Michelson* (born 1852) at the laboratory of the Naval Academy at Annapolis.[3] A gift of $2000 enabled him to continue experimentation. Measurements were taken in 1879. At Newcomb's request Michelson, in 1882, made a determination at the Case Institute in Cleveland, Ohio. The main difficulty in Foucault's experiments had been that the deflection was too small to be measured accurately. His distance between the fixed and the rotating mirror was only 4 metres (though, by using five fixed mirrors, this was virtually increased to 20 metres), and the displacement of the return image was only .7 millimetre. In Michelson's improved arrangement the return image was displaced through 133 millimetres, or nearly 200 times that obtained by Foucault.

In March, 1879, Congress voted an appropriation of $5000 for experiments to be made under the direction of Simon New-

[1] *Philos. Trans.*, Part I., 1882.

[2] A. A. MICHELSON, *Astr. Papers for the Am. Ephem. and Naut. Almanac*, Vol. II., Part IV., p. 237, 1885.

[3] JOSEPH LOVERING, "Address on Presentation of Rumford Medal to Prof. A. A. Michelson," in *Am. Acad. of Arts and Science*, New Series, Vol. 16, 1888–89, p. 384. We have taken several details from this source.

comb.   The movable mirror was mounted at Fort Meyer.   The fixed mirror was placed at one time at the Naval Observatory (distance, 2550.95 metres), and at another time at Washington Monument (distance, 3721.21 metres).   Michelson assisted in the operations until he removed to Cleveland in the autumn of 1880.   Observations began in the summer of 1880, and were continued until the autumn of 1882, the most favourable days in spring, summer, and autumn being selected.   Only during the hour after sunrise or the hour before sunset were the atmospheric conditions such that a steady image of the slit could be obtained.   Altogether 504 sets of measurements were made; 276 by Newcomb, 140 by Michelson, 88 by Holcombe.[1]

The results in kilometres per second obtained for the velocity of light *in vacuo* are as follows: Fizeau, in 1849, 315,000; Foucault, in 1862, 298,000; Cornu, in 1874, 298,500; Cornu, in 1878, 300,400; Young and Forbes, in 1880–1881, 301,382; Michelson, in 1879, 299,910; Michelson, in 1882, 299,853; Newcomb, in 1882, 299,860, when using only results supposed free from constant error, and 299,810 when including all observations.[2]

The earliest observation of *dark lines* in the solar spectrum was made by *William Hyde Wollaston* (1766–1828), a London physician.[3]   In 1802 he saw seven lines; the five most promi-

---

[1] Consult S. Newcomb, *Astr. Papers for the Am. Ephem. and Naut. Alm.*, Vol. III., Part III., 1885.

[2] These figures and some other details have been taken from Preston, *Theory of Light*, Ch. XIX.   For a fuller account of researches on light the reader is referred to R. T. Glazebrook, "Report on Optical Theories," in *Report of British Association*, 1885, abstracted in *Nature*, Vol. 48, pp. 473–477; Humphrey Lloyd, "Report on the Progress and Present State of Physical Optics," in *Report of British Association*, 1834.

[3] His invention of the process of rendering platinum malleable brought him a considerable annual royalty.   He invented the *camera lucida* and cryophorus; he discovered palladium and rhodium.

nent ones were considered by him to be the natural boundaries or dividing lines of the pure simple colours of the spectrum.[1] His explanation is of interest, for it shows how a most plausible theory may be destitute of all truth. Says Wollaston: " . . . The colours into which a beam of white light is separable by refraction, appear to me to be neither *seven*, as they usually are seen in the rainbow, nor reducible by any means (that I can find) to *three*, as some persons have conceived; but . . . *four* primary divisions of the prismatic spectrum may be seen, with a degree of distinctness that, I believe, has not been described nor observed before."[2]

The first great research on solar dark lines was made by Fraunhofer, who had no knowledge of Wollaston's discovery. *Joseph Fraunhofer* (1787–1826) was born at Straubing in Bavaria. He was the son of a poor glazier, and early in life began to assist his father in his trade. Skilled in glass-grinding, he secured a place in the optical institute of Utzschneider in the village of Benediktbeuern. In 1818 he took charge of the institute, which, soon after, was moved to Munich. Fraun-

---

[1] Mrs. MARY SOMERVILLE, the mathematician and physicist, gives the following recollections : "One bright morning Dr. Wollaston came to pay us a visit in Hanover Square, saying, 'I have discovered seven dark lines crossing the solar spectrum, which I wish to show you;' then, closing the window shutters so as to leave only a narrow line of light, he put a small glass prism into my hand, telling me how to hold it. I saw them distinctly. I was among the first, if not the very first, to whom he showed these lines, which were the origin of the most wonderful series of cosmical discoveries, and have proved that many of the substances of our globe are also constituents of the sun, the stars, and even the nebulæ. Dr. Wollaston gave me the little prism, which is doubly valuable, being of glass manufactured at Munich by Fraunhofer, whose table of dark lines has now become the standard of comparison in that marvellous science, the work of many illustrious men, brought to perfection by Bunsen and Kirchhoff." *Personal Recollections of Mary Somerville*, by her daughter MARTHA SOMERVILLE, Boston, 1874, p. 133.

[2] *Philos. Trans.*, 1802, p. 378.

hofer became a member of the Munich Academy of Sciences, and conservator of its physical cabinet.[1]

In his optical work, Fraunhofer combined to a rare degree theoretic insight with practical skill. "By his invention of new and improved methods, machinery, and measuring instruments for grinding and polishing lenses, by his having the superintendence, after 1811, also of the work in glass-melting, enabling him to produce flint and crown glass in larger pieces, free of veins, but especially by his discovery of a method of computing accurately the forms of lenses, he has led practical optics into entirely new paths, and has raised the achromatic telescope to, until then, undreamed-of perfection."[2]

In the endeavour to determine indices of refraction of glass for particular colours, to be used in the design of more accurate achromatic lenses, Fraunhofer accidentally discovered in the spectrum of a lamp the double line in the orange, now known as the sodium line. In oil and tallow light and, in fact, in all firelight, he saw this sharply defined, bright, double line, "exactly in the same place and consequently very useful" in the determination of indices. A ray from a narrow slit was allowed to fall upon a distant flint-glass prism, placed in the position of least deviation in front of the telescope of a theodolite. Fraunhofer proceeded to use sunlight. "I wished to find out," he says, "whether a similar bright line could be seen in the spectrum of sunlight as in the spectrum of lamplight, and I found, with the telescope, instead of this, an almost countless number of strong and feeble vertical lines, which, however, were darker than the other parts of the

[1] ROSENBERGER, III., p. 189.
[2] E. LOMMEL in preface, p. vii., to *Joseph von Fraunhofer's Gesammelte Schriften*, München, 1888.

spectrum, some appearing to be almost perfectly black."[1]
On examining other substances, like hydrogen, alcohol, sulphur, he found the bright line again. This must have been
due, of course, to the presence of sodium as an impurity,
the minutest quantity of which will exhibit its spectrum.
Fraunhofer examined also starlight, and recognized in Venus
some of the solar lines.[2]

He was the first to observe spectra due to gratings, and
with them he made the earliest determination of wave-lengths.
His gratings were of wire .04 to .6 mm. thick. The grating
space varied from .0528 to .6866 mm. He made ten gratings
and found the wave-length for D with each. The results ranged
from .0005882 to .0005897, giving a mean value of .0005888
mm., which is remarkably accurate, if we consider the crude-
ness of his gratings.[3] A paper of 1823 contains experiments
with two glass gratings having spaces of .0033 and .0160 mm.,
respectively.

Fraunhofer's publication of 1814 did not receive prompt
recognition, nor did his papers of 1821 and 1823. Physicists
were fighting over the emission and wave theories of light.
The attention of chemists was concentrated upon Dalton's
atomic theory and the Berthollet-Proust controversy over the
law of definite proportions. The full explanation of the
new fact brought forth by Fraunhofer was not given for

---

[1] *Gesammelte Schriften, op. cit.,* p. 10. Quoted from the memoir,
" Bestimmung des Brechungs- und des Farbenzerstreuungs-Vermögens
verschiedener Glasarten, in Bezug auf die Vervollkommnung achroma-
tischer Fernröhre," which appeared first in *Denkschriften der Münchener
Akad.,* Band V., 1814–1815.

[2] G. W. A. KAHLBAUM, *Aus der Vorgeschichte der Spectralanalyse,*
Basel, 1888, p. 12.

[3] See FRAUNHOFER, *Neue Modification des Lichtes,* 1821 ; also LOUIS
BELL, "The Absolute Wave-Length of Light" in *Philos. Magazine* (5),
Vol. 25, 1888, p. 245.

nearly forty years. He himself had failed to find the key
to the hieroglyphics of the solar lines, the "Fraunhofer lines,"
nor had he clearly defined the rôle which the spectral lines
were destined to play in chemical analysis.

After Fraunhofer, the first researches were made in England. *J. F. W. Herschel* examined bright-line spectra of several substances, stated that the colours of the bright lines were
a means of detecting small quantities of a substance, and in
1827 touched on this subject in his work *On Light*. *Charles
Wheatstone* published, in 1835, a paper on spectra of the
electric arc passing between metals. *William Henry Fox
Talbot* (1800–1877), a rich citizen, expressed the belief that
every homogeneous ray, whatever its colour, always indicates
the presence of a definite chemical compound. Yet none of
these investigators arrived at clear notions on the subject.
Talbot, for instance, falls into an error which inexperienced
students in our laboratories frequently commit: he looks upon
certain bright-line spectra as being really dark-line spectra.
"Copper-salts give spectra so covered with dark lines as to
resemble the solar spectrum."[1] Kirchhoff points out that the
English investigators did not establish the strict dependence
of the spectral lines upon the particular element in the flame;[2]
thus Talbot ascribes the *D* line to both sulphur and the salts
of sodium. *Sir David Brewster*, in 1832, described dark-line
spectra, formed by absorption of rays passing through coloured
glass and through certain gases. These spectra simulated the
solar spectrum. In the fact that fuming nitric acid absorbs
lines, while the liquid does not, Brewster saw an argument
against the wave theory of light; for a gas ought to offer less
impedance to motion of the ether than its denser liquid. The

[1] KAHLBAUM, *op. cit.*, p. 18.

[2] G. KIRCHHOFF, "Zur Geschichte der Spectralanalyse," *Gesammelte
Abhandlungen*, Leipzig, 1882, pp. 625–641 ; ROSENBERGER, III., p. 313.

exact coincidence of the bright lines of sodium with the dark
D lines of the sun was established by *William Allen Miller* of
Kings College, and by *Foucault* in Paris.   The latter did this
by introducing simultaneously into the spectroscope sunlight
and the electric light displaying the sodium lines.   The possible production of the Fraunhofer lines through absorption of
certain rays by the solar atmosphere was then under consideration, but no definite conclusion was reached as to the validity
of this explanation.

A great aid to the study of spectra was the discovery of the
art of photography by *Joseph Nicephore Niepce* (1765–1833),
who produced photographic pictures on metal in 1827.   *Louis
Jacques Mandé Daguerre* (1789–1851) was for some years
Niepce's coadjutor, and subsequently improved the method of
the latter, announcing in 1839 the new process known as the
"daguerreotype."   This famous process was at once taken up by
J. W. Draper in New York, who was the first to apply it to
individuals.   In the first trials, "the face of the sitter . . .
was dusted with white powder," and on a bright day a picture
was taken in five or seven minutes.   In 1840 Draper photographed the moon; in 1842 he photographed the Fraunhofer lines, only a few months after a similar achievement
by *Edmond Becquerel* in France.   In 1843 Joseph Saxton, a
mechanician of the United States mint in Philadelphia, ruled
for Draper a diffraction grating of glass, and the latter photographed the diffraction spectrum.   We will now sketch the
life of this assiduous investigator.

John William Draper (1811–1882) was born at St. Helen's,
near Liverpool, and studied at the London University.   He
came to the United States in 1833.   After studying medicine
at the University of Pennsylvania, he was chosen to the chair
of chemistry and physiology at Hampden-Sidney College, Virginia, and later to the same chair at the University of New

York, where he remained until the end of his long life. For many years he dwelt in a quiet retreat at Hastings-on-the-Hudson, near New York, surrounded by everything which could minister to the tastes of a veteran in science.[1]

In 1847, Draper published an important memoir,[2] in which he concluded from experiment that all solid substances and probably liquids become incandescent at the same temperature, viz., red hot at 525° C.; that below 525° C. invisible rays are emitted, and as the temperature rises above 525°, rays of greater refrangibility are added successively and continuously; that all spectra of incandescent solids are continuous, that gases give continuous spectra too, but may have bright lines superposed. The last statement is incorrect. The error originated in his use of bright flames giving, in addition to the line spectrum of the salt placed in the flame, the continuous spectrum of solid carbon; a luminous gas ordinarily gives only bright lines.

Thirteen years later Draper's correct conclusions were deduced independently from theoretical considerations by Kirchhoff, who started out from the relation between emitting and absorbing powers possessed by different bodies for radiant energy. This relation had been established in 1854 by Ångström (and later by Balfour Stewart).

An exhaustive account of spectrum analysis before Kirchhoff and Bunsen would call for further reference to researches made by *Andreas, Ångström, Balfour Stewart, Sir David Brewster, J. H. Gladstone, Julius Plücker* (the inventor of "Plücker

---

[1] *Am. Jour. of Science* (3), Vol. 23, 1882, p. 163; see also *Nat. Acad. of Sciences, Biographical Memoirs*, Vol. II., 1886, p. 351.

[2] *Philos. Magazine*, May, 1847; J. W. DRAPER's *Scientific Memoirs*, New York, 1878, "Memoir I."; see also J. W. DRAPER, "Early Contributions to Spectrum Photography and Photo-Chemistry," *Nature*, Vol. X., 1874.

tubes "), *V. S. M. van der Willigen, Edmond Becquerel,* and many others.[1]

Gustav Kirchhoff (1824–1887) was born at Königsberg; he became privat-docent in Berlin, then extraordinary professor at Breslau, ordinary professor at Heidelberg in 1854, and professor in Berlin after 1875. The rich period of his life was the twenty years he taught at Heidelberg, where he worked conjointly with the great chemist, *Robert Wilhelm Bunsen* (born 1811).[2] It was during the years 1859–1862 that these great investigators together made the great discoveries of spectrum analysis. At that time the physical laboratory at Heidelberg was very unpretentious, being located in a house, the "Riesengebäude," then 150 years old. The memorable researches were carried on in a small room. Illuminating gas had been introduced into the building in 1855.[3] In 1857 Bunsen and Roscoe first described the "Bunsen burner."[4] This new burner furnished Bunsen and Kirchhoff with a non-luminous gas-flame of fairly high temperature, in which chemical substances could be vaporized and a spectrum could be obtained, due purely and simply to the luminous vapour. In this way some of the errors of earlier experimenters were avoided.

In October, 1859, Kirchhoff and Bunsen published their first paper,[5] which contains their later researches *in nuce*. From experiments the conclusion is drawn by Kirchhoff "that a coloured flame, the spectrum of which contains bright sharp

---

[1] Consult KAHLBAUM, *op. cit.;* KIRCHHOFF, "Zur Geschichte der Spectralanalyse."

[2] For his contributions to chemistry, see *Nature*, Vol. 23, 1881, p. 597.

[3] GEORG QUINCKE, *Gesch. d. Physik. Instituts d. Univ. Heidelberg,* Heidelberg, 1885, p. 16.

[4] *Poggendorff's Annalen,* C, pp. 84–86; ROSENBERGER, III., p. 484.

[5] "Ueber die Fraunhoferschen Linien," in *Monatsberichte d. Akad. d. Wissensch. zu Berlin,* October, 1859, p. 662.

lines, so weakens rays of the colour of these lines, when they pass through it, that dark lines appear in place of the bright lines as soon as there is placed behind the flame a light of sufficient intensity, in which the lines are otherwise absent;" "that the dark lines of the solar spectrum, which are not caused by the terrestrial atmosphere, arise from the presence in the glowing solar atmosphere of those substances which in a flame produce bright lines in the same position." Kirchhoff concluded that sodium, iron, magnesium, copper, zinc, barium, nickel, existed in the solar atmosphere.

The two investigators advanced, as scientifically established, the law that the bright lines in the spectrum may be taken as a sure sign of the presence of the respective metals. This conclusion was rendered doubly sure by the discovery in the mineral water at Dürkheim, through the spectrum, of two new metals. From the blue and the red lines, by which they were recognized, they were named "Cæsium" and "Rubidium." While spectrum analysis, as a terrestrial science, was due equally to Kirchhoff and Bunsen, its celestial applications belong to Kirchhoff alone. Kirchhoff's explanation of the Fraunhofer lines was epoch-making. Says Helmholtz:[1] "It had in fact most extraordinary consequences of the most palpable kind, and has become of the highest importance for all branches of natural science. It has excited the admiration and stimulated the fancy of men as hardly any other discovery has done, because it has permitted an insight into worlds that seemed forever veiled for us." In this connection Kirchhoff frequently related the following story:[2] "The question whether Fraunhofer's lines reveal the presence of

---

[1] "A Memoir of Gustav Robert Kirchhoff," *Deutsche Rundschau*, February 1888, Vol. 14, pp. 232–245; translated in *Smithsonian Report*, 1889, pp. 527–540.

[2] *Smithsonian Report*, 1889, p. 537.

gold in the sun was being investigated. Kirchhoff's banker
remarked on this occasion: 'What do I care for gold in the
sun if I cannot fetch it down here?' Shortly afterwards
Kirchhoff received from England a medal for his discovery,
and its value in gold. While handing it over to his banker,
he observed, 'Look here, I have succeeded at last in fetching
some gold from the sun.'"

It has been said that Kirchhoff's gift as an investigator was
not to *initiate*, but to *complete*.[1] This is plainly seen in his
work on spectrum analysis. The threads of his discovery had
been seized upon by great men before him. So nearly had
English, French, and American scientists attained to Kirchhoff's results, that prolonged discussions have arisen on questions of priority. "All had seen something, made guesses,
considered as possible or probable (without Kirchhoff having
been aware of it at the time, however)." But it remains the
great merit of Kirchhoff to have established a solid basis, to
have arrived at sure knowledge.

One claim of priority was made in favour of *William Hallows
Miller* of Cambridge, who, it was argued, "anticipated by
nearly sixteen years the remarkable discovery, ascribed to
Kirchhoff, of the opacity of certain coloured flames to light of
their own colour."[2] Another claim was made soon after Kirchhoff's paper of 1859 by William Thomson (now Lord Kelvin)
in favour of *George Gabriel Stokes* (born 1819) of Pembroke
College, Cambridge, who, before Kirchhoff (perhaps about the
year 1849), in course of a conversation, explained the formation of absorption lines as follows: "Vapour of sodium must
possess by its molecular structure a tendency to vibrate in the

[1] W. VOIGT, *Zum Gedächtniss von G. Kirchhoff*, Göttingen, 1888,
p. 9.
[2] CROOKES in *Chemical News*, May 18, 1862; *Philos. Magazine* (4),
Vol. 25, 1863, p. 261.

periods corresponding to the degree of refrangibility of the double line D. Hence the presence of sodium in a source of light must tend to originate light of that quality. On the other hand, vapour of sodium in an atmosphere round a source must have a great tendency to retain itself, *i.e.* to absorb and have its temperature raised by light from the source of the precise quality in question. In the atmosphere round the sun, therefore, there must be present vapour of sodium, which, according to the mechanical explanation thus suggested, being particularly opaque for light of that quality, prevents such of it as is emitted from the sun from penetrating to any considerable distance through the surrounding atmosphere."[1] Stokes did not ascertain experimentally whether or not the vapour of sodium has the special absorbing power anticipated, but he remembered a test, showing this power, made in France by Foucault.[2] He did not attach sufficient importance to his mechanical theory to have it appear in print. Sir William Thomson, however, adds this: "I have given it in my lectures regularly for many years, always pointing out along with it that solar and stellar chemistry were to be studied by investigating terrestrial substances giving bright lines in the spectra of artificial flames corresponding to the dark lines of the solar and stellar spectra." Stokes himself generously published the following disclaimer: "I have never attempted to claim for myself any part of Kirchhoff's admirable discovery, and cannot help thinking that some of my friends have been over zealous in my cause."[3]

Since the creation of the science of spectrum analysis by Kirchhoff and Bunsen, scientists have been busy perfecting the details of the theory, improving methods of experimenta-

[1] *Philos. Magazine* (4), Vol. 25, 1863, p. 261.

[2] *L'Institut*, Feb. 7, 1849, p. 45.

[3] *Nature*, Vol. 13, 1875, p. 189.

tion, and enlarging our knowledge of celestial chemistry. It soon became evident that great caution must be exercised in deducing the chemical constitution and physical characteristics of bodies from the spectra which they give. Confusion is introduced by the occurrence of multiple spectra. As early as 1862, *Julius Plücker*, in Bonn, pointed out that the same substance may give different spectra at different temperatures. He and *W. Hittorf* found for hydrogen, nitrogen, and sulphur fumes two kinds of spectra, namely, a weak band spectrum and a bright line spectrum. *Adolph Wüllner* of the Technicum in Aachen, in 1868, discussed the variation in the spectra of hydrogen, oxygen, nitrogen, when subjected in Plücker tubes to different degrees of pressure.[1] For oxygen he observed three spectra under different conditions of pressure. As in a denser gas the electric resistance to the discharge through the tube was greater, the temperature was probably higher. Hence Wüllner thought that in Plücker tubes variations in pressure of the gas were accompanied by changes in the temperature, and that the spectral changes resulted from alterations in both pressure and temperature. Ångström combated Wüllner's position, arguing that while a rise in temperature may bring out new lines and an increase in pressure may widen the lines, nevertheless a spectrum never changes into another of entirely new characteristics.[2] Some of Wüllner's results were attributed by Ångström to the presence of impurities in the gases. However, more extended research revealed that spectral changes depend not only upon variations in temperature and pressure, but also upon molecular constitution. The effect of molecular structure was investigated by *Al. Mitscherlich*, *Clifton*, *H. E. Roscoe*, and by

---

[1] *Poggendorff's Annalen*, Vol. 135, p. 497.

[2] *Recherches sur le Spectre Solaire*, Upsala, 1868. See ROSENBERGER, III., p. 701.

J. Norman Lockyer.[1]   Lockyer, in 1873 and 1874, advanced the view that each composite body has as definite a spectrum as a simple one; that line spectra are due to the free atoms, band spectra to molecules or groups of molecules.   Lockyer's theory was regarded favourably by Ångström, but was opposed by Wüllner, who in 1879[2] made experiments on nitrogen, showing that by gradual change of temperature the band spectra passed gradually into the line spectra.   He argued that Lockyer's theory of the dissociation of molecules was not needed to explain the facts.   Lockyer observed that line spectra (of calcium, for instance) change as the temperature rises.   He then advanced the bold theory that just as the transition of band spectra into line spectra may be explained by the dissociation of molecules into atoms, so the changes in the line spectra, due to rise in temperature, may be explained by the breaking up of the atoms into still more elementary substances, thus indicating the compound nature of the chemical elements themselves.[3]

The Germans, *H. Kayser* and *C. Runge*, in a series of researches, beginning in 1890, have shown that the distribution of lines in the spectra of the elements is by no means so irregular as it at first seems.   They find that in the spectra of the common elements there are line series.   At one time the presence in argon of more than one series was supposed to indicate that it was a mixture of elements; but as the same reasoning applied to oxygen, which has six series, leads to conclusions presumably erroneous, this hypothesis has been abandoned.

[1] Consult J. N. LOCKYER, *Studies in Spectrum Analysis*, New York, 1893, Chap. VII.

[2] ROSENBERGER, III., p. 706.   Consult report "On the Present State of Spectrum Analysis," *Report of Brit. Ass.*, Swansea meeting, 1880; abstracted in *Nature*, Vol. 22, p. 522.

[3] LOCKYER, *op. cit.*, p. 189.

It is still doubtful whether increased pressure augments the breadth of lines. *G. D. Liveing* and *J. Dewar* have combated the theory that the continuous spectra are produced by the broadening of the lines of the same gas at low pressure.[1] An important observation was made in 1895 by *W. J. Humphreys* and *J. F. Mohler* in the Johns Hopkins University laboratory. Certain discrepancies noticed by *L. E. Jewell* led them to undertake experiments which demonstrate that the lines in the arc spectra of metals shift appreciably toward the red when the pressure of the atmosphere surrounding the arc is increased. This may be distinguished from the Doppler effect by the fact that the displacement is different for every metal and for different spectral series of the same metal.[2] Another interesting phenomenon, showing the influence of magnetization on light, was observed in 1896 by *P. Zeeman*, now professor at the University of Amsterdam. In 1862 Faraday had examined the sodium lines when the flame was placed between the poles of a magnet, but had failed to notice any effect; Zeeman, by means of modern appliances, noticed a change. Light from an electric arc was sent through a heated tube containing sodium vapour and placed between the poles of an electro-magnet. When acted upon by the magnet a slight broadening of the lines was seen.[3] *A. A. Michelson* of the University of Chicago, using his new echelon spectroscope, showed that the phenomenon is much more complex. For instance, "all spectral lines are tripled when the radiations emanate in a magnetic field."

The spectroscope has been used extensively in the chemical

---

[1] W. HUGGINS, Inaugural Address, *Nature*, Vol. 44, 1891, p. 373.

[2] *Astrophys. Jour.*, Vol. III., 1896, pp. 114–137 ; *Johns Hopkins Univ. Circular*, No. 130 ; *Nature*, Vol. 56, 1897, pp. 415, 461.

[3] *P. Zeeman* in *Phil. Mag.*, Vol. 43, pp. 226–239 ; *Nature*, Vol. 55, pp. 192, 347 ; consult O. LODGE in *Electrician* (London), Vol. 38, pp. 568, 643.

analysis of heavenly bodies,[1] but it has received also an indirect application, which promises to become hardly less important. A telescope gives us no direct evidence of stellar motion in a direction toward us or from us, but now the spectroscope has placed in our hands the means of detecting such motion. The principle involved was first worked out for sound by *Johann Christian Doppler* (1803–1853), a native of Salzburg, Austria. In 1835, having been unable to secure a suitable situation, he was about to emigrate to America, when he was made professor of mathematics at the Realschule in Prague.[2] He called attention, in a paper of 1842, to the fact that the colour of a luminous body, just like the pitch of a sounding body, must be changed by motion of the body to or from the observer. In the year 1845, *Christoph Heinrich Dietrich Buys-Ballot* (born 1817), director of the royal meteorological institute at Utrecht, experimented on railroad trains, and verified the theory as applied to sound. A person on a train rushing through a station finds the pitch of a sounding bell at the station higher on approach and lower on recession than it actually is. Doppler argued that most probably all stars emitted white light, and that the colour of some of them was due to their motion toward us or away from us. As Buys-Ballot pointed out, this conclusion is erroneous. The approach of a star would simply produce a slight shift of the entire spectrum in the direction of the ultra-violet region, some infra-red rays becoming visible and some violet rays becoming invisible. No change in colour could take place. But in 1848

---

[1] For the history of astrophysics consult A. M. CLERKE, *History of Astronomy during the Nineteenth Century.* For "Literature of the Spectroscope," see *Smithsonian Miscellaneous Collections*, Vol. 32, 1888.

[2] Before his death he was professor of experimental physics at the University of Vienna. See F. POSKE, *Zeitsch. f. d. Physik. u. Chem. Unterricht*, Vol. 9, 1896, p. 248.

Fizeau pointed out that this shifting must become noticeable through the examination of the lines of the spectrum. For instance, if the hydrogen lines of an approaching star are compared with those of a hydrogen tube in the laboratory, the former are moved toward the violet, while the latter are fixed. The displacement is so slight that many years elapsed before instruments were devised by which accurate measurements could be taken. The initiative in this delicate work was taken in 1868 by the English astronomer, *William Huggins* (born 1824), and, in 1871, *H. C. Vogel* of Potsdam detected the shifting effects due to the sun's rotation. In recent years Doppler's principle has been applied with great success to the motions of stars and to the discovery of double stars by Vogel, *Edward C. Pickering* of Harvard, *James E. Keeler* of the Lick Observatory, and others. Some double stars discovered by this method are so close to each other that they appear like a single star even when examined by our most powerful telescopes.

There are two methods of obtaining spectra: one is by the aid of a prism or a train of prisms, the other by the use of a grating. The former means was employed by Kirchhoff and Bunsen; the latter was used to some extent by Fraunhofer and by J. W. Draper. The theory of the grating ("striated surfaces") had been outlined by Thomas Young. After Fraunhofer the first improvement in the art of manufacturing gratings was made by the optician, *F. A. Nobert*, of Greifswald in Pomerania. He made glass micrometers, which were used to determine the magnifying power of microscopes, and he furnished gratings to *E. Mascart* and *Ångström*. The latter published at Upsala, in 1868, in his *Recherches sur le Spectre Solaire*, a table of wave-lengths which for a long time served as a standard. All the measurements are in error by about one part in seven or eight thousand, owing mainly to the fact that the metre which he used as the standard of length was a trifle too short.[1] Ångström became aware of this as early as 1872, but he did not live to make the needed alterations. The corrections were made by his pupil, *R. Thalén*, in a publication of 1885.

Nobert's method of ruling diffraction gratings was jealously guarded by him as a trade secret. Since his time the best gratings have been made in the United States. About 1863 *Lewis Morris Rutherfurd* (1816–1892), a graduate of Williams College, and a lawyer, who studied astronomy in his own private observatory near New York, became interested in the preparation of gratings. Rutherfurd, after numerous preliminary experiments, constructed a machine of his own device, and ran it by means of a small water motor. " A diamond point traced parallel lines upon a glass plate pushed regularly forward by a system of levers acting on au acute glass wedge, this in its turn pushing the plate sideways." [2] Except for occasional slight changes in the intervals between the lines the gratings were admirable. Following the advice of *Ogden N. Rood* of Columbia College, he constructed, in 1867, a machine in which the plate was moved by a screw in place of levers. After several years' effort he produced gratings far superior to Nobert's. In 1875, or earlier, Rutherfurd silvered the gratings with the view to their more convenient spectroscopic use, but later he made gratings upon speculum metal in order to avoid the great wear upon the diamond.[3] In 1877 the ruling machine was enlarged. Armed with Rutherfurd's superior gratings, *Charles Saunders Peirce*, then of the United States Coast

---

[1] L. BELL, " The Absolute Wave-Length of Light," *Phil. Mag.* (5), Vol. 25, 1888, p. 245.

[2] B. A. GOULD in *Nat. Acad. of Sciences, Biographical Memoirs*, Vol. 3, p. 428.

[3] For details, consult article, " Ruling Machines," in *Johnson's Universal Cyclopædia.*

Survey, again attacked the problem of wave-lengths where
Ångström had left it ten years previously.[1]

The best gratings of the present time are those of *Henry A.
Rowland* of the Johns Hopkins University. His attention
was first called to the construction of dividing engines by the
inspection of an engine made by *William Augustus Rogers*
(1832–1898), at Waltham, Mass.[2] Rogers's aim was to produce
lines of extreme fineness for recticules in optical instruments,
and for delicate tests of microscope objectives. He was able
to rule as many as 4800 lines to the millimetre. Rowland
devoted about one year to the construction of a dividing
engine. The making of an accurate screw was the most delicate part of the task. The process consisted in grinding
the screw in a long nut in which it was constantly reversed.
When it was finished, there was not an error of half a wave-
length, although it was nine inches long.[3] Rowland invented
concave gratings, and ruled them on his engine. The colli-
mator could thereby be dispensed with. A second and a third
engine have been prepared under Rowland's direction, and at
present Rowland's gratings have no rival.[4] He has made large
photographic maps of the solar spectrum, and has prepared a
system of standard wave-lengths which is now universally
adopted. Under his direction, the wave-length of every line
in the solar spectrum is being measured, and the chemical
element to which it belongs is being determined.

That the solar spectrum is not confined to the visible part,

[1] *Am. Jour. Sci.* (3), Vol. 18, 1879, p. 51.

[2] *Proc. Am. Acad. of Arts and Sci.*, New Series, Vol. II., 1883–1884,
p. 482.

[3] Consult Rowland's article, "Screw," in *Encyclopædia Britannica*,
9th ed.

[4] For a biographical sketch of Rowland, and a picture of his second
dividing engine, see *Appleton's Pop. Sci. Month.*, Vol. 49, 1896,
pp. 110–120.

extending from the red to the violet, was first shown by *Sir William Herschel* (1738-1822), who in 1800 discovered that there are infra-red solar rays. Placing the thermometer in successive colours, he discovered the unequal distribution of heat in the solar spectrum, the heating being greatest below the red. Before him no one had suspected such an inequality. "It is sometimes of great use in natural philosophy," says the veteran astronomer,[1] "to doubt of things that are commonly taken for granted; especially as the means of resolving any doubt, when once it is entertained, are often within our reach." He speaks of solar heat as occasioned by "rays," subject to the laws of reflection and refraction." Thomas Young, in his *Lectures* of 1807, says, "This discovery must be allowed to be one of the greatest that has been made since the days of Newton." Nevertheless, the mass of physicists and text-book writers, for over half a century, failed to see the truth foreshadowed by W. Herschel, and afterwards established more clearly by Melloni. Herschel's views were attacked by *John Leslie* (1766-1832) of Edinburgh, the inventor of the differential thermometer. This able and earnest investigator, like all seekers after the truth, fell into error. He saw no affinity between radiant heat and light. He says: "What, then, is this calorific and frigorific fluid after which we are inquiring? It is no light, it has no relation to ether, it bears no analogy to the fluids, real or imaginary, of magnetism and electricity. But why have recourse to invisible agents? *Quod petis, hic est.* It is merely the ambient air." Thus Herschel's heating effects in the infra-red were attributed to currents of air from the visible part of the spectrum. However, Leslie found no followers, after *Sir Humphry Davy* had shown that in a partial vacuum the radiation was three times greater than

<hr />

[1] *Phil. Trans.*, 1800, p. 255.

in air at ordinary pressure, and after *Johann Wilhelm Ritter* (1776–1810) and *Wollaston* had discovered dark chemical rays in the ultra-violet.[1] In 1811 a young Frenchman, *De la Roche*, showed that, of two successive screens of the same kind, the second absorbs heat in a less ratio than the first, and he concluded that radiant heat is of different kinds.[2] W. Herschel had previously shown that "radiant heat is of different refrangibility."

But no marked progress was made in the knowledge of radiant heat until *Macedonio Melloni* (1798–1854)[3] began his researches. From early boyhood he displayed great love for science. He "was born a physicist," and began to teach physics as soon as he left the school-bench. For seven years he taught at the University of Parma. Political troubles banished him from Italy. In France he found in Arago a good friend. Melloni accepted a professorship in the Department of the Jura, but in 1837 he was permitted to return to his native country, where, in 1839, he was appointed Director of the Cabinet of Arts and Trades in Naples.[4] In 1850 Melloni published a great work, *La Thermochrôse, ou la coloration calorifique*, in which he embodied his researches on radiant energy. In the preface he gives the story of his early passion for nature. The passage is, in part, as follows:

"I was born at Parma, and when I got a holiday used to go into the country the night before, and go to bed early, so as to get up before the dawn. Then I used to steal silently out of the house, and run, with bounding heart, till I got to the

---

[1] ROSENBERGER, III., p. 67.

[2] S. P. LANGLEY, *Address* before A.A.A.S., 1888, p. 14.

[3] We have taken these dates from ROSENBERGER. MARIE and LAROUSSE give 1801–1853.

[4] J. LOVERING's biographic sketch in *Proc. of the Am. Acad. of Arts and Sci.*, Vol. III., 1857, p. 164.

top of a little hill, where I used to set myself so as to look toward the east." There, he tells us, he used to wait the rising sun and enjoy the glorious spectacle. "But nothing," he continues, "so rapt my imagination as the bond, so intimate, which unites the phenomena of life to the brilliant star of day," whose beams are accompanied by mysterious heat.[1]

To insure progress in the study of radiant heat it was necessary that the thermometer used by Herschel be superseded by a more delicate instrument. Such a one was the thermo-multiplier,[2] or thermopile, invented by *Leopoldo Nobili* (1784–1835), professor in Florence, and perfected by him and Melloni. One of the results, recognized more or less clearly by W. Herschel, De la Roche, and others, was emphasized by Melloni; viz. that radiant heat is of different kinds, that there is variety among heat rays just as there is variety among the visible rays. The colour of heat, as the phenomenon is metaphorically called by Melloni, is not perceived by the eye, but can be detected, as can colours of light, by prismatic dispersion or by experiments in which some colour varieties are absorbed more than others. Melloni invented the word *thermochrôse*, signifying "heat-colour." He arrived at a close realization of the identity of radiant heat and light. In 1843 he said, "Light is merely a series of calorific indications sensible to the organs of sight, or *vice versa*, the radiations of obscure heat are veritable invisible radiations of light."[3] But if it is true that where light is there must be radiant heat, then lunar rays must exhibit heat-effects. He tried the experiment, failed at first, but succeeded afterwards. On Mount Vesuvius, in 1846, by the employment of a polyzonal lens, one metre in

[1] LANGLEY, *op. cit.*, p. 16.
[2] *Pogg. Annal.*, Vol. 20, 1830, p. 245 ; Vol. 24, 1831, p. 640.
[3] Translated by LANGLEY, *op. cit.*, p. 18.

diameter, together with a thermopile and galvanometer, he succeeded in getting feeble indications of heat from lunar rays. Melloni made numerous experiments on the absorption of radiant heat by solids and liquids. He coined the word *diathermancy*, which has the same significance for radiant heat that the word *transparency* has for visible light. In his experiments, the radiation from a lamp, or other source, was allowed to pass through the air to the thermopile; the deflection of the galvanometer was then noted. Next, the substance whose diathermancy was to be tested (water, rock-salt, glass, or ice) was placed in the path of the rays directed upon the pile, and the consequent deflection noted. Melloni's tests seemed to show that rock-salt was perfectly transparent to all kinds of calorific rays—a conclusion now known to require some qualification. Ice and glass absorb most of these rays. Melloni demonstrated clearly that different solids and liquids possess different transmissive powers and that (except in rock-salt) the diathermancy varies with the source of the heat. Glass transmits 39% of the radiation from a Locatelli lamp, but only 6% of that from copper at 400° C.

While Melloni measured the diathermancy of different thicknesses of solids and liquids, *John Tyndall* (1820–1893) effected the same for gases and vapours. Tyndall was born near Carlow in Ireland. When about twenty-one years old he went to England and attached himself to a Manchester firm of railway engineers. In 1847 he accepted a position as teacher of mathematics and surveying in the newly established Greenwood College, where science was to be taught experimentally. About one year later he went to the University of Marburg to study mathematics, physics, and chemistry. The last study was taken under Bunsen. A strong influence toward physics was exerted upon him by *Karl Hermann Knoblauch*, born 1820, who had verified and extended Mel-

loni's work on radiant energy. After graduating in 1850,
Tyndall went to Berlin and worked one year in Magnus's
laboratory on diamagnetism and magne-crystallic action.
After his return to England he delivered, in 1853, a lecture
at the Royal Institution which "took his audience by storm."[1]
He was elected professor of natural philosophy in the Royal
Institution, which had become famous through the labours of
Thomas Young, Sir Humphry Davy, and Faraday. It was
in the laboratory of that place that Tyndall's subsequent
researches were made, except his observations of natural phenomena in the Swiss Alps during his vacations. His most
important original work was in the domain of heat. He possessed extraordinary powers of popularizing difficult subjects.
Perhaps his greatest services to science are through his books,
Heat a Mode of Motion, Six Lectures on Light (delivered in
America in 1872–1873), *Forms of Water*, etc., which are models
of popular exposition.

Melloni had concluded from experiments with his thermo-
electric apparatus that, for a distance of 18 or 20 feet, the
absorption of radiant heat by atmospheric air is perfectly in-
sensible. Tyndall, with more delicate appliances, verified this
conclusion: dry air is a practical vacuum, as regards the rays
of heat. In general, the elementary gases absorb scarcely
perceptible amounts of radiant heat. But Tyndall found it
different with compound gases; they absorb portions varying
directly with the complexity of their molecules. Thus the
vapour of ether, having fifteen atoms in one molecule, absorbed

[1] E. FRANKLAND, "John Tyndall," in *Proc. Royal Soc. of London*,
Vol. 55, 1894, p. xviii. For Tyndall's celebrated "Prayer-test" see
Contemporary Review, Vol. 20, 1872, pp. 205–210. The same volume
contains replies by *James M'Cosh* and others. Tyndall's "Belfast
Address," which, at the time, brought upon him the charge of "infi-
delity," is given in *Report of British Association*, 1874.

for equal volumes at maximum density, 100 times the quantity of radiant heat intercepted by the vapour of carbon disulphide, containing only three atoms. Tyndall found that the radiating powers follow precisely the same order as the powers of absorption. Thus, oxygen, hydrogen, and nitrogen do not radiate heat, while ammonia will show decided effects. The same subject was investigated by *II. G. Magnus* of Berlin, and the agreement between the two investigators was very close, except in case of aqueous vapour. Magnus found that it had little or no action; Tyndall found it to be considerable for heat rays of low refrangibility. The question is an important one in meteorology. The controversy lasted many years.[1] But in 1881 Tyndall published a paper[2] which finally proved that he was right. At that time *Alexander Graham Bell* had obtained musical sounds through the action of an intermittent beam of light falling upon solid bodies enclosed in a glass flask. The ear was placed in communication with the interior of the flask by means of a hearing tube. When a beam of light fell upon the substance in the tube, it expanded and a pulse of air was expelled. When the light was cut off, the opposite effect took place. Thus, sound was produced. Bell showed some of these experiments to Tyndall in the laboratory of the Royal Institution, whereupon Tyndall made experiments on flasks filled with different gases.[3] He says that when a flask containing moist air was placed in the intermittent beam, "I heard a powerful musical sound produced by

---

[1] For historic remarks on this point, consult TYNDALL, *Contributions to Molecular Physics in the Domain of Radiant Heat*, London, 1872, pp. 59-64.

[2] "Action of an Intermittent Beam of Radiant Heat upon Gaseous Matter," *Proc. Roy. Soc.*, Vol. 31, 1881, p. 307; *Nature*, Vol. 25, 1882, pp. 232-234.

[3] A. G. BELL, *Upon the Production of Sound by Radiant Energy*, Washington, 1881, p. 19.

the aqueous vapor. I placed the flask in cold water until its temperature was reduced from about 90° to 10° C., fully expecting the same sound would vanish at this temperature; but . . . the sound was distinct and loud. Three empty flasks filled with ordinary air were placed in a freezing mixture. On being rapidly transferred to the intermittent beam, sounds much louder than those obtained from dry air were produced." Thus the aqueous vapour showed absorption, and the controversy was finally ended.

Leslie, Melloni, and Tyndall pointed out an error of wide prevalence regarding the influence of colour on absorption. Benjamin Franklin had placed cloths of various colours upon snow and allowed the sun to shine upon them. They absorbed solar rays to different degrees and sank to different depths in the snow. From this Franklin concluded that dark colours were the best absorbers, and light colours the worst. But this generalization requires qualification. Did the radiation from the sun or other luminous body consist exclusively of visible rays, then the problem would be simpler, but the invisible rays often produce effects exactly opposite to what Franklin's theory would lead us to expect. Tyndall coated the bulb of a delicate mercury thermometer with alum (a white powder), and the bulb of a second thermometer with iodine (a dark powder). On exposing the bulbs at the same distance to the radiation from a gas flame, the alum-covered thermometer rose nearly twice as high as the other; alum was a better absorber than iodine. Tyndall says that "radiation from the clothes which cover the human body is not at all, to the extent sometimes supposed, dependent on their color. The color of animal's fur is equally incompetent to influence radiation. These are the conclusions arrived at by Leslie and Melloni *for obscure heat.*"[1]

[1] TYNDALL, *Heat a Mode of Motion*, New York, 1897, p. 299.

Important contributions to our knowledge of radiant energy were made by *Samuel Pierpont Langley* (born 1834). In 1867 he became professor of astronomy in the Western University of Pennsylvania, with charge of the observatory at Allegheny City. Since 1887 he has been connected with the Smithsonian Institution as secretary. To make marked progress in the study of radiation it seemed necessary to invent a more delicate instrument than the thermopile of Melloni and Tyndall. Langley's new device was the bolometer, first described in 1881.[1] A very fine strip of platinum (at first iron was used) serves as a conducting wire in a circuit. If radiation falls upon it, its temperature is raised and its electric resistance increased. A delicate galvanometer records the resulting disturbance in the electric current. The bolometer has been made to indicate a change of temperature of .0000001 of a degree centigrade. Some of its first results were to show that the maximum heat in the solar spectrum was in the orange, not in the infra-red, as claimed by W. Herschel and others. The earlier observers had used the prismatic spectrum, which is subject to two important errors: (1) the prism absorbs part of the radiation, exercising so-called "selective absorption"; (2) the prism concentrates the rays in the lower part of the spectrum as compared with the upper, thus falsifying the true distribution of heat. These errors are avoided by the use of a grating, which yields a "normal spectrum." For many years the belief (unsupported by experiment) was prevalent that our atmosphere acted exactly the part of glass in a hot-bed, and that it kept the planet warm by absorbing the *infra-red* rays radiated by the earth. Langley proved experi-

---

[1] *Am. Jour. Sci.* (3) Vol. 21, pp. 187–198. The latest form of it is described in the same journal, (4) Vol. 5, 1898, pp. 241–245. For a biographical sketch of Langley, see *Popular Science Monthly*, Vol. 27, 1885, pp. 401–409.

mentally that this was not true. The infra-red rays pass through with comparative ease. His experiments at Allegheny City, continued in 1881 on the crest of Mount Whitney in the Sierra Nevadas,[1] showed that the atmosphere acts "with selective absorption to an unanticipated degree, keeping back an immense proportion of the blue and green." The atmosphere not only keeps back a part of the solar radiation, but totally changes its composition in doing so. By taking out more of the blue and green, the residue coming down to us produces the sensation of what is familiarly known as "white" light, so that "white" is *not* the sum of all the radiation from the sun. Could we rise above the earth's atmosphere, then the sun would appear to us greenish blue. The pure original sunlight is no more like the radiation falling upon the earth's surface than the electric light is like that which reaches the eye through reddish glasses.

Assisted by F. W. Very, Langley experimented on the temperature of the moon.[2] The bolometer "gave indications of two maxima in the heat-curve, the first corresponding to the heat from the solar reflected rays, the second (indefinitely lower down in the spectrum) corresponding to a greater amount of radiant heat emitted from a source at a far lower temperature," viz. from the surface of the moon itself. The mean temperature of the sunlit lunar soil "is most probably not greatly above zero centigrade." The determination is founded on the fact, experimentally established by Langley, "that the position of the maximum in a curve, representing invisible radiant heat, furnishes a reliable criterion as to the temperature of the radiating (solid) body."

[1] *Am. Jour. Sci.* (3), Vol. 25, 1883, pp. 169–196.
[2] *Am. Jour. Sci.*, Vol. 38, 1889, pp. 421–440. This is only in abstract. The full memoir appeared in *Memoirs of the National Acad. of Sciences*, Vol. IV.

By the study of the radiation of the fire-fly, Langley and Very showed[1] "that it is possible to produce light without heat, other than that in the light itself; that this is actually effected now by nature's processes"; "that nature produces this cheapest light at about one four-hundredth part of the cost of the energy which is expended in the candle-flame, and at but an insignificant fraction of the cost of the electric light."

Langley demonstrated that the visual effect produced by any given constant amount of energy varies enormously according to the colour of the light in question. For the same colour, it varies with eyes of different individuals. The sensation of crimson light ordinarily requires that the energy of the waves arrested by the retina, during the act of perception, be about .001 of an erg, while the sensation of green can be produced by .000,000,01 of an erg. In other words, about 100,000 times the energy is demanded to make us see red that is needed to make us see green.[2]

Langley explored widely the infra-red region of the solar spectrum. J. W. Draper had, in his photograph of 1842, observed three wide bands in this region. The same were noticed by Foucault and Fizeau in 1846. *Captain W. de W. Abney* in 1880 mapped by photography the infra-red prismatic spectrum as far as 1.075^{μ}. Langley got heating effects of more than twice that wave-length; his delicate filament of platinum groping its way down to nearly 3^{μ}, that is, nearly to rays of .003 mm. wave-length. At this place solar heat seems to be abruptly cut off. The visible part of the solar spectrum extends from about the line $H = .39^{\mu}$ to $A = .76^{\mu}$; the invisible spectrum, as explored by Langley, reaches from $.76^{\mu}$ to

[1] *Am. Journ. Sci.* (3), Vol. 40, 1890, pp. 97–113.
[2] LANGLEY, *Phil. Mag.*, Vol. 27, 1889, p. 23.

nearly 3$^\mu$. Langley studied also invisible infra-red radiations from terrestrial sources, and has learned with certainty of wave-lengths greater than .005 mm., and has grounds for estimating that he has recognized radiations whose wave-length exceeds .03 mm., so that, while he has directly measured nearly eight times the wave-length known to Newton, he has probable indications of wave-lengths much greater.[1] In place of the bolometer, *Rubens* and *E. F. Nichols* have used a modified form of Crookes's radiometer. They have isolated and identified rays from hot zirconia of .05 mm. wave-length.[2] These are about $\frac{1}{100}$ the length to the shortest Hertzian waves. Thus, homogeneous radiation of nearly every wave-length from Hertzian waves, several kilometers long, down to ultra-violet rays, less than .0002 mm., is definitely known.

The ultra-violet rays in the solar spectrum, the existence of which was discovered by *Ritter* and *Wollaston*, were studied by Biot, who found that the absorptive power of glass, rock-salt, and quartz for these rays is independent of their absorptive power for visible rays. *A. C. Becquerel* showed that quartz is especially transparent to these rays; even a dark piece will let more through than a clear pane of glass. The ultra-violet region has been studied both for solar and artificial radiation. *Franz Exner* and *E. Haschek*, using a Rowland grating, in 1896 studied the spark spectra of eleven metals by photography, and took measurements on more than 19,000 ultra-violet lines.[3]

Curious observations have been made on "anomalous dispersion." The existence of this phenomenon was first dis-

---

[1] *Am. Jour. Sci.* (3), Vol. 32, 1886, p. 24. For still more recent results, see *Nature,* Vol. 51, pp. 12–16, 1894.

[2] *Physical Review,* Vol. IV., 1897, pp. 314–323.

[3] *Sitzungsberichte d. K. Akad. d. W. Wien,* Vol. 105, pp. 389–436, 503–574, 707–740; *Astrophys. Jour.,* Vol. 5, 1897, p. 290.

covered by *Fox Talbot* about 1840. The term was invented in 1862 by *Le Roux*,[1] who noticed that the vapour of iodine absorbs the middle part of the visible spectrum; and that, as compared with other bodies, it refracts the blue to a less degree than the red. In 1870 *C. Christiansen* saw that a hollow glass prism filled with a solution of fuchsine gave the order of the colours, violet, red, yellow, instead of red, yellow, violet. *August Kundt* (1839–1894), professor at Würzburg, after 1888 professor in Berlin, has described a similar behaviour in cyan, mauve anilin, anilin blue, and other substances[2] whose colour by reflection is different from their colour by transmission. His observations were not confined to substances in the liquid state. In 1880 he accidentally discovered anomalous dispersion in the vapour of sodium. In the dispersion, caused by very thin films of certain metals, Kundt noticed a strange fact. In gold, silver, and copper the ray was bent away from the normal, on passing from air into the film; that is, the index of refraction turned out to be less than unity. For gold and copper the red ray was bent further from the normal than the blue ray. For platinum, iron, nickel, bismuth, the index was greater than unity, and in each case greater for the red light than the blue, showing that the red was deviated further toward the perpendicular than the blue. The preparation of the metallic prisms of very small angle and of sufficient transparency for these experiments was effected by electrolytic deposition upon platinized glass. This work occupied two years, and the small number of usable prisms was chosen out of more than 2000 made. The velocity of light in these metals stands in close relationship to their power of conducting electricity and heat; the greatest velocity being

[1] *Compt. Rend.*, Vol. 55, p. 126.

[2] *Pogg. Ann.*, Vol. 142, p. 163; Vol. 143, pp. 149, 259; Vol. 144, p. 128; Vol. 145, pp. 67, 164.

through the best conductors.[1] The phenomena of anomalous dispersion play an important rôle in modern theories of dispersion, advanced by Ketteler, Helmholtz, and others.

The nomenclature of the subject of radiant energy is in need of revision. The expression "radiant heat" is still much used; but the term is self-contradictory, if by heat we mean a form of energy due to molecular motion in ponderable matter. Where there are no molecules there can be no heat. The phenomena of "radiant heat" do not belong to the science of heat at all, unless we resort to the objectionable course of attaching a double meaning to the word "heat" by allowing it to designate a form of energy due to ethereal waves as well as that due to molecular agitation.[2] The terms "diathermanous" and "athermanous" are ill chosen, because they etymologically refer to thermic or heat phenomena, when really we are dealing with ether-waves.[3]

The problem of photography in natural colours is as old as photography itself. The first efforts at solution were by the chemical method. The trials which are best known are those made by *Edmond Becquerel*, who succeeded in obtaining upon a silver plate covered with a film of violet subchloride of silver the impression of all the colours of the solar spectrum. But they vanished as soon as they were exposed to the light.[4]

In the second method of colour photography three separate colourless negatives are taken of an object by light passing through three differently coloured screens. From these, three colourless positives are made. Then each positive is dyed with the colour corresponding to the light used in obtaining its

[1] KUNDT, *Phil. Mag.* (5), Vol. 26, 1888, p. 2.

[2] The word "heat" is so defined in the *Standard Dictionary*.

[3] The nomenclature of radiant energy is discussed in *Nature*, Vol. 49, 1893, pp. 100, 149, 389.

[4] L. WEILLER in *Pop. Sci. Monthly*, Vol. 45, 1894, p. 539.

negative. On superimposing the coloured positives and viewing them by transmitted light, the object photographed is seen in its natural colours. This process was invented in France by *Charles Cros* and at the same time (1869) by *Ducos du Hauron*. The Germans claim the priority of the idea for *Baron Bonstetten*. The process has been improved by *J. Joly*.[1]

The third method, due to interference of light, was published by *G. Lippmann* of Paris.[2] A transparent photographic film is placed in contact with a layer of mercury. The light reflected from the mercury interferes with the incident light so as to form standing waves in the film. In this way the film is divided into a number of thin, equidistant strata, parallel to the surface of the glass. The distance between these layers is half the wave-length of the incident light. They act as reflecting surfaces, and appear coloured when viewed at the proper angle. Thus, if the strata at any point are formed by violet light, they will reflect only violet light. It is interesting to notice that Lippmann was led to these experiments through an effort to transport into the domain of light the acoustic property of an organ-pipe, according to which the fundamental pitch which it gives forth depends only upon its length.

The unique idea of adopting the wave-length of some particular ray of light as a "standard of length" was first advanced in 1829 by the Frenchman *Jacques Babinet* (1794–1872).[3] The wave-lengths of light were assumed to be of constant value. The first attempt to carry out this plan was made by *C. S. Peirce*, in conjunction with *Rutherfurd*.[4] The scheme approached more nearly to a practical realization in the hands of *A. A. Michelson* and *Edward W. Morley*, who in 1887 sug-

[1] *Nature*, Vol. 53, 1896, p. 617.   [2] *Nature*, Vol. 53, pp. 617, 618.

[3] ROSENBERGER, III., p. 193.   [4] *Nature*, Vol. 20, 1879, p. 99.

gested the wave-length of sodium light as the standard and explained their inferential comparator for determining the length of the metre in terms of the wave-length.[1] Later a green mercury ray was tried in place of the sodium light.[2] In 1892 Michelson, by invitation, took his apparatus from Clark University to Paris, for the purpose of instituting a comparison of the length of the new international metre, with the wave-lengths of certain cadmium lines which were found to be preferable to others on account of their great homogeneity. This delicate undertaking was carried out in the Pavillon de Breteuil.[3] Thus the fundamental unit of the metric system was compared "with a natural unit with the same degree of approximation as that which obtains in the comparison of two standard metres. This natural unit depends only on the properties of the vibrating atoms and of the universal ether; it is thus, in all probability, one of the most constant dimensions in all nature."

The first step toward modern theories of vision was taken by Thomas Young in 1801 in his article on *Light and Colours*. He there makes the hypothetical statement that each part of the retina has three particles, sensitive respectively to the colours *red, yellow,* and *blue*.[4] Thereupon Wollaston made his celebrated observation of dark lines in the solar spectrum, which he supposed to be the dividing lines of the pure simple colours. This misconception led Young to choose *red, green,* and *violet* as colours primarily perceived, in place of *red, yellow,* and *blue*.[5] Later, Young found, by the rotation of coloured

---

[1] *Am. Jour. Sci.*, Vol. 34, 1887, pp. 427–430.

[2] *Am. Jour. Sci.*, Vol. 38, 1889, p. 181.

[3] *Compt. Rend.*, Vol. 116, 1893, pp. 790–794; *Astronomy and Astro-Physics*, Vol. XII., 1893, pp. 556–560.

[4] *Miscellaneous Works*, Vol. I., p. 147.

[5] *Ibidem*, I., p. 177.

disks, that a mixture of red, green, and violet produces gray.[1]
Young's theory was elaborated by two of the greatest physicists of the century, — *Helmholtz*[2] and *Maxwell*. It is mainly
owing to their labours that it received the careful consideration
of physicists. The main support for the selection of red,
green, and violet as the fundamental triad has been sought in
the phenomenon of colour-blindness. Blindness to *red* is the
most common; blindness to *green* is not uncommon; to *violet*,
has been known to exist. But this argument is not so conclusive as might be desired, for the reason that a deficiency in
colour sense for red is at times accompanied by a deficiency
for yellow, green, and blue. The so-called "Young-Helmholtz
theory" has been extended by *Ogden N. Rood*, of Columbia
College, and *W. de W. Abney*. But it has not met with universal acceptation. A rival theory was advanced by *E. Hering*[3]
of Vienna, who accepts three elementary sensations, viz. black
and white, red and green, blue and yellow. Since 1887 the
physiological psychologists have begun investigating the subject, and half a dozen new theories have been advanced.
Among physicists the Young-Helmholtz theory, on account of
its simplicity, is meeting with greater favour than any other.[4]
A strong committee of English physicists, a few years ago,
reported on colour-vision. It adopted the Young-Helmholtz
theory, but pointed out that it fails to explain some curious
cases of diseased vision in which the sensation of colour is confined to the blue end of the spectrum. On the other hand,

---

[1] *Natural Philosophy*, 1807. See also A. M. MAYER in *Phil. Mag.*
(5), Vol. I., 1876.

[2] See HELMHOLTZ, *Physiologische Optik*, 1856; L. CAMPBELL and
W. GARNETT, *The Life of James Clerk Maxwell*, London, 1882, pp.
466-483.

[3] *Lehre vom Lichtsinne*, Vienna, 1878.

[4] Consult W. LE CONTE STEVENS in *Science*, N. S., Vol. 7, 1898, pp.
513-520; F. P. WHITMAN in *Science*, N. S., Vol. 8, 1898, pp. 306-316.

Hering's theory was also declared to fail to account for some known facts.[1]

Once there was a wide-spread conviction that the human eye was an optical instrument of such great perfection that none formed by human hands could rival it. Actual examination of the action of the eye, carried on mainly by Helmholtz, has brought about a change in these views. Says he, "Now it is not too much to say that if an optician wanted to sell me an instrument which had all these defects, I should think myself quite justified in blaming his carelessness in the strongest terms, and giving him back his instrument."[2] This statement is supported by passages like the following:[3] "A refracting surface which is imperfectly elliptical, an ill-centred telescope, does not give a single illuminated point as the image of a star, but according to the surface and arrangement of the refracting media, elliptic, circular, or linear images. Now the images of an illuminated point, as the human eye brings them to focus, are even more inaccurate: they are irregularly radiated. The reason of this lies in the construction of the crystalline lens, the fibres of which are arranged around six diverging axes, so that the rays which we see around stars and other distant lights are images of the radiated structure of our lens; and the universality of this optical defect is proved by any figure with diverging rays, being called 'starshaped.' It is from the same cause that the moon, while her crescent is still narrow, appears to many persons double or threefold." The mechanism by which the eye accommodates itself to viewing objects at various distances was a great riddle until the French surgeon, *Louis Joseph Sanson*, first observed

[1] See *Proc. Roy. Soc. of London*, Vol. 51, 1892, pp. 281–395.

[2] H. HELMHOLTZ, *Popular Lectures*, trans. by *E. Atkinson*, London, 1873, p. 219.

[3] *Ibidem*, p. 218.

very faint reflection of light through the pupil from the two surfaces of the crystalline lens. *Max Lagenbeck* found that this reflection altered during the act of accommodation. Helmholtz and others, by these alterations, studied the changes of the lens, and arrived at the conclusion that the eye adjusts itself by the contraction of the ciliary muscle, causing the tension of the lens to be diminished and its surfaces (chiefly the front one) to become more convex than when the eye is at rest, the images of near objects being thus brought to a focus on the retina.[1]

Helmholtz irreverently disclosed the fact that in blue eyes there is no real blue colouring matter whatever; the deepest blue is nothing but a turbid medium. The optic action is the same as in case of smoke which appears blue on a dark background, though the particles themselves are not blue; or in case of the sky, which, according to Newton, Stokes and Rayleigh,[2] looks blue through the agency of extremely fine dust suspended in the air.[3] This dust, when illuminated by sunlight, reflects a greater proportion of the shorter waves of bluish light and transmits a greater proportion of longer waves of reddish light.

Helmholtz and Maxwell experimented on the effects produced by mixing colours. That a mixture of yellow and blue light produces gray and not green was probably first pointed out by *James D. Forbes.*[4]

---

[1] H. Helmholtz, *Popular Lectures*, trans. by *E. Atkinson*, London, 1873, p. 205.

[2] *Phil. Mag.*, Vol. 41, pp. 107, 275.

[3] James Dewar attributes the blueness of the sky to the oxygen in the air; liquefied oxygen is blue.

[4] Campbell and Garnett, *The Life of James Clerk Maxwell*, London, 1882, p. 214. Maxwell "was fond of insisting, to his female cousins, aunts, etc., on the truth that blue and yellow do not make green. I remember his explaining to me [L. Campbell] the difference between

HEAT

The first prominent physicist who endeavoured to overthrow the caloric theory of heat was *Benjamin Thompson, Count Rumford* (1753–1814).[1]   He was born at North Woburn in a humble New England home, within two miles of the native place of another great Benjamin, — Franklin.   These men never met, but both achieved great things in physical investigation.   In Benjamin Thompson a taste for research displayed itself early.   An old note-book of his contains the entry : " An account of what work I have done towards getting an Electrical Machine.   Two or three days' work making wheels.   One half day's work making pattern for small Conductor.   Making pattern for Electrometer."   At one time he walked eight miles from Woburn to Cambridge to attend the lectures on natural philosophy of Professor John Winthrop at Harvard College.[2]   At the age of nineteen he taught school in the

pigments and colors " (p. 198).   While Maxwell sometimes mixed colours by rotation, he usually used a " colour-box " which he perfected in 1862. " A beam of sunlight is to be divided into colors by a prism, certain colors selected by a screen with slits.   These gathered by a lens, and restored to the form of a beam by another prism, and then viewed by the eye directly " (p. 334).   While he was professor at King's College, he resided at 8, Palace Gardens Terrace, Kensington, " where he carried on many of his experiments in a large garret which ran the whole length of the house. When experimenting at the window with the color-box (which was painted black, and nearly eight feet long), he excited the wonder of his neighbors, who thought him mad to spend so many hours in staring into a coffin " (p. 318).

[1] G. E. ELLIS, *Memoir of Sir Benjamin Thompson, Count Rumford,* with notices of his daughter, published in connection with an edition of Rumford's complete works, by the American Academy of Arts and Sciences, Boston.

[2] It was as a grateful return for the favours he had thus enjoyed at the college that Count Rumford later gave to it the endowment which founded the professorship that bears his name.   *Ibidem,* p. 36.

district at Wilmington. At the outbreak of the War of the
Revolution Thompson seemed to favour the Tory party; he
was viewed with suspicion as being an enemy to his country;
was arrested and confined in Woburn. Yet no positive and
direct evidence has ever been found of any unfriendly act done
by Thompson, or even of any speech of such a character
attributed to him.[1] At the age of twenty-two, Thompson fled
to England, leaving behind him a wife and daughter. As far
as known he never even wrote to his wife. In this prominent
scientist, "the life of the intellect appeared to have interfered
with the life of the affections." For a time he participated in
the war on the side of the British.

In 1777 he began his career as an experimental scientist by
a research on the cohesive strength of different substances.
The following year he was admitted as a fellow of the Royal
Society. Having a strong predilection for a military life, he
left England in 1783 to serve with the Austrians in a war then
meditated against the Turks. As war did not break out, he
entered into the service of the Elector of Bavaria, who, in
1790, made him a count. He established houses of industry,
schools of industry, founded a military academy at Munich,
and at the same time continued his physical researches.[2] On
the death of the elector, in 1799, Rumford went to London,
where he founded the *Royal Institution* for the diffusion of a
knowledge of applied science. It is pleasant to contemplate
that, while the Royal Institution was founded by an American,
the *Smithsonian Institution*, in Washington, owes its origin to

---

[1] *Memoir of Sir Benjamin Thompson, Count Rumford*, p. 58.

[2] "His labors in the production of cheap and nutritious food necessarily directed Rumford's attention to fireplaces and chimney flues.
When he published his *Essays* [1795–1800, 4 volumes], in London, he
reported that he had not less than 500 smoky chimneys on his hands." —
JOHN TYNDALL, *New Fragments*, New York, 1892, p. 123.

an Englishman.   In 1803 Rumford went to France, and married the widow of the chemist Lavoisier.   A divorce soon followed.   He died at Auteuil, near Paris.

Of his various experiments, the ones on the source of heat excited by friction, published in 1798, are of the greatest interest.   While engaged at Munich in the boring of cannon, he was surprised at the heat generated.   Whence comes this heat?   What is its nature?   He arranged apparatus so that the heat generated by the friction of a blunt steel borer raised the temperature of a quantity of water.   In his third experiment,[1] water rose in one hour to 107° F.; in one hour and a half to 142°; "at the end of two hours and thirty minutes the water *actually boiled!*"   "It is difficult to describe the surprise and astonishment," says Rumford, "expressed in the countenances of the bystanders, on seeing so large a quantity of cold water (18¾ pounds) heated, and actually made to boil, without any fire . . . yet I acknowledge fairly that it afforded me a degree of childish pleasure, which, were I ambitious of the reputation of a *grave philosopher*, I ought most certainly rather to hide than to discover."   The source of heat generated by friction "appeared evidently to be *inexhaustible.*"   The reasoning by which he concluded that heat was not matter, but was due to motion, we can give only in part.   He says, "It is hardly necessary to add, that anything which any *insulated* body, or system of bodies, can continue to furnish *without limitation*, cannot possibly be *a material substance;* and it appears to me to be extremely difficult, if not quite impossible, to form any distinct idea of anything capable of being excited and communicated in the manner in which heat was excited and communicated in these experiments, except it be *motion.*"

[1] *The Complete Works of Count Rumford*, published by the American Academy of Arts and Sciences, Boston, Vol. I., pp. 481–488.

In 1804 Rumford wrote in a letter to Marc Auguste Pictet, of Geneva, " I am persuaded that I shall live a sufficient long time to have the satisfaction of seeing caloric interred with phlogiston in the same tomb." This hope was hardly realized. For nearly half a century later the large majority of physicists and chemists continued in the belief that heat was a substance.

In the accurate measurement of heat Rumford was less successful than in his qualitative work. In his experiments on heat from friction he himself says that no estimate was made of the heat accumulated in the wooden box holding the water, nor of that dispersed during the experiment. From Rumford's data we may make a rough estimate of the dynamical equivalent of heat. He estimated the thermal capacity of the water and metal as the equivalent to that of 26.58 pounds of water. Enough heat could be generated in $2\frac{1}{4}$ hours, by the use of one horse, to raise the temperature from 33° to 212° F. Hence, the rate of increase in temperature was 1.2° per minute; the number of calories of heat generated per minute was 1.2×26.58, or 31.92, which must be equivalent to one horse-power, or 33,000 foot-pounds per minute. Hence one calorie, using Fahrenheit degrees, is equivalent to 1034 foot-pounds. Joule's estimate was 772 foot-pounds.

Rumford's conclusion regarding the nature of heat was vigorously attacked by the calorists, but it was confirmed in 1799 by *Sir Humphry Davy*.[1] By means of clockwork he rubbed two pieces of ice against one another in the vacuum of an air-pump. Part of the ice was melted, although the temperature of the receiver was kept below the freezing-point. From this he concluded that friction causes vibration of the corpuscles of bodies, and this vibration is heat. However, he

---

[1] DAVY's *Complete Works*, Vol. II., p. 11.

was not so confident of the correctness of this view as Rumford, and it was not till 1812 that he felt sure in asserting that "the immediate cause of the phenomenon of heat is motion, and the laws of its communication are precisely the same as the laws of the communication of motion."[1] Arguing from Rumford's experiments, a conclusive refutation of the caloric theory was given in 1807 by Thomas Young in his *Natural Philosophy*. But Rumford, Davy, and Young made, at the time, but few converts.[2]

An important observation bearing on exact thermometry was announced in 1822 by *Flaugergues*,[3] who observed the gradual change of the zero point of mercury in glass thermometers. Glass does not immediately return to its original volume on cooling from a high temperature. In course of time the capacity of the bulb diminishes a little, rather rapidly at first, and then very slowly for years afterwards. This property has been the source of an untold amount of annoyance to persons aiming to secure very accurate determinations of temperature. Joule examined the "zero reading" of a delicate thermometer at intervals over a period of thirty-eight years, with the following results: April, 1844, $0°$ F.; February, 1846, $.42°$; January, 1848, $.51°$; April, 1848, $.53°$; February, 1853, $.68°$; April, 1856, $.73°$; December, 1860, $.86°$; March, 1867, $.90°$; February, 1870, $.93°$; February, 1873, $.94°$; January, 1877, $.978°$; November, 1879, $.994°$; December, 1882, $1.020°$.[4] Researches on glass, carried out in Europe, have resulted in the discovery of a material free from many of the objections to ordinary glass, and the accuracy of mercury thermometers

[1] Davy, *Elements of Chemical Philosophy*, p. 94.

[2] For details consult G. Berthold, *Rumford und d. Mechanische Wärmetheorie*, Heidelberg, 1875.

[3] *Ann. de Chimie et de Physique*, Vol. 21, p. 333.

[4] Joule, *Scientific Papers*, p. 558.

has been increased fivefold.[1] Wiebe and Schott of Jena have shown that glass containing either sodium or potassium, but not both, gives the least displacement of the zero.[2]

Recently platinum thermometers have been recommended for accurate research.[3] They may be made by welding a coil of fine platinum wire to leads of relatively low electric resistance. The coil and leads must be suitably insulated and supported. It is an improved form of William Siemens's electrical pyrometer. The platinum thermometer shows comparative freedom from change of zero. It indicates temperature by its change of electrical resistance, which is always very nearly the same at the same temperature.[4]

The first careful comparison of the mercury thermometer with the air thermometer was made in 1815 by *Dulong* and *Petit*.[5] They assumed that mercury thermometers agreed among themselves, so that a table of corrections carefully prepared for one mercury thermometer was applicable to all. That this is not the case was shown by *Regnault*.[6] Not only have different kinds of glass different coefficients of expansion, but they have different laws of expansion. More than this, *I. Pierre*[7] has shown that two mercury thermometers, made of the same piece of glass with equal care, did not agree exactly with each other. Regnault showed that, between 0°

---

[1] *Nature*, Vol. 55, 1897, p. 368.   [2] *Nature*, Vol. 52, 1895, p. 87.

[3] H. L. CALLENDAR, *Phil. Mag.* (5), Vol. 32, 1891 ; E. H. GRIFFITHS, *Science Progress*, Vol. II., 1894–1895, article, "The Measurement of Temperature."

[4] For detailed information, consult "Metals at High Temperatures," *Nature*, Vol. 45, 1892, pp. 534–540; "Long-range Temperature and Pressure Variables in Physics," *Science*, N. S., Vol. VI., 1897, pp. 338–356.

[5] *Ann. de Chimie et de Physique*, Vol. 2, 1815, pp. 240–254 ; reprinted in *Ostwald's Klass.*, No. 44, pp. 31–40.

[6] *Ann. de Chimie et de Physique* (3), Vol. 5, p 83 ; *Ostwald's Klass.*, No. 44, pp. 164–181.

[7] *Ann. de Chimie et de Physique* (3), Vol. 5, 1842, p. 427.

and 100° C., the air thermometer and the mercury thermometer
of ordinary soft glass agree very closely, though at about the
middle of the scale the air thermometer lags behind the other
by about .2°.   Above 250° C. the mercury thermometer reads
considerably higher; at 300° the difference is 1°; at 350° it
is 3°.   Olzewski showed that in low temperatures hydrogen
thermometers are still quite reliable; at − 220° C. its error is
not more than 1°.   In recent years, perhaps the most careful
work on exact thermometry has been carried on in connection
with determinations of the mechanical equivalent of heat, by
Rowland and others.

Considerable confusion existed at one time in the minds of
leading physicists, and still exists in some of our text-books,
on the subject of temperature.   It was stated as a merit of
the mercurial thermometer that mercury "expands uniformly,"
or of the air thermometer that air "expands uniformly" or
"expands nearly uniformly," and yet no standard of reference
was given by which this uniformity was supposed to have
been established.   As a matter of fact, we may take any substance as a standard and then define equal increments of temperature as those which give equal increments of that substance.
But, if mercury be so taken, then the assertion that mercury
expands "uniformly" is destitute of good sense.   Mercury
gives us an arbitrary scale of temperature differing, probably,
from every other similar scale.   Air does not expand quite
uniformly, if mercury is the arbitrary standard, and *vice
versa*.   One of the first to possess clear notions on this subject was Lord Kelvin, who, in 1848, established the "absolute
thermodynamic scale" of temperature,[1] which is independent

---

[1] WILLIAM THOMSON, *Proc. Cambridge Phil. Soc.*, 1848.   Consult also
his article "Heat" in *Encycl. Brit.*, 9th ed.   For a "Kritik des Tempera-
turbegriffes," see MACH, *Principien d. Wärmelehre*, Leipzig, 1896, pp.
39-57.

of the particular properties of any particular substance and, therefore, constitutes a much more satisfactory foundation for thermometry than any arbitrary scale. It is now our ultimate scale of reference. The air thermometer gives indications agreeing very closely with the absolute thermodynamic scale.

The propagation of heat in solid bodies was investigated mathematically by *Joseph Fourier* (1768–1830), who published, in 1822, a work entitled, *La Théorie Analytique de la Chaleur*, which not only marked an epoch in the history of mathematical physics, but stimulated experimental inquiry. Fourier assumed the conductivity of a substance for heat to be constant for all temperatures. But *James David Forbes* (1809–1868), professor at Edinburgh, showed that this is not true, that from 0° to 100° the conductivity of iron diminishes 15.9%; of copper, 24.5%. He noticed at the same time that there was an accompanying decrease in electric conductivity.

At the beginning of the nineteenth century, the laws of gases were diligently studied. Amontons had arrived at an approximate value for the coefficient of expansion of air under constant pressure, but the measurements made by about twenty physicists of the eighteenth century differed very widely from each other. The first to deduce the law as we now know it was *Jacques Alexandre César Charles* (1746–1823), who was professor of physics at the Conservatoire des Arts et Métiers in Paris. He was best known for his improvements in the design of balloons. At his suggestion, hydrogen, then a new gas (discovered by Henry Cavendish in 1766), was used in filling balloons. In 1773 the two brothers *Montgolfier* had raised the first balloons at Annonay in southern France, and had caused a great sensation. They used hot air. Charles, assisted by the mechanic Robert, in 1783, raised the first hydrogen balloon from the *Champ de Mars* in Paris. Later he and Robert made balloon ascensions together.

This bold navigator of the air busied himself also with the expansion of gases and discovered what is known as the "law of Charles" or "law of Gay-Lussac." Charles failed to publish his results and it was only by accident that they became known to Gay-Lussac. Gay-Lussac's researches were published in 1802.[1] He attributed the want of agreement in earlier experiments to the presence of moisture. His own elaborate investigation led him to the conclusion "that in general all gases by equal degrees of heat, under the same conditions, expand proportionately just alike."

Joseph Louis Gay-Lussac (1778–1850) was educated at the Polytechnic School, became assistant to the chemist Berthollet, and later professor of chemistry at the Polytechnic School, of Physics at the Sorbonne. His physical researches are mainly on the expansion of gases. To ascertain the chemical and electric condition of the air in the upper strata, and also to measure the force of terrestrial magnetism at great elevations, he and Biot ascended in a balloon which had survived Napoleon's campaign in Egypt. "Supplied with a full complement of barometers, thermometers, hygrometers, electrometers, and instruments for measuring magnetic force and dip, as well as frogs, insects, and birds for galvanic experiments, the scientific voyagers embarked on August 23, 1804. They began their experiments at an altitude of 6500 feet and continued them to the altitude of 13,000 feet, and with a success commensurate with their wishes. The last part of the excursion, and especially the landing which they made, was so difficult . . . that . . . Biot, though a man of activity and not deficient in personal courage, was so much overpowered by the alarms of their descent, as to lose for a time the entire

[1] *Annales de Chimie*, Vol. 43, pp. 137–175 ; *Ostwald's Klass.*, No. 44, pp. 3–25.

possession of himself."[1]   Gay-Lussac made another balloon
excursion the same year. Air bottled at a height of 6300
metres was found to have the same composition as air near
the surface.

The expansion of gases was investigated also by *John
Dalton* (1766–1844) of Manchester, the great founder of the
chemical atomic theory.[2] His conclusions did not quite agree
with Gay-Lussac's. The latter had shown that, using a mercury thermometer, the expansion per degree is a constant
fraction of the volume at some arbitrary fixed temperature.
Dalton, on the other hand, claimed that the increment of
volume for each equal rise of temperature is a constant fraction of the volume at the temperature immediately preceding.
The question was decided by Dulong and Petit in favour of
Gay-Lussac.[3] The value of the coefficient of expansion for
the interval from 0° to 100°, as determined by Gay-Lussac and
Dalton, was .375; as determined in 1837 by *Fredrik Rudberg*
(1800–1839), professor at Upsala, it was .365; as determined
by *Magnus* and *Regnault*, it was between .366 and .367. The
whole subject of the expansion of gases was independently
re-investigated with the aid of more refined methods by the
two experimentalists last named.

We pause a moment to catch a glimpse of some of the men
just mentioned. *Alexis Thérèse Petit* (1791–1820) was professor
of physics at the Polytechnic School in Paris. *Pierre Louis
Dulong* (1785–1838) held the same position for some years
after 1820. At first Dulong practised medicine, but as he not
only treated the poor free of charge, but also bought medicine
for them, he found his vocation too expensive. As a physicist,

---

[1] *Proc. of the Am. Acad. of Arts and Sci.*, Vol. VI., p. 20.

[2] Consult H. E. ROSCOE, *John Dalton and the Rise of Modern Chemistry*, 1895.

[3] *Ostwald's Klass.*, No. 44, pp. 28, 40.

his wealth was absorbed by the cost of his expensive apparatus.[1] Most of his researches were carried on in conjunction
with other men. Some were carried on with Petit; others with
Arago, Berzelius, Despretz. *Henri Victor Regnault* (1810–
1878) was professor in Lyons, then in Paris at the Polytechnic
School, and at the *Collège de France*. After 1854 he was
director of a porcelain manufactory at Sèvres. He displayed
wonderful patience and skill in the execution of careful measurements. His numerical tables on the dilatation of elastic
fluids, on the elastic force of steam, on the heat of vaporization
of water, on the specific heat of water at different temperatures,
etc., still rank among the best. But he lacked that creative
genius which enables its possessor not only to experiment but
to grapple with great questions of theoretical science. Regnault proved that all gases do not possess quite the same
coefficient of expansion; that, except for hydrogen, it increases
with the initial pressure; that no gas obeys Boyle's law
exactly.[2]

Regnault's experiments showed that, as the pressure increased, the product of the pressure and volume, pv, diminished
in all gases except hydrogen. If Boyle's law were followed,
this product would be constant. Regnault's observations extended over a comparatively small range of pressures. That

[1] ROSENBERGER, III., p. 221.

[2] Three papers by Regnault and two by Magnus, on the expansion of
gases, are reprinted in *Ostwald's Klass.*, No. 44. Regnault's most valuable experimental results are collected in Vols. 21 and 26 of the *Mémoires*
of the French Academy. At the close of the Franco-Prussian War Regnault found, on returning to his laboratory at Sèvres, that the results of
his last great research on the phenomena of heat accompanying the expansion of gases, derived from over 600 observations, had been destroyed.
The announcement of this loss was his last communication to the scientific world. One of his sons, a promising artist, died on the battle-field.
See *Nature*, Vol. 17, 1878, pp. 263, 264.

pv, as p increases, does not diminish for all pressures beyond this range, but reaches a minimum, and then increases, as in case of hydrogen, was first shown by the Vienna physician, *Johann August Natterer*, in the years 1850–1854,[1] while he was endeavouring to liquefy oxygen, hydrogen, and air. For twenty years this interesting observation was not extended. In 1870 the subject was taken up by *Cailletet* and later by *E. H. Amagat.* The experiments of the latter are particularly instructive.[2] For an increase of pressure from 30 to 320 atmospheres, pv increases continually in hydrogen; it first diminishes a trifle and then increases in nitrogen (at 17.7° C.); it diminishes greatly and then increases rapidly in ethylene and carbon dioxide. The variations of pv are very rapid near the critical point; they are more pronounced for low temperatures.

The first important work on the liquefaction of gases was performed by *Faraday.*[3] His experiments, begun in 1823, showed that the capability of being liquefied was a property common to most gases. A bent glass tube was taken; into its longer leg, which was closed, there was introduced a substance which would evolve, when heated, the particular gas to be tested. The shorter leg of the tube was then sealed up, and cooled by being placed in a freezing mixture. When the longer leg was heated, and gas was generated, the pressure in the tube increased, and in many cases the gas condensed in the shorter leg. Thus, by heating sodium bicarbonate, car-

[1] *Pogg. Ann.*, Vol. 62, p. 139; Vol. 94, p. 436.

[2] AMAGAT, *Ann. de Chimie et de Physique* (5), Vol. 19, 1880, p. 435, and other articles in the same journal. Summaries of his work are found in PRESTON, *Theory of Heat*, London, 1894, pp. 403–410; OSTWALD, *Lehrb. d. Allgem. Chemie*, Vol. I., 1891, pp. 146–159.

[3] Before Faraday, several gases had been liquefied by cooling: *Marum*, liquefied ammonia; *Monge* and *Clouet*, sulphurous acid; *Northmore*, chlorine (in 1805); *Stromeyer*, arsenic trihydride. See OSTWALD, *op. cit.*, Vol. I., p. 294; *Nature*, Vol. 17, 1878, p. 177.

bonic acid gas was obtained, which was liquefied in the short leg. By this method Faraday liquefied H_2S, HCl, SO_2, C_2N_2, NH_3, Cl_2. *Thilorier* in 1835 produced in larger quantities liquid and solid CO_2. By mixing solid CO_2 with ether, he obtained low degrees of temperature previously undreamed of. Notwithstanding the researches of Thilorier, of Natterer, and of Faraday in 1845, several gases still resisted liquefaction. They were classed under the name of "permanent gases," a title which they bore over a quarter of a century, until 1877.

Meanwhile new things were being ascertained regarding the continuity of the gaseous and liquid states of matter. As early as 1822 *Charles Cagniard-Latour* (1777–1859), an engineer, later attaché to the Ministry of the Interior in Paris, observed that ether, alcohol, and water, when heated in hermetically sealed tubes, were apparently totally changed into vapour occupying only from two to four times the original volume of the liquid. But the discovery of the continuity of the liquid and gaseous states belongs to *Thomas Andrews* (1813–1885), the vice-president and professor of chemistry in the college at Belfast. In his experiments pressure was produced by screwing up mercury into a capillary tube, in which the gas was kept at the desired temperature. In 1863 he wrote: "On partially liquefying carbonic acid by pressure alone, and gradually raising at the same time the temperature to 88° F. [30.92° C.], the surface of demarcation between the liquid and gas became fainter, lost its curvature, and at last disappeared. The space was then occupied by a homogeneous fluid, which exhibited, when the pressure was suddenly diminished or the temperature slightly lowered, a peculiar appearance of moving or flickering striæ throughout its entire mass. At temperatures above 88° F. no apparent liquefaction of carbonic acid, or separation into two distinct forms of matter, could be effected, even when a pressure of 300 or 400 atmospheres was

applied."[1]   This temperature of 30.92° C., at which the liquid
and the gaseous states of CO_2 merge into one another, has been
called by Andrews the "critical point." Every gas has its
own critical temperature. Below this the substance may exist
partly as a vapour, partly as a liquid. Above it this is not
true; the substance may be made to pass from a gas to a
liquid without a break of continuity, so that it is impossible
to state when it ceases to be a gas and begins to be a liquid.
J. D. van der Waals treated the subject from the standpoint of
the mathematical theory of gases. *William Ramsay*, in 1880,
concluded that "the critical point is that point at which the
liquid owing to expansion, and the gas owing to compression,
acquire the same specific gravity, and consequently mix with
each other."[2]   Three years later the same result was obtained
by *Jules Celestin Jamin*.[3]

Andrews had, in 1869, expressed the opinion that the failure
to liquefy the "permanent gases" was due to the fact that their
critical temperatures were much lower than the lowest temperature hitherto obtained. Taking this hint, two young
investigators — Pictet and Cailletet — made the year 1877
memorable in the history of science by their brilliant demonstration that the "permanent gases" may be liquefied, and
that molecular cohesion is a property of all bodies without
exception. The means at the command of both experimenters
arose from their industrial equipments, one for making iron,
the other for making ice. *L. Cailletet*, one of the greatest iron-
masters of France, employed the enormous resources at his
disposal at the Châtillon-sur-Seine in Paris.[4]   *Raoul Pictet* of
Geneva was interested in the artificial production of ice, and

[1] MILLER's *Chemical Physics*, 3d ed., p. 328.
[2] *Nature*, Vol. 22, 1880, p. 46.
[3] *Compt. Rend.*, Vol. 96, 1883, p. 1448.
[4] *Nature*, Vol. 17, 1878, pp. 177, 178.

now has a laboratory in Berlin for experimentation on low temperatures. Low temperatures find industrial application; for instance, in the purification of chloroform. On December 24, 1877, at the same meeting of the French Academy, it was announced that, working independently and by different methods, Cailletet and Pictet had liquefied oxygen. A week later Cailletet performed a series of experiments in the laboratory of the *École Normale* at Paris in the presence of leading French scientists. He then and there liquefied hydrogen, nitrogen, and air. The same result was achieved by Pictet. Cailletet's process consists in compressing the gas into a small tube, cooling it, and then suddenly allowing it to expand by removal of the pressure. This instantaneous expansion of the gas causes such a low degree of cold that a large portion of the gas is condensed into a cloud of vapour. In case of oxygen the temperature of the tube was reduced to $- 29°$ C. by the application of sulphurous acid. The pressure was 300 atmospheres. The sudden expansion probably lowered the temperature as much as $200°$.[1] Pictet used more elaborate apparatus (costing about 50,000 francs), and obtained the condensed gases on a larger scale. The low temperatures were obtained on the principle of evaporation. A vacuum pump withdrew from a tube the vapour above liquid sulphurous acid; the vapour was then liquefied, cooled, and returned to the tube. Thus a complete circulation was maintained. In this way the temperature of the liquid fell to about $- 70°$ C. Within this tube was another thinner tube containing liquid carbonic acid. The object of the former liquid was to keep the latter cool. The carbonic acid was let into another tube, where its temperature was reduced by evaporation, brought

[1] A large figure of Cailletet's apparatus will be found in *Nature*, Vol. 17, p. 267.

about as before by a vacuum pump, to $-140°$ C.   The vapour
of CO_2 was condensed by the sulphurous acid.   Thus by compression, liquefaction, and exhaustion, there was a circulation
of CO_2 like that of sulphurous acid.   A tube containing oxygen
passed inside the tube of solidified CO_2 at $-140°$.   The
oxygen was generated by heating chlorate of potash in a strong
shell at one end of the last-mentioned tube.   The other end of
that tube was furnished with a stop-cock.   The oxygen was condensed in the tube by the combined action of its own pressure
of several hundred atmospheres and the intense cold.   On opening the stop-cock a small stream of oxygen escaped.   In its
central portion it was white, indicating the liquid or solid condition.   In case of hydrogen, the escaping stream was steel-blue.

In larger quantities the three gases, oxygen, nitrogen, and
hydrogen, have been liquefied by *Sigmund v. Wroblewski* (1848–
1888) and *Karl Olszewski* of the University of Cracow in
Austria-Hungary, and by *James Dewar* of the Royal Institution in London.   Their apparatus is based on the general
principle of that designed by Pictet, only it has been found
better to use other liquids, like ethylene or oxygen.   Olzewski
determined   critical   points,   boiling-points,   freezing-points,
and densities.   He found boiling-points as follows: oxygen,
$-182.7°$ C.; argon, $-187°$; nitrogen, $-194.4°$; hydrogen,
$-243.5°$.   Freezing-points: argon, $-189.6°$; nitrogen, $-214°$.[1]
James Dewar succeeded in 1898 in obtaining liquid hydrogen
in larger quantities (half a wine glass), and in liquefying
helium.   In 1891 he announced that liquid oxygen and liquid
ozone are attracted by the poles of a magnet.   J. Dewar and
J. A. Fleming have examined the electric resistance of metals
at low temperatures.   The resistance of some pure metals
(platinum, for instance) diminishes at low temperatures at

---

[1] See table in *Nature*, Vol. 51, 1895, pp. 355, 356.

such a rate that, if the rate is kept up in the lower temperatures not yet reached, it will vanish at the absolute zero. The study of phenomena of heat led to a better comprehension of meteorological phenomena. At one time it was believed that dew fell from the stars, or, at any rate, from great heights. The first scientific study of the formation of dew was made by the London physician, *William Charles Wells* (1757–1817), and the results published in his *Essay on Dew*, 1814. In a clear, quiet night, the grass radiates heat into free space, whence no heat returns. Being a poor conductor, the lower parts of the grass receive little heat from the earth. The grass cools and vapour condenses upon it. Good conductors, like metals, receive heat from surrounding bodies, and, therefore, are not covered with dew. A cloudy sky hinders the formation of dew by returning the radiated heat. Winds are unfavourable, because they carry heat to the cooling objects. Wells supposed that only a very small part of the dew deposited comes from vapour rising from the earth or the evaporation from plants. Recent investigations by *Badgeley*[1] and *R. Russell*[2] have shown that Wells underestimated the rôle played by both the earth and the plant. The vapour has been shown by experiment to come largely from the earth beneath, and not from the air above. This is contrary to the commonly received view.

New information has been obtained in recent years on the formation of rain and fog, which has hardly yet found its way into elementary text-books. It has been shown by *Coulier, E. Mascart*,[3] and especially by *John Aitken*,[4] that in the de-

[1] *Proc. of the Royal Meteor. Soc.*, April, 1891.

[2] *Nature*, Vol. 47, 1892, pp. 210–213.

[3] *Naturforscher*, 1875, p. 400; *Journal de Pharmacie et de Chimie* (4), Vol. 22, p. 165; *Nature*, Vol. 23, 1881, p. 337.

[4] *Nature*, Vol. 23, p. 196; Vol. 41, p. 408; Vol. 44, 1891, p. 279; Vol. 45, p. 299; Vol. 49, 1893, p. 544.

velopment of fogs and clouds, the presence of dust is essential. That is, "whenever water vapour condenses in the atmosphere, it always does so on some solid nucleus;" "dust particles in air are nuclei on which vapour condenses;" except for dust we should have no fogs, no clouds, no mists, and probably no rain. City fogs are due to dust. It is not true that dust is always absolutely essential for cloudy condensation; it may be brought about by the presence of hydrochloric, sulphuric, or nitric acids, or by very high degrees of supersaturation. Yet the conditions in the atmosphere are such that, except for dust, we could hardly have rain. Aitken invented a dust counter; he made extensive observations in England and in Switzerland. By observations on the Rigi he concluded "that whenever a cloud is formed, it at once begins to rain, and the small drops fall into the drier air underneath, where they are evaporated, the distance to which they will fall depending on their size and the dryness of the air."

One of the earliest recorded experiments on the heating and cooling of a gas, by condensation and rarefaction, respectively, was made by a workman in a French gun factory, who ignited tinder by compression of air. An account of this experiment was sent to Paris by Mollet, professor at Lyons. The subject was carefully examined by John Dalton, who, in 1800, read a paper "on the heat and cold produced by the mechanical condensation and rarefaction of air."[1]

The science of thermodynamics had its origin in attempts to determine mathematically how much work can be gotten out of a steam-engine. The first impulse to this was given by *Nicolas Léonard Sadi Carnot* (1796–1832), who, in 1824, published his *Réflexions sur la puissance motrice du feu*.[2] Carnot

[1] Rosenberger, III., p. 224.
[2] Reprinted in German in *Ostwald's Klass.*, No. 37 ; an English translation by R. H. Thurston appeared in 1890.

introduced the consideration of cyclic operations, in which a
working substance, after a series of changes, is brought back to
its initial condition.   He also advanced the principle of revers-
ibility, by which the heat may be taken from the condenser
and restored to the source by the expenditure of an equal
quantity of work.   Assuming perpetual motion to be impossible, he concluded that no engine can have a greater efficiency
than a reversible engine.   At this time Carnot was an adherent
of the caloric theory; he believed in the doctrine of the conservation of caloric; he compared the motive power of heat
with that of falling water.   Both, he says, have a maximum
power, independent, in one case, of the machine upon which
the water acts, and, in the other case, of the nature of the
substance receiving the heat.   The motive power of water depends upon the amount of water and the height through which
it falls; the motive power of heat depends upon the quantity
of caloric and the difference in temperature between the source
and the receiver.   But some years later Carnot became convinced of the falsity of the caloric theory.   His later writings,
which have remained unpublished until recent times, prove
that he was finally persuaded of the truth of the dynamical
theory of heat.   More than this, he had grasped the law of
the conservation of energy.   "Motive power is in quantity invariable in nature; it is, correctly speaking, never either produced or destroyed."

Though the importance of Carnot's work of 1824 was emphasized by B. P. E. Clapeyron, it did not meet with general
recognition until it was brought forward by William Thomson,
who pointed out the necessity of modifying Carnot's reasoning
so as to bring it into accord with the new theory of heat.   In
1848 Thomson showed that Carnot's principle of cyclic transformations leads to the conception of an absolute thermodynamic
scale of temperature.   In 1849 he published "an account of

Carnot's theory of the motive power of heat, with numerical results deduced from Regnault's experiments." In February, 1850, *Rudolph Clausius* (1822–1888) communicated to the Berlin Academy a paper on the same subject, which contains the Protean second law of thermodynamics: " Heat cannot, of itself, pass from a colder to a hotter body." Clausius was at this time professor in Zürich; later he went to Würzburg, and, after 1869, was at Bonn. He was no great experimenter, but ranked very high as a mathematical physicist.[1] In the same month of February, 1850, *William John M. Rankine* (1820–1872), professor of engineering and mechanics at Glasgow, read before the Royal Society of Edinburgh a paper in which he declares heat to consist in the rotational motion of molecules, and arrives independently at some of the results reached previously by Clausius. He does not mention the second law of thermodynamics, but in a subsequent paper he declares that it can be derived from equations contained in his paper. His proof of the second law is not free from objections. In March, 1851, there appeared a paper by William Thomson which contained a perfectly rigorous proof of the second law. He obtained it before he had seen the researches of Clausius. The statement of this law, as given by Clausius, has been much criticised, particularly by Rankine, *Theodor Wand, P. G. Tait,* and *Tolver Preston.* Repeated efforts to deduce it from general mechanical principles have remained fruitless. The science of thermodynamics was developed with great success by Thomson, Clausius, and Rankine. As early as 1852 Thomson discovered the law of the dissipation of energy, deduced at a later period also by Clausius.

---

[1] During the Franco-Prussian War, his burning patriotism did not permit him to stay at home. He undertook the leadership of an ambulance corps, which he formed of Bonn students. See *Proc. of Roy. Soc. of London,* Vol. 48, 1890, p. II.

The first law of thermodynamics is merely the application of the principle of the conservation of energy to heat-effects. This principle is the greatest generalization in physics of the nineteenth century. Its history is remarkable from various points of view. Several thinkers arrived at this great truth at about the same time; and, at first, all of them were either met with a very cold reception or were completely ignored. The principle of the conservation of energy was established by the Heilbronn physician, Robert Mayer, and again independently by Ludwig August Colding of Copenhagen, Joule in England, and Helmholtz in Germany.

Robert Mayer (1814–1878) was born in Heilbronn. In the gymnasium and the theological school he gave no evidence of great intellectual power. In 1832 he entered upon the study of medicine at Tübingen, and in 1838 began to practise, but he never found the work of a practising physician agreeable to his tastes. He travelled considerably and engaged in the study of physiology. An observation made in 1840, on the blood of a patient in a tropical climate, was the origin of his scientific writings. It led him to the study of those physical forces on which the phenomena of vitality depend. Thus, he was led from the contemplation of organic nature to the preparation of a paper, "On the Forces of Inorganic Nature," 1842. It was refused publication in *Poggendorff's Annalen*, but was accepted by *Liebig* for the May number of his *Annalen*. It attracted no attention, though containing the great principle that the energy of the world is constant. A second paper, 1845, could be published only at his own expense. Several other papers were published later.[1] The following story, related by Mach, shows Mayer's alertness of

[1] See J. J. WEYRAUCH, *Robert Mayer*, Stuttgart, 1890. Consult also WEYRAUCH, *Die Mechanik der Wärme von ROBERT MAYER*, 3d ed., 1893; WEYRAUCH, *Kleinere Schriften und Briefe von Robert Mayer*, 1893.

mind:[1] "During a hurried meeting with Mayer in Heidelberg once, Jolly remarked, with a rather dubious implication, that if Mayer's theory were correct, water could be warmed by shaking. Mayer went away without a word of reply. Several weeks later . . . he rushed into the latter's presence exclaiming: 'Es ischt so!' (It is so, it is so!) It was only after considerable explanation that Jolly found out what Mayer wanted to say." The mind of Robert Mayer became seriously affected by the lack of appreciation of his ideas, by controversies regarding his rights of priority, as well as by the death of two of his children. On May 28, 1849, he unsuccessfully attempted suicide by jumping from a second-story window. After a seeming recovery, he wrote a paper on the mechanical equivalent of heat. In 1851 he was placed in an insane asylum, where he was cruelly treated. In 1853 he was set free, but he never again regained complete mental equilibrium. In 1858 a few voices were heard in Germany in praise of Mayer, but the one who did most to bring him historical justice was John Tyndall, who in 1862 lectured before the Royal Institution on Robert Mayer and also translated several of Mayer's papers. William Thomson and Tait, placing a much lower estimate on Mayer's researches, brought the charge that Tyndall was belittling the work of Joule.[2]

James Prescott Joule (1818–1889) was born at Salford, near Manchester, where he was the proprietor of a large brewery. At an early age he engaged in electromagnetic researches. After laborious tests he succeeded in showing that during electrolytic action there was an absorption of heat equivalent to the heat evolved during the original combination of the

[1] "On the Part played by Accident in Invention and Discovery," *Monist*, Vol. 6, 1896, p. 171.

[2] Consult "Notes on Scientific History" by TYNDALL in *Phil. Mag.*, July, 1864.

constituents of the compound body. He studied the relations between electrical, chemical, and mechanical effects, and was led to the great discovery of the mechanical equivalent of heat. In a paper read before the British Association, in 1843, he gave the number as 460 kilogramme-metres. Friends who recognized the physicist in the young brewer persuaded him .to become a candidate for the professorship of natural philosophy at St. Andrews, Scotland, but his slight personal deformity was an objection in the eyes of one of the electors, and he did not receive the appointment. He remained a brewer, but continued scientific research throughout life. In April, 1847, Joule gave a popular lecture in Manchester, delivering "the first full and clear exposition of the universal conservation of that principle now called energy."[1] The local press would at first have nothing to do with it. One paper refused to give even a notice of it; the *Manchester Courier*, after long debate, published the address in full. In June, 1847, the subject was presented before the British Association meeting at Oxford. The chairman suggested that the author be brief; no discussion was invited. In a moment the section would have passed on to other matters without giving the new ideas any consideration, "if a young man had not risen in the section, and by his intelligent observations created a lively interest in the new theory. The young man was William Thomson." The result was that the paper caused a great sensation; Joule had attracted the attention of scientific men. After the meeting Joule and Thomson discussed the subject further, and the latter "obtained ideas he had never had before," while through him Joule heard for the first time of Carnot's theory.[2]

---

[1] A. W. RÜCKER in *Fortnightly Review*, 1894, p. 652. We are making considerable use of this article, entitled, "Hermann von Helmholtz." It is reprinted in *Smithsonian Report*, 1894.

[2] *Nature*, Vol. 49, 1893, p. 164.

Joule experimented on the mechanical equivalent of heat for about forty years. By magneto-electric currents he got, in 1843, the value of 460 kilogramme-metres as the equivalent of the large French calorie. By the friction of water in tubes, he got 424.9; by the compression of air, in 1845, 443.8; by the friction of water he got, in 1845, 488.3; in 1847, 428.9; in 1850, 423.9; in 1878, 423.9.[1]

The mechanical equivalent of heat is such an important constant in nature that several physicists since Joule have thought it desirable to redetermine it. One of the most accurate determinations was made in 1879 by *Henry A. Rowland* of Baltimore.[2] The part of the work which received greater attention than Joule had given it, was the subject of themometry. Joule used mercury thermometers. Rowland, for convenience, used a mercury thermometer too, but compared it with an air thermometer and then reduced his data to the absolute scale. Rowland paid attention also to variations in the specific heat of water for different temperatures. Starting with the water at different temperatures, he obtained by friction of water in a calorimeter different values for the mechanical equivalent. This variation in the values he attributed to changes in the specific heat of water. The latter was found by him to reach a minimum at 30° C. More recently the mechanical equivalent of heat has been measured by D'Arsonval, Miculescu, E. H. Griffiths, and others. Joule's estimate of this constant has been raised somewhat by the later determinations.[3]

The same year, 1847, in which Joule announced his views

---

[1] Consult *The Scientific Papers of James Prescott Joule*, in two volumes, London, 1884 ; *Nature*, Vol. 43, 1890, p. 112.

[2] *Proc. of the Am. Acad. of Arts and Sciences*, N. S., Vol. 7, 1880.

[3] Consult E. H. GRIFFITHS in *Science Progress*, Vol. 1, 1894, p. 127 ; *Johns Hopkins Circulars*, 1898, No. 135.

on energy, Helmholtz read before the Physical Society in Berlin a paper on the same subject. *Hermann von Helmholtz* (1821-1894) was born at Potsdam, studied medicine in Berlin, became assistant at the charity hospital there, then military surgeon in Potsdam (1843-1847), teacher of anatomy at Berlin, of physiology at Königsberg, later at Bonn and Heidelberg (1858-1871). In 1871 he accepted the chair of physics at the University of Berlin. He possessed an intellect of extraordinary breadth and depth. He was of the first rank as a physiologist, as a physicist, and as a mathematician. A few years ago W. K. Clifford, in his article "Seeing and Thinking," spoke of him as follows: "In the first place he began by studying physiology, dissecting the eye and the ear, and finding out how they acted, and what was their precise constitution; but he found that it was impossible to study the proper action of the eye and ear without studying also the nature of light and sound, which led him to the study of physics. He had already become one of the most accomplished physiologists of this century when he commenced the study of physics, and he is now one of the greatest physicists of this century. He then found it was impossible to study physics without knowing mathematics; and accordingly he took to studying mathematics and he is now one of the most accomplished mathematicians of this century."

His famous paper on energy, entitled "Die Erhaltung der Kraft,"[1] which the youth of twenty-six read before the Physical Society of Berlin in 1847, was at first looked upon as a fantastic speculation. The editor of *Poggendorff's Annalen*, who in 1843 declined Mayer's paper, rejected Helmholtz's also. As Joule had been supported by William Thomson, so

---

[1] Reprinted in *Ostwald's Klass.*, No. 1. In Note 5 Helmholtz outlines the history of the new principle of energy.

Helmholtz was defended by his fellow-student Du Bois-Reymond and by the mathematician C. G. J. Jacobi. Helmholtz's paper was published in pamphlet form in 1847. For a time it attracted little notice, but in 1853 it was vigorously attacked by Clausius. Later it subjected its author to virulent attacks from Eugen Karl Dühring and others, who accused him of being a dishonest borrower from his forerunner, Robert Mayer.[1] In 1847 Helmholtz, like Joule, had not heard of Robert Mayer, but later he cheerfully acknowledged Mayer's priority.

By the word *Kraft*, used by Mayer and Helmholtz, we must understand *energy*. For a time great confusion existed in text-books between the terms "force" and "energy." The two terms were frequently used synonymously and continue to be so used by some psychological writers. The use of the word "energy" to denote the quantity of work which a material system can do was introduced by Thomas Young in Lecture VIII. of his *Natural Philosophy*. With him it designated mv^2; Lord Kelvin in 1849 used it for $\frac{1}{2}mv^2$. The expression "conservation of energy" is due to Rankine.[2]

---

[1] *Physical Review*, Vol. 2, 1894, p. 224.

[2] Students desiring more detailed information on heat may consult, besides ROSENBERGER, POGGENDORFF, and HELLER, MACH, *Principien der Wärmelehre*, Leipzig, 1896 ; GEORG HELM, *Lehre von der Energie historisch-kritisch Entwickelt*, Leipzig, 1887 ; M. P. DESAINS, *Rapport sur les progrès de la théorie de la chaleur*, Paris, 1868 ; M. BERTIN, *Rapport sur les progrès de la thermodynamique en France*, Paris, 1867 ; JOSEPH PEVELING, *Gesch. d. Gesetze von d. Erhaltung d. Materie und Energie*, Aachen, 1891.

ELECTRICITY AND MAGNETISM

Electrical progress, both theoretical and practical, has been so rapid that this has been called the age of electricity. After the discovery of current electricity by Galvani and the construction of the voltaic pile, Carlisle and Nicholson decomposed water by *low pressure currents.* This feat caused great excitement. In September, 1800, *Johann Wilhelm Ritter* (1776–1810), of Silesia, announced that he had succeeded in collecting the two gases separately and that copper could be precipitated from blue vitriol.

Sir Humphry Davy (1778–1829) was among the early workers in this line. While a poor boy, Davy attained notoriety for being "so fond of chemical experiments." After serving as assistant in the Pneumatic Institution at Bristol, he in 1801 became lecturer in chemistry at the Royal Institution in London. His lectures delighted the fashionable audiences. Said Coleridge, "I go to Davy's lectures to increase my stock of metaphors." It has been said that, if Davy had not been one of the first chemists, he would have been one of the first poets of his age.[1]

Davy showed that in the decomposition of water, the volume of hydrogen is double that of oxygen. His most striking discoveries were the resolution, by electrolysis, of the fixed alkalies, potash and soda. In 1807 the elements sodium and potassium were thus discovered, and the rapid advance of chemistry was aided by electricity.

The apparent migration of the products of electric decomposition called forth several curious theories, but the one which held its ground for over half a century and is still described in text-books was proposed by *Ch. J. D. von Grothuss*[2] (1785–

[1] *The Gallery of Portraits, with Memoirs*, London, 1883, Vol. I., p. 12.
[2] Or Grotthuss.

1822). In his boyhood Grothuss was forbidden the study of chemistry, but later he pursued scientific courses at Leipzig, Paris (at the Polytechnic School), and Naples. After 1808 he lived on his estate in Lithauen, Prussia, giving his leisure time to chemical research. During his last years he suffered intensely from some organic trouble which finally drove him to suicide. He is best known by his paper, first published at Rome in 1805, when he was only twenty years old, "Mémoire sur la décomposition de l'eau et des corps, qu'elle tient en dissolution, à l'aide de l'électricité galvanique."[1] In a quantity of water (Fig. 14), composed of oxygen (marked −) and hydrogen (marked +), electric polarity manifests itself as soon as an electric current is established in the water. All oxygen atoms in the path of the current receive a tendency to move toward the positive pole, while all hydrogen atoms in the same path tend toward the negative pole. Consequently, if the molecule *oh* gives off its oxygen *o* to the positive wire, then the hydrogen *h* soon gets oxidized by the arrival of another oxygen atom *o'*, whose hydrogen *h'* combines with *r*, etc. The same action, in the opposite sense, occurs in the molecule *QP*. Thus, there is a progressive alternate separation and union of atoms. That such separation and recombination should go on, without the

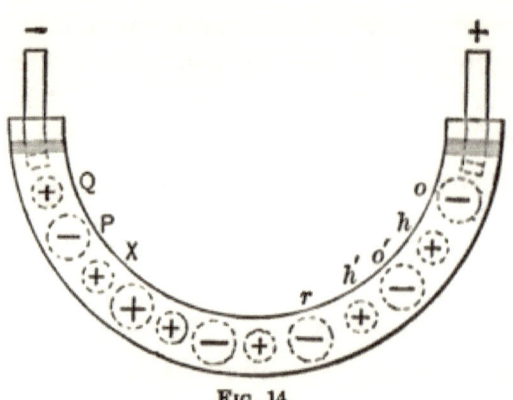

FIG. 14.

[1] Reprinted in 1806 in *Annales de Chimie*, Vol. 58, pp. 54–74. A German translation in full is given in OSTWALD, *Elektrochemie*, Leipzig, 1896, pp. 309–316.

expenditure of work, is contrary to the laws of energy. As Ostwald puts it, energy in a condition of rest cannot of itself become active; a stone lying on the ground cannot of itself rise and then fall again. Grothuss supposed "that at the moment of the segregated appearance of the hydrogen and oxygen, there takes place a division of their natural electricity, either by their contact or by mutual friction, so that the former assumes the positive, the latter the negative condition." On this point the first differences of opinion arose. Modified hypotheses were suggested by *H. G. Magnus* of Berlin, by the Swede chemist *Jöns Jacob Berzelius* (1779–1848), and by *Auguste Arthur de la Rive* (1801–1873) of Geneva. As to the mechanism of electrolytic conduction, the molecular chain of Grothuss was modified somewhat by *Faraday* and *W. Hittorf* (born 1824), professor of physics at Münster. But the first radical modification of Grothuss's theory was made by Clausius in 1857.[1] He argued that, according to the electrolytic theories then held, the E. M. F. first turns the molecules, so that the positive ions face the kathode and the negative ions the anode, and then pulls asunder the ions which were previously firmly united in the molecule. Now, to separate these ions requires a force of definite intensity. Hence, if the electrolytic force acting upon the ions is less than the attraction between the ions, there can be no segregation whatever; if this force increases, many molecules will be broken up at once. This is contrary to fact. Experiment shows that the weakest E. M. F. causes decomposition, and that the action is proportional to the intensity of the current. To remove this difficulty, Clausius assumed that the ions are not permanently united with each other; that part of them exist in the liquid in an uncombined state wandering about seeking partners. The

[1] *Pogg. Ann.*, Vol. 101, p. 338.

electromotive force of the current acts upon these loose atoms. Some of the ions being free to begin with, the weakest current can act. Thus Clausius advanced the idea of dissociation to explain electrolysis. This dissociation hypothesis was modified by *G. Quincke* of Heidelberg to better explain the migration of ions. It was used by *F. Kohlrausch* (born 1840; formerly professor at Strassburg, now Helmholtz's successor at the Reichsanstalt in Berlin) to explain the facts of electrolytic conductivity. Yet Clausius's dissociation theory of the constitution of electrolytes met with little favour until 1887, when *Svante Arrhenius* in Stockholm brought new arguments to support it, based on *J. II. van't Hoff's* theory of solutions and the phenomena of osmotic pressure.[1] From certain new considerations the conclusion was reached that in solutions there exists a partial dissociation of the dissolved substances.[2] Important researches on this subject have been carried on by *Wilhelm Ostwald* of Leipzig, and *Walter Nernst* of Göttingen.

In these researches there are exemplified the beneficial results arising from an intimate reunion of the two branches of science, physics and chemistry. At the beginning of the century many scientists contributed original researches in both sciences; they were chemists as well as physicists. But about 1835 a separation took place; men were known only as physicists or only as chemists. About 1885, after half a century of separation, a tendency to reunion became apparent in what is known as the "Leipzig School," with Ostwald, Nernst, and Arrhenius at the head.

One of the most interesting results achieved by this school is the solution of a problem which has been under discussion a

---

[1] ARRHENIUS, *Zeitschr. f. Physik. Chemie*, Vol. 1, p. 631.

[2] For a systematic and historical exposition of osmotic pressure and the theory of solutions, see W. OSTWALD, *Allgemeine Chemie*, Vol. 1, 1891, Viertes Buch, or P. MUIR's English translation of the same.

whole century, viz. the source or seat of the electromotive force in a voltaic cell. It will be remembered that Volta's contact theory did not meet with general acceptation. The theory that the origin and maintenance of the power of the voltaic pile resided in the contact of different metals was opposed by *Giov. Val. Mattia Fabbroni* (1752–1822) of Florence, Italy; by *Wollaston* in England, and by *Ritter* in Germany. They held that the real source of voltaic electricity was chemical action. This view was taken also by *A. C. Becquerel* in Paris, *A. A. de la Rive* of Geneva, and particularly by *Faraday* in London, who, in 1837 and 1840, published many experiments which seemed to disprove the contact theory. Volta's contact theory received strongest support in Germany. It was advocated by Fechner, Poggendorff, C. H. Pfaff, Ohm, and others. When the principle of the conservation of energy was established, this theory, as originally taught, had to be modified; the mere contact of metals could not give rise to an inexhaustible supply of electric energy. It became evident that in the voltaic cell there took place a transformation of energy. Nevertheless, the seat of the electromotive force might still be at the points of metallic contact. The question appears at last to have been settled in a paper by *Walter Nernst* on the electromotive action of ions.[1] The seat of the electromotive force coincides with the seat of the chemical phenomena, and lies in the surfaces of contact between the metals and the electrolytes. Nernst has established the following fundamental formula:

$$E = K \text{ nat. } \log \frac{P}{p},$$

where E is the potential difference between the metal and electrolyte under consideration; p is the osmotic pressure of

---

[1] *Zeitschr. f. Physik. Chemie*, Vol. 4, 1889, p. 129.

the metal ions in the solution; K is a constant depending on
the units used; P is a constant of integration, to be physically
interpreted as a pressure. This theory of the voltaic cell rests
on *van't Hoff's* ideas of osmotic pressure and the views of
Arrhenius on dissociation in electrolytes.[1] Nernst gives the
following comparison with the action of a Daniell cell: "Given
a reservoir containing liquid carbonic acid and another containing a substance, for instance, caustic potash, absorbing this
one rapidly, and between the two a cylinder and piston contrivance to turn the difference of pressure into work. The
machine does work until all the carbonic acid is absorbed;
just so a Daniell cell acts till the zinc is used up."

Volta's pile and crown of cups, or slight modifications
thereof, were for a long while the only means known for the
generation of current electricity. They laboured under the
defect of a rapid diminution in current on account of polarization. The amalgamation of the zincs, first practised by
Sturgeon in 1830, was a step in advance. A year previous
A. C. Becquerel constructed a cell yielding a somewhat steadier
current. A glass trough was divided into three partitions by
two layers of gold-beater's skin. The middle portion between
the two membranes was filled with a salt; into the outer portions containing appropriate solutions, dipped copper and zinc
plates, respectively. With such a cell a tangent galvanometer
deflection of 84° fell to 68° in half an hour. Better success in
inventing a constant cell crowned the efforts of *John Frederic
Daniell* (1790–1845), who was professor of chemistry at King's
College, London. He contributed to science not only the
"Daniell cell," but also "Daniell's hygrometer." The inven-

---

[1] For an exposition of the theory see W. Ostwald, *Elektrochemie*,
1896, pp. 1133–1148; W. Ostwald, *Allg. Chemie*, Vol. 2, I., 1893; W.
Nernst, *Theoretical Chemistry*, trans. by C. S. Palmer, 1895, pp. 609–
616; A. Wüllner, *Experimentalphysik*, Vol. 3, 1897, pp. 909–919.

tion of the cell, in 1836, grew out of his contact with Faraday. In a letter describing the cell he wrote Faraday as follows: "You know how deep an interest I have taken in your *Experimental Researches in Electricity*, and how zealously I have availed myself of the opportunities which you have ever kindly offered me, of profiting by your oral explanation of such difficulties as occurred to me in the study of your last series of papers."[1] In his original cell the concentrated copper sulphate and dilute sulphuric acid were separated from each other by an animal membrane — the windpipe of an ox. Soon after *J. P. Gassiot* suggested the use of an earthen porous cup in place of the windpipe. In 1839 *Sir William Robert Grove* (1811–1896) communicated to the British Association a paper, entitled "On a Small Voltaic Battery of Extraordinary Energy," and exhibited a battery "hastily constructed." In 1840 Grove was appointed professor of experimental philosophy at the London Institution. Later he entered upon the practice of law,[2] but retained his interest in science. Still another battery,[3] in which the polarization was prevented mechanically by giving the electronegative plate a rough surface, was designed by the London surgeon, *Alfred Smee*[4] (1818–1877). In Grove's cell the great cost of the platinum was an objection; so Bunsen and

[1] *Phil. Trans.*, Part I., 1836, p. 107.

[2] *Electrician* (London), Vol. 37, 1896, p. 483; *Nature*, Vol. 54, 1896, p. 393.

[3] *Phil. Mag.* (3), Vol. 16, 1840.

[4] The reader may be interested in the following *jeu d'esprit*, being part of an electric valentine, written by Clerk Maxwell:

> "Constant as Daniell, strong as Grove;
>   Ebullient through all its depths like Smee;
>   My heart pours forth its tide of love,
>   And all its circuits close in thee."

All four stanzas are given in L. CAMPBELL and W. GARNETT, *Life of J. C. Maxwell*, 1882, p. 630.

others suggested the use of carbon in place of the platinum. Descriptions of " Bunsen's cell" appeared in 1841.[1] Among the numerous open circuit batteries of the present time a prominent one is that brought forth in 1867 by *Georges Leclanché* (1839–1882), a Parisian chemist. A cell whose electromotive force is even more constant than that of the Daniell was suggested in 1873 by *Latimer Clark*, modified forms of which have been used by Lord Rayleigh, Helmholtz, and Henry S. Carhart. The Clark cell has been adopted as the international standard of electromotive force, and official specifications for its preparation have been issued.

In 1803 *Ritter* described the first secondary or storage battery. He found that when two platinum wires were dipped in water and a battery current passed through so that hydrogen appeared at one wire and oxygen at the other, then, if the wires were disconnected from the battery and connected with each other by a conductor, the two wires acted like the plates of a battery, and a current passed for a short time in this new circuit. Its direction was opposite to that of the original current. The subject was studied in 1843 by Grove, who constructed a gas battery to illustrate the phenomenon of "polarization." In 1859 *Gaston Planté* (1834–1889), a pupil of A. C. Becquerel, made a thorough study of this method of storing energy, and devised a secondary cell consisting of two pieces of sheet lead rolled up and dipping into dilute sulphuric acid. The lead plates had to be "formed" (coated at the anode with a semi-porous film of dioxide of lead, and at the kathode with a spongy metallic surface) by sending a current through the cell, and reversing its direction several times. His cell had a higher electromotive force than any primary battery, nevertheless it hardly reached commercial

---

[1] *Pogg. Ann.*, Vol. 54, 1841, p. 417.

efficiency on account of the tedious process of "forming." Little attention was paid to it. The operation of "forming" was avoided in 1881 by *Camille A. Faure*.[1] This was accomplished by coating the lead plates with red lead. Thereby the capacity of the cell was also increased. After this improvement commercial circles suddenly became interested. Four cells were sent from Paris to London in 1881 weighing only 75 pounds, yet it was said they were charged with 1,000,000 foot-pounds of energy! After all, this was no more than the energy stored up in a few ounces of coal. Filled with hope, inventors put forth extraordinary effort to make storage batteries, or "accumulators," commercially available. While they are now used quite extensively, nevertheless the results are disappointing.

The science of electromagnetism originated in 1819 in what is known as "Oersted's experiment." *Hans Christian Oersted* (1777–1851) was born at Rudkjöbing, Langeland, attended the University of Copenhagen, and later was professor at the university and polytechnic school there. Regarding Oersted's great discovery, Hansteen wrote Faraday in 1857 as follows:[2] " Already in the former century there was a general thought that there was a great conformity, and perhaps identity, between the electrical and magnetical force; it was only the question how to demonstrate it by experiments. Oersted tried to place the wire of his galvanic battery perpendicular (at right angles) over the magnetic needle, but marked no sensible motion. Once, after the end of his lecture, as he had used a strong galvanic battery in other experiments, he said: ' Let us now once, as the battery is in activity, try to place the wire parallel with the needle; ' as this was made, he was quite struck with perplexity by seeing the needle making

[1] Born 1840, died 1898.
[2] B. Jones, *Life and Letters of Faraday*, London, 1870, Vol. II., p. 390.

a great oscillation (almost at right angles with the magnetic meridian). Then he said: 'Let us now invert the direction of the current,' and the needle deviated in the contrary direction. Thus the great detection was made; and it has been said, not without reason, that 'he tumbled over it by accident.' He had not before any more idea than any other person that the force should be *transversal.* But as Lagrange has said of Newton on a similar occasion: 'Such accidents only meet persons who deserve them.'"[1]

"Professor Oersted was a man of genius, but he was a very unhappy experimenter; he could not manipulate instruments. He must always have an assistant, or one of his auditors who had easy hands, to arrange the experiment; I have often in this way assisted him as his auditor."[2]

Oersted placed different media between the needle and the wire carrying the current, and concluded that the current "acts upon the needle through glass, metals, wood, water, resin, earthen jars, stones; for when we placed between the two a plate of glass, or of metal, or a board, the result was not cancelled; indeed all three combined hardly lessened the effect."

---

[1] In 1876 H. A. Rowland showed that a magnetic needle is affected also by a rotating body carrying an *electrostatic charge.* The latter acts like a true current.

[2] For Oersted's paper see *Gilbert's Ann.*, Vol. 66, 1820, p. 295; Ostwald, *Elektrochemie*, 1896, p. 367; *Ostwald's Klass.*, No. 63. F. A. P. Barnard said of this discovery: "When Oersted, in 1819, observed the disturbance of the magnetic needle by the influence of a neighbouring magnetic current, how wild and visionary would not that have been pronounced to be, who should have professed to read, in an indication so slight, the grand truth that science had, that day, stretched out the sceptre of her authority over a winged messenger, whose fleetness should make a laggard even of Oberon's familiar sprite, and render the velocity which could 'put a girdle round the earth in forty minutes' tardy and unsatisfactory?"

Oersted's experiment was repeated everywhere. *Dominique François Jean Arago* (1786–1853), the noted Parisian astronomer and physicist, observed the following year (1820) that iron filings were attracted by the current. He concluded that the wire carrying the current must be considered a magnet, even if it is not of iron. In 1822 Davy proved that this apparent attraction of the filings was really due to their peripheral arrangement around the wire; opposite poles of the filings attracting each other and establishing a chain around the wire. The fact that the magnetizing force acts in a plane at right angles to the wire induced Ampère to twist the wire into a spiral in order to intensify the effect upon a needle placed inside. *André Marie Ampère*[1] (1775–1836) was born at Lyons, and early displayed mathematical power. During the Revolution his father was beheaded. In consequence, young Ampère was mentally crushed; hour after hour was passed in silence, while he was staring into the sky, or mechanically heaping sand into little piles. After a year he awoke from his mental stupor and his love for science was rekindled by his reading Rousseau's work on botany. After his marriage in 1799, his religious emotions became very strong. His intense catholicism, though weakened in the middle of his career, again asserted itself later in life. He became professor of physics and chemistry at Lyons. After his wife's death, Ampère, depressed and melancholy, wished to leave Lyons. "Ampère, celebrated, overwhelmed with honourable distinctions, the great Ampère! apart from his mental labours, became once more hesitating and fearful, uneasy and troubled, and more disposed to place confidence in others than in himself."[2] In 1805 he

---

[1] Consult ARAGO, "Eulogy on Ampère," *Smithsonian Report*, 1872, p. 111.

[2] *The Story of his Love, being the journal and early correspondence of André Marie Ampère, edited by Madame H. C.*, London, 1873, p. 164.

became connected with the Polytechnic School in Paris, where, for twenty years, he engaged in important researches.[1]

While Oersted had discovered simply the action of a current on a magnet, Ampère discovered the action of a current upon another current: parallel currents in the same direction attract each other; those in opposite directions repel each other.[2] In these beautiful phenomena some critics saw nothing more than the old electric attractions and repulsions. To this Ampère replied that while equal electric charges repel each other, conductors carrying parallel currents attract each other. Another critic aimed to belittle the discovery by asserting that, since it was known that two currents acted upon one and the same magnet, it was evident, to begin with, that they would act upon each other. Upon hearing this, Arago drew two keys out of his pocket and replied, "Each of these keys attracts a magnet; do you believe that they, therefore, also attract each other?"

Ampère gave a rule — "Ampère's rule" — for the direction in which a magnet is deflected by a current. Faraday arrived

[1] The following extract from a letter of 1805 gives a vivid picture of the man: "My life is a circle, with nothing to break its uniformity. . . . I have but one pleasure, a very hollow, very artificial one, and which I rarely enjoy, and that is to discuss metaphysical questions with those who are engaged in this science at Paris, and who show me more kindness than the mathematicians. But my position obliges me to work at the pleasure of the latter, a circumstance which does not contribute to my diversion, for I have no longer any relish for mathematics. Nevertheless, since I have been here I have written two treatises on Calculation which are to be printed in the journal of the Polytechnic School. It is seldom, except on Sunday, that I can see the metaphysicians, such as M. Maine de Biran, with whom I am very intimate, and M. de Tracy, with whom I dine occasionally at Auteuil, where he resides. It is almost the only place in Paris where the country reminds me of the banks of the Saône." — *Ibidem*, p. 322.

[2] *Annales de Chimie et de Physique*, Vol. 15, 1820.

at a more comprehensive conception of the relation, and devised experiments showing that current and magnet have a tendency to encircle each other. This result was extended by Ampère. Contrary to the opinion of *Thomas Johann See-beck*, who looked upon the electric current as a magnetic action, Ampère considered a magnet as primarily due to the action of electric currents. Each particle in a magnet has an equatorial current, producing magnetic poles. To magnetize a magnet is to cause all these hypothetical mo-lecular currents to flow in the same direction. Terrestrial magnetism, according to Ampère, is due to electric currents around the earth. In 1823 Ampère published a paper giving a mathematical theory of the new phenomena. Maxwell describes this research as "perfect in form and unassailable in accuracy."

Georg Simon Ohm[1] (1789–1854) was an ingenious investi-gator who, although removed from the influence of personal contact with the great physicists of his time, yet working independently and alone, discovered the great law bearing his name. He was born in Erlangen, attended the university at his native place, then taught school at Gottstadt, Neufchâtel, and Bamberg. At the age of thirty he became teacher of mathematics and physics at the gymnasium in Cologne. He taught there nine years with great success. A pupil of that time, who attained great celebrity as a mathematician, was Lejeune Dirichlet. Ohm became ambitious to engage in research, but the want of leisure and books, as well as the lack of suitable apparatus, rendered progress difficult. The mechanical skill which he had acquired as a boy through his father, a locksmith, enabled him to construct much apparatus

---

[1] Consult EUGENE LOMMEL, "The Scientific Work of George Simon Ohm" in *Smithsonian Report*, 1891, pp. 247–256.

for himself. . His first experiments[1] were on the relative conductivity of metals. Taking wire of different material, but
of the same thickness, he found that the following lengths
possessed equal conductivities: copper 1000, gold 574, silver
356, zinc 333, brass 280, iron 174, platinum 171, tin 168, lead
97. Observe that his measurements made silver a much
poorer conductor than copper, though it is actually a better
conductor. Later, Ohm tried to verify his results and found
the mistake. The silver wire first used, in being drawn,
became covered with oily leather, so that, while both wires
were drawn so as to be apparently of equal thickness, the
first one was really much thinner. Further experiments with
wires of the same material, but of different thicknesses, yielded
him the result that they have the same conductivity if their
lengths are proportional to their cross-sections. In these tests
he was greatly troubled by variations in his batteries (" Wogen
der Kraft "). Finally, at the suggestion of Poggendorff, he
adopted thermo-electric elements as the sources of current.
These were free from this source of trouble.

In the experiments by which Ohm established his law, he
used two tin vessels A and B, Fig. 15. In A he kept boiling
water; in B snow or ice. He prepared a bar of bismuth $abb'a'$;
to this he fastened by screws strips of copper, whose two
free ends dipped into two cups filled with mercury. The
thermo-electric couple was, therefore, bismuth and copper.
To generate current, junction ab was placed in the hollow
cylinder x of vessel A, while junction $a'b'$ was placed in the
corresponding position in vessel B. The difference in temperature gave rise to an electric current whenever the two

---

[1] G. S. Oнм, "Bestimmung des Gesetzes, nach welchem Metalle die
Contaktelectricität leiten, etc.," in *Schweigger's Journal f. Chemie u.
Physik*, Vol. 46, 1826, p. 144. This article contains, among other
things, the experimental proof of Ohm's law.

mercury cups were connected with each other by a conductor, so as to complete the circuit. Ohm had a torsion balance constructed by a mechanic under his direction. A magnetic needle was suspended from a torsion-head by a flattened wire five inches long. When the needle was deflected by the cur-

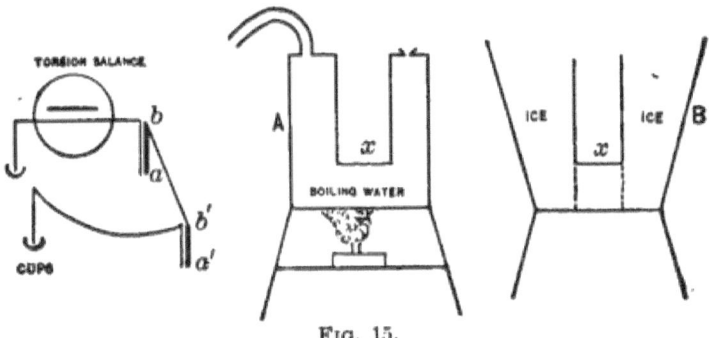

FIG. 15.

rent from its position of rest in the magnetic meridian, it was brought back to its original position by torsion. The angle through which the torsion-head must be deflected was measured in centesimal divisions of the circle. The force tending to deflect the needle from its initial position was proportional to this angle. Hence the strengths of currents could be compared by measuring the angles through which the torsion-head was turned, in each case, in order to bring the needle back to zero.

Ohm prepared eight copper wires of equal thickness ($\frac{7}{8}$ of a line) and, respectively, 2, 4, 6, 10, 18, 34, 66, 130 inches long. These were inserted as part of the electric circuit, one after the other. For each, measurements were taken of the strength of current. On January 8, 1826, he obtained the following data:

Number of conductor,	1,	2,	3,	4,	5,	6,	7,	8.
Angle of torsion in centesimal divisions,	$326\frac{3}{4}$,	$300\frac{3}{4}$,	$277\frac{3}{4}$,	$238\frac{1}{4}$,	$190\frac{3}{4}$,	$134\frac{1}{4}$,	$83\frac{1}{4}$,	$48\frac{1}{4}$.

On the 11th and 15th of the month he took, each day, two more sets of readings. He tabulates his readings and then says: "The above numbers can be represented very satisfactorily by the equation,

$$X = \frac{a}{b+x},$$

where X designates the intensity of the magnetic effect of the conductor whose length is x, a and b being constants depending on the exciting force and the resistance of the remaining parts of the circuit." He gave the quantity b the value $20\frac{1}{4}$, and, for the set of measurements given above, the quantity a the value 7285. These numbers reproduce very closely all the angular numbers given above. Take, for instance, the third conductor, for which $x = 6$, then, by computation, X becomes 277.53, its measured value being $277\frac{3}{4}$. The experiments were varied by selecting brass wire resistances, and again by taking for the two temperatures of the thermo-electric couples those of melting ice and of the room (7.5° C.). By this change in the range of temperature Ohm secured a variation in the electromotive force, which yielded a different value for a, but did not affect b. In all cases the above formula was satisfied. Thus, the new law was established, for a represents the electromotive force, $b + x$ the total resistance of the circuit, X the strength of current. Ohm then established experimentally the formulæ giving the strength of current for the cases when cells are grouped in series and when in multiple arc. These results were published in 1826. Ohm deserves great credit for introducing and defining the accurate notions of electromotive force, strength of current, and electric resistance.

The following year Ohm published a book, entitled *Die Galvanische Kette, mathematisch bearbeitet* (Berlin, 1827). It contained a *theoretic* deduction of Ohm's law, and became far more widely known than his article of 1826, giving the experimental deduction. In fact, his experimental paper was so little known that the impression long prevailed and still exists that he based his law on theory and never established it empirically. This misapprehension accounts, perhaps, for the unfavourable reception of Ohm's conclusions. Professor H. W. Dove, of Berlin, says that "In the Berlin *Jahrbücher für wissenschaftliche Kritik*, Ohm's theory was named a web of naked fancies, which can never find the semblance of support from even the most superficial observation of facts; 'he who looks on the world,' proceeds the writer, 'with the eye of reverence must turn aside from this book as the result of an incurable delusion, whose sole effort is to detract from the dignity of nature.'" [1]

As Ohm's great ambition was to secure a university professorship, we may readily imagine how this lack of appreciation affected him. In order to write his book of 1827, he had secured leave of absence and had gone to Berlin, where the library facilities were better than at Cologne. Not only did he fail to secure promotion by the publication of this book, but he incurred the ill-will of a certain school official (who was a supporter of Hegelianism and, therefore, opposed to experimental research) and, in consequence, he resigned his position in Cologne.

For six years Ohm lived in Berlin, giving three mathematical lessons a week in the *Kriegsschule*, at a yearly salary of 300 thaler. In 1833 he secured an appointment at the polytechnicum in Nürnberg. Gradually his electric researches called forth respect and appreciation. Poggendorff and Fechner in Germany, Lenz in Russia, Wheatstone in England, Henry in America expressed their admiration for his work. The Royal

[1] *Memorial of Joseph Henry*, 1880, p. 489.

Society of London in 1841 awarded him the Copley medal. In 1849, at the age of sixty-two, the ambition of his youth was finally attained. He was appointed extraordinary professor at the University of Munich, and in 1852 ordinary professor. He died two years later.

Wheatstone, the great admirer of Ohm, perceiving the necessity of more accurate means of measuring resistances, invented what is known as "Wheatstone's bridge." *Charles Wheatstone* (1802–1875) was born near Gloucester. He became a manufacturer of musical instruments, but in 1834 accepted the chair of experimental physics at King's College, London. Later he retired to private life, living on the income from his inventions, particularly that of the telegraph. He was an experimentalist of extraordinary skill, but disliked to speak in public. "In fulfilment of the duties of his office at King's College he delivered a course of eight lectures on sound . . . but his habitual though unreasonable distrust of his own powers of utterance proved to be an invincible obstacle, and he soon afterwards discontinued his lectures, but retained the professorship for many years. Although any one would be charmed by his able and lucid exposition *in private*, yet his attempt to repeat the same process *in public* invariably proved unsatisfactory."[1] For this reason some of his more important investigations were brought before the public by Faraday in the theatre of the Royal Institution.

It is interesting to note that the measurement of resistance has been brought to perfection chiefly by those interested in the development of the telegraph. Wheatstone invented the rheostat, but this has been superseded by the resistance box, which was first used by Werner Siemens. The earlier methods of measuring resistance laboured under the defect of depending

[1] *Proc. Roy. Soc. of London*, Vol. 24, p. xviii.

on the constancy of the batteries used. This source of trouble was removed by Becquerel, who introduced the differential galvanometer, and by Wheatstone, who adopted a method suggested by Hunter Christie, and was led to the invention of "Wheatstone's bridge." In 1843 Wheatstone describes two forms, differing merely in the arrangement of the wires.[1] The second is shown in Fig. 16. Resistances Za and aC are constructed equal to each other; resistances Zc, db, be, fC are also equal to each other. The battery is connected at Z and C, the galvanometer at a and b. The gap cd may be bridged by the resistance to be measured; the gap ef by a rheostat, the resist-

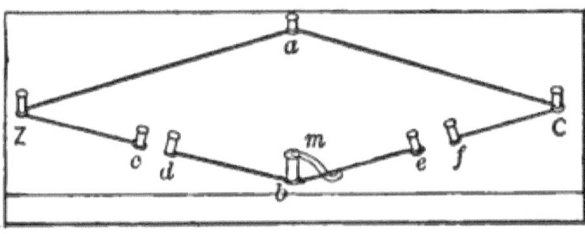

FIG. 16.

ance of which is adjusted until the galvanometer deflection is reduced to zero. Then the required resistance equals the known rheostat resistance. Wheatstone's new instrument was modified by Kirchhoff, who introduced a platinum wire of uniform thickness with which movable contact was made. Kirchhoff gave it a triangular shape; Siemens adopted the long, rectangular form.

The galvanometer was invented by *J. S. C. Schweigger* (1779–1857), professor at Halle, in 1820, immediately after Oersted's experiment became known. Schweigger increased the effective action of the current by carrying the wire many times round the magnetic needle. In 1825 *Leopoldo Nobili*

[1] *Phil. Trans.*, Vol. 133, pp. 303–327; *Scientific Papers of Sir Charles Wheatstone*, London, 1879, p. 127.

(1784–1835) of Florence used the astatic multiplier, having two needles rigidly connected with each other, and with the south pole of the one pointing the same way as the north pole of the other. In 1839 *Claude Servais Mathias Pouillet* (1790–1868), professor in Paris, invented the tangent and the sine galvanometers. Great improvements in the promptness and delicacy of action of galvanometers were effected by *Sir William Thomson,* who devised mirror galvanometers for signalling through submarine cables. In recent years a galvanometer designed by *A. D'Arsonval* is meeting with great favour. In principle it is the same as the "siphon recorder" of Sir William Thomson, employed in submarine telegraphy, and as the suspended coil galvanometer, used as early as 1836 by Sturgeon. About 1890 *C. Vernon Boys* recommended the use of quartz fibres in place of silk for needle suspension in delicate experimentation.

Michael Faraday (1791–1867), the greatest experimentalist of the nineteenth century in the field of electricity and magnetism, was born at Newington in London, and was the son of a blacksmith. "My education," he says, "was of the most ordinary description, consisting of little more than the rudiments of reading, writing, and arithmetic at a common day-school. My hours out of school were passed at home and in the streets."[1] In 1804 he served as errand boy at a bookstore and bookbindery near his home. The following year he became an apprentice to the bookbinder. At this time he liked to read scientific books which happened to pass through his hands. "I made such simple experiments in chemistry," he says, "as could be defrayed in their expense by a few pence per week, and also constructed an electrical machine." At the age of nineteen he sometimes in the evening attended lectures

---

[1] B. Jones, *Life and Letters of Faraday*, 1870, Vol. I., p. 9.

given by Mr. Tatum on natural philosophy, his brother pay-
ing the admission fee for him.   In 1812 he had the good
fortune to hear four lectures delivered at the Royal Institution
by Sir H. Davy, the great chemist.   About this time Faraday
went as a journeyman bookbinder to a Frenchman in London.
His new work was uncongenial.   " My desire," he said later,
" to escape from trade, which I thought vicious and selfish,
and to enter into the service of science, which I imagined made
its pursuers amiable and liberal, induced me at last to make
the bold and simple step of writing to Sir H. Davy, expressing
my wishes, and a hope that if an opportunity came in his way
he would favour my views; at the same time, I sent the notes
I had taken of his lectures."   Davy replied, " I am far from
displeased with the proof you have given me of your confidence. . . ."   Faraday became Davy's assistant at the Royal
Institution in 1813.   In the autumn of that year Davy and his
wife started on a tour abroad, Faraday going with them as
amanuensis.   After being with Davy in France, Italy, Switzerland, he returned to the Royal Institution in 1815.   Soon after
his return he began original researches, and published his first
paper in 1816.   He also commenced to lecture before the
" City Philosophical Society."   In a letter he wrote of " the
glorious opportunity I enjoy of improving in the knowledge of
chemistry and the sciences with Sir H. Davy."   In 1821 Faraday married, and brought his wife to his rooms at the Royal
Institution, where they lived together for forty-six years.   In
1824 he was elected member of the Royal Society at a time
when Davy was its president.   It is sad to relate that jealousy
on the part of Davy led him to oppose Faraday's election.
Nevertheless, Faraday always spoke with respect and admiration for the talents of the man who had done so much to start
him in his early scientific career.   In 1825 Faraday became
director of the Royal Institution.

Oersted's memorable experiment of 1820 was studied in England by Wollaston, who in 1821, in the presence of Davy in the laboratory of the Royal Institution, sought by experiment to convert the deflection of the needle by the current into a permanent rotation. He also hoped to produce the reciprocal effect of a current rotating around a magnet. His experiments failed. As previously noted, Faraday began to study magnetic rotations, and on the morning of Christmas Day, 1821, he showed his wife for the first time the revolution of a magnetic needle around an electric current.[1] Faraday was blamed for not mentioning Wollaston in his paper describing the experiments, but Faraday justly claimed that he was in no way indebted to Wollaston.[2]

His next investigations were on the liquefaction of gases, on vibrating surfaces, and chemical subjects. In 1831 came the discovery of magneto-electricity and induction currents. As early as 1824 he had argued that as a voltaic current affects a magnet, so a magnet ought to react upon an electric current. But he could obtain no experimental evidence of this effect. Again, he knew that an electrified body acts upon an unelectrified body, that a wire carrying an electric current is electrified. Could that wire excite in other wires a state similar to its own? In 1825 he passed a current through one wire which was lying close to another wire connected with a galvanometer, but obtained no result. The momentary existence of the phenomena of induction then escaped him. In 1828 he again experimented without result.[3]

---

[1] JOHN TYNDALL, *Faraday as a Discoverer*, New York, 1877, p. 12. A work on *Michael Faraday* by S. P. THOMPSON is to appear soon.

[2] Faraday explains all in his " Historical Statement respecting Electromagnetic Rotation," *Experimental Researches*, Vol. II., pp. 159–162.

[3] B. JONES *op. cit.*, Vol. II., p. 2. What follows is taken from this source.

But Faraday persisted.   In August, 1831, he took a ring of
soft iron (Fig. 17), and wound coils A and B around it.   Coil
B was connected with a galvanometer.
When coil A was connected with a
battery of ten cells, the galvanometer
needle oscillated and settled at last
in the original position.   On discon-
necting the battery the needle was
again disturbed.   Faraday did not at

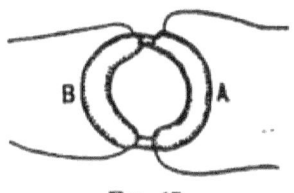

Fig. 17.

once grasp the full significance of this.   On September 23 he
says in a letter, "I am busy just now again on electromagnetism, and think I have got hold of a good thing,
but can't say.   It may be a weed instead of a fish
that, after all my labour, I may at last pull up."
Next day he took an iron cylinder, surrounded by
a helix connected with a galvanometer.   Then the
cylinder was placed between the poles of a bar
magnet, as in Fig. 18.   "Every time the magnetic
contact at N and S was made or broken, there was
magnetic motion at the indicating helix [galva-
nometer] — the effect being, as in former cases,
not permanent, but a mere momentary push or
pull. . . .   Hence here [was] distinct conversion
of magnetism into electricity."   This experiment
is the converse of Oersted's experiment; an electric current was excited by a magnet.

Fig. 18.

On October 1, 1831, Faraday discovered induced
electric currents.   A helix, wound with insulated
copper wire 203 feet long, was connected with a
galvanometer.   Another coil of the same length
and wound around the same block of wood was
joined to the poles of a battery of ten cells.   "A
sudden jerk was perceived when the battery communication

was *made* and *broken*, but it was so slight as to be scarcely visible. It was one way when *made*, the other way when *broken*, and the needle took up its natural position at intermediate times." On October 17 he produced the same effects by merely thrusting a permanent steel magnet into a coil of wire. The unexpected phenomenon in these experiments was that the induced effect was not continuous; it was instantaneous "and partook more of the nature of the electrical wave passed through from the shock of a common Leyden jar, than the current from a voltaic battery."[1]

These epoch-making results threw light upon the mysterious experiment of Arago, who in 1824 had observed the motion of a magnet caused by rotating a copper disk in its neighbourhood.

Faraday then, for a time, dropped electromagnetism and entered upon the study of electrolysis and the voltaic cell. He discovered the laws of electrolysis. The amount of water decomposed is proportional to the quantity of electricity passing through the liquid, no matter what the electric pressure or the area of the electrodes or the conductivity of the liquid may be. Thus, the amount of gas set free is an exact measure of the quantity of electricity passing through. He next ascertained that equal quantities of electricity decompose in different electrolytes equivalent amounts. In 1834 he introduced the terms "anode" and "kathode."

In 1834 *William Jenkin* observed that, if the wire which surrounds an electromagnet be used to join the plates of a single cell, a shock is felt each time contact is broken, provided the ends of the wire are grasped one in each hand. *A. P. Mas-*

---

[1] Faraday describes his tests in *Experimental Researches in Electricity*, London, 1839, Vol. I. See also *Ostwald's Klass.*, No. 81. The order in which the experiments are described by Faraday is not quite the order of discovery.

son in Paris had observed similar phenomena. Unaware of Henry's researches on self-induction, Faraday began in 1834 to study this action, and he recognized it as one of "induction of an electric current on itself"; he succeeded in showing the presence of an "extra current." The "extra current" at the "break" had the same direction as the original current and strengthened it; the "extra current" at the "make" flowed in the same direction and weakened the original current. This theory of the existence of an "extra current" met at first with considerable opposition, but was finally verified by other workers.

On contemplating Faraday's experiments on electromagnetism, Tyndall writes enthusiastically as follows: "I cannot help thinking . . . that this discovery of magneto-electricity is the greatest experimental result ever obtained. It is the Mont Blanc of Faraday's own achievements. He always worked at great elevations, but higher than this he never attained."

The lofty heights which were scaled by the bold English explorer were at the same time reached by an American explorer, neither being conscious of the other's efforts until the summit was reached. In the discovery of magneto-electricity the name of Faraday must be accompanied by that of Joseph Henry.

Joseph Henry (1799–1878) was born at Albany, New York. At the age of fifteen he entered the shop of a watchmaker as an apprentice, although his chief ambition then was to excel as an actor and dramatic writer. Accidentally he came across Gregory's *Lectures on Experimental Philosophy*, the perusal of which created a love for science. He entered the Albany Academy as a pupil, and in 1826 became professor of mathematics there. He was appointed in 1832 professor of natural philosophy at Princeton College, and in 1846 secretary of the newly established Smithsonian Institution in Washington.

He first engaged in original investigation at Albany in 1827. Both as professor and as secretary his time was so largely taken up with teaching or routine work, that but little time was left for research. At the Albany Academy seven hours of daily teaching and the want of a room which could be used for experimentation prevented nearly all research, except during vacation time — the month of August. His researches were carried on in the large hall of the Academy, and invariably came to a stop with the first of September, the time when the Academy reopened.[1] Henry was the first to undertake important original electrical experimentation in the United States since the time of Franklin.

Henry's first improvements were in the electromagnet. We must here premise that in 1820 Arago and Ampère magnetized steel needles by placing them in a helix carrying an electric current, that in 1825 Sturgeon described the earliest electromagnet worthy of the name. *William Sturgeon* (1783–1850), the son of an idle shoemaker in Lancashire, was a self-taught scientist, the founder of a monthly periodical, the *Annals of Electricity*.[2] Sturgeon's electromagnet of 1825 could lift nine pounds, or about twenty times its own weight. He used soft iron in place of steel, bent the iron in form of a horseshoe, and varnished the iron in order to insulate the single layer of naked copper wire wound around it in a loose spiral of eighteen turns. The current was obtained from a copper-zinc cell of small internal resistance. The fact that this horseshoe became a strong magnet as soon as the current started and lost its power the moment the current stopped made it the object of general interest. Professor Moll of Utrecht constructed a

[1] MARY A. HENRY, "A Study of the Work of Faraday and Henry," *Electrical Engineer*, Vol. 13, p. 28.

[2] Consult a sketch of his life in S. P. THOMPSON, *The Electromagnet*, New York, 1891, pp. 412–418.

horseshoe magnet supporting 154 pounds. But the one who introduced radical improvements was Henry at Albany. Instead of varnishing the iron, he insulated the copper wire by covering it with silk; instead of a few turns of wire about the core, he put on many turns. His first magnet, having 400 turns, was exhibited in March, 1829. A further improvement consisted in winding the core with several coils, the ends of which were left free. Thereby the battery current could be made to subdivide, the coils being arranged in parallel. He experimented on the proper size of coil to be used with batteries of different kinds, and arrived at the highly important conclusion that one may use an "intensity" magnet with a long single wire, receiving current from an "intensity" battery, with cells grouped in series; or one may use a "quantity" magnet with many short wires, to be excited by a "quantity" battery of a single large pair of plates. The former magnet was to be preferred when the current was carried over considerable distances from the cell to the magnet, as in case of telegraphy. Henry's electromagnets were capable of sustaining fifty times their own weight under the stimulus of a single cell with plates hardly a hand's breadth in length and width.[1]

The originality of these results is the more conspicuous when we remember that Henry was at this time unacquainted with the law discovered by Ohm in 1826. In 1833 Henry asked Dr. Bache, "Can you give me any information about the theory of Ohm? Where is it to be found?" It was not till 1837, during his visit to London, that he became acquainted with Ohm's theory.[2]

---

[1] Henry published his results in the *Am. Jour. of Sci.*, Vol. 19, January, 1831, pp. 404, 405. Consult also the "Scientific Writings of Joseph Henry," in *Smithsonian Miscellaneous Collections*, Vol. 30, 1887, Part I., p. 37.

[2] MARY A. HENRY, *op. cit.*, p. 30.

In August, 1829, while he was testing the lifting power of magnets with different lengths of wire, and by means of his "intensity" magnet and battery had made the actual combination which constitutes the electric telegraph of to-day, he noticed an unexpected spark resulting from the break of a long coiled wire through which the battery current had been passing. "Nature . . . had lifted her veil for a moment to lure him in a different direction, and so it happened that when vacation came round again in August, 1830, he had taken up the investigation of this new phenomenon." He recognized its nature, and in 1832 published it under the heading "Electrical Self-induction in a Long Helical Wire."[1] Faraday's investigation on "extra current" was made in 1834 and published in 1835. The priority of the discovery of self-induction plainly belongs, therefore, to the American physicist.

Henry asked himself the question, if electricity can produce magnetism, cannot magnetism produce electricity? He took his "quantity" magnet at the Albany Academy, wound around the middle of its armature a coil of thin copper wire, the ends of which were connected with a galvanometer, forty feet away. The armature was placed across the ends of the magnet; the plates of the battery were dipped into the dilute acid, the magnet was excited, and the needle of the galvanometer swerved; the answer came, magnetism can produce electricity. Like Faraday, Henry was surprised to find only momentary effects, and that the deflection of the needle at "break" was in the opposite direction to that at "make." There is almost conclusive evidence to show that this experiment was performed in August, 1830, or one year before Faraday made his first experiment on magneto-electricity.[2] Henry was enthu-

---

[1] *Am. Jour. Sci.*, Vol. 22, 1832, p. 408.
[2] MARY A. HENRY, *op. cit.*, pp. 53 *et seq.*

siastic, and was getting ready for an exhaustive series of experiments in August, 1831. He started to make a much larger electromagnet, also a great "reel," aiming to secure a machine capable of powerful work — he was endeavouring to make a dynamo. But vacation drew to a close before it was completed.[1]

He resumed work, not in August, 1832, but in June! And why? By chance he had come upon a paragraph in a periodical, stating that Faraday had shown that magnetism can produce electricity. Faraday's experimentation was given only in outline. Henry could not tell to what extent he was anticipated. He immediately went to work. Using his old apparatus, he repeated the experiments mentioned in the notice, and hastily prepared a paper, printed in the *American Journal of Science*, July, 1832. This paper contains tests made before he had heard of Faraday's work, and also tests made after that. Faraday had published his discovery of magneto-electricity in 1831. While it is almost certain that Henry's discovery antedated Faraday's, Henry was anticipated in the date of publication. Hence the priority rightly belongs to Faraday. In 1837 Henry was in Great Britain, and became personally acquainted with England's great physicists. Henry loved to dwell on the hours he spent in Faraday's society. Faraday and Wheatstone expressed great esteem for the American physicist. At King's College, in London, Faraday, Wheatstone, Daniell, and Henry once tried to evolve the electric spark from the thermopile. The Englishmen attempted it and failed. Henry, calling in the aid of a discovery he had made of the effect of a long interpolar wire wrapped around a piece of soft iron, succeeded. Faraday became as wild as a boy, and, jumping up, shouted, "Hurrah for the Yankee experiment."[2]

[1] MARY A. HENRY, *op. cit.*, p. 54.
[2] *A Memorial of Joseph Henry*, Washington, 1880, p. 506.

Henry carried on original researches in various departments of physics, but of all his investigations the most finished are those on induced currents of different orders, made in the summer of 1838 at Princeton. As we have seen, currents induced by currents were observed by Faraday. As Faraday's secondary current was but momentary, it was by no means self-evident that it could act as a primary current and itself induce a current in a third circuit. Henry proved that induced currents of higher order are possible. "It was found that with a small battery a shock could be given from the current of the third order to twenty-five persons joining hands; also shocks perceptible in the arms were obtained from a current of the fifth order."[1]

An observation which has an important bearing on recent electromagnetic theories was made by Henry in 1842. He showed that the discharge of the Leyden jar did not consist of a single restoration of the equilibrium, but of a rapid succession of librations back and forth, gradually diminishing to zero. That the Leyden jar discharge is oscillatory was shown again in 1847 by Helmholtz in his paper "Ueber die Erhaltung der Kraft." But both Helmholtz and Henry were anticipated by *Felix Savary*, who drew this conclusion from an experiment as early as 1827.[2] In 1853 *Sir William Thomson*, unaware of the earlier researches, concluded from theory and mathematical deduction that the discharge must be oscillatory.

Henry's "quantity" magnet and coiled armature of 1830 (?), and Faraday's ring (Fig. 17), used in 1831, may be looked upon as the first *transformers*. Inspired by Henry's researches, *Charles Grafton Page* (1812–1868), a native of Salem and

---

[1] *Trans. Am. Phil. Soc.*, Vol. VI. (N. S.), p. 303. Quite full accounts of Henry's work on induced currents are given in J. A. FLEMING, *The Alternate-current Transformer*, Vol. I.

[2] *Memorial of Joseph Henry*, 1880, pp. 255, 396, 448.

graduate of Harvard College, after 1840 examiner in the patent office in Washington, invented what is now known as the Ruhmkorff's Coil. His earliest research was published in 1836. In 1838 he had constructed an induction coil[1] of a high degree of perfection. The primary was of thick copper wire; the secondary of very thin wire. The vibrations of an automatic hammer made and broke a mercury contact. To shorten the time of contact at break, Page poured oil or alcohol over the mercury. Later this device was suggested by others and is usually attributed to Foucault. The platinum contact, in place of the mercurial break, was first suggested in Germany in 1839 by J. P. Wagner and by Neef. Of Page's coil Uppenborn says: "The effects which Page produced by means of this instrument were much more intense than those produced by Ruhmkorff with his, as Page succeeded with only a single Grove element in inducing in the second circuit such a high electromotive force as produced sparks 4½ inches in length through a vacuum tube — a result which Ruhmkorff, although his invention created such a great and well-deserved attention, did not attain." In the year 1850 Page produced a coil yielding sparks through the air, eight inches in length. Says Uppenborn, "All things considered, it is not a little surprising that while the invention of the Ruhmkorff's coil was still in its infancy, the wonderful output of Page's apparatus was still, even in the year 1851, quite unknown in Europe." Evidently the coil should have been named after Page and not after Ruhmkorff.

Heinrich Daniel Ruhmkorff or *Rühmkorff* (1803–1877) was born at Hanover in Germany. In 1819 he went to Paris

---

[1] Described in *Am. Jour. Sci.*, Vol. 35, 1839, p. 250. A drawing of the coil is given there, also in BEDELL, *Principles of the Transformer*, 1896, p. 291; in FLEMING, *Alternate-current Transformer*, Vol. II., 1892, p. 26; and in F. UPPENBORN, *History of the Transformer*, 1889, p. 7.

where, later, he started a manufactory of physical apparatus. A long series of experiments resulted in the appearance in 1851 of the famous "Ruhmkorff coil." It gave sparks in air two inches in length. In 1858 one of his coils received the first prize of 50,000 francs at the French Exposition of Electrical Apparatus.[1] Jamin says that Ruhmkorff died almost a poor man, because he had spent all his earnings in behalf of science and in works of benevolence.[2]

The Ruhmkorff coil is a transformer of the "open magnetic circuit" type, while the commercial transformer of our day, like Faraday's original ring (Fig. 17), has a "closed magnetic circuit"; that is, in the latter the magnetic lines of force nowhere pass through air, but follow the easier iron path throughout. The transformer or converter used in systems of electric lighting or long-distance power transmission, has been developed by Cromwell Fleetwood Varley, Paul Jablochkoff, C. W. Harrison, C. T. and E. B. Bright, S. Z. de Ferranti, Carl Zipernowsky, Max Déri, Otto Titus Bláthy, Gaulard and Gibbs, William Stanley, and others. Thus, the theoretical researches of Faraday and Henry, carried on out of pure love for science, have become the foundation of one of the most extensive commercial developments of modern times, and are contributing vastly toward the progress of civilization and the comfort of mankind.

---

[1] It has been claimed by some that this prize should have been awarded to *Edward Samuel Ritchie* (1814–1895), the American philosophical instrument maker, who improved on Ruhmkorff's instrument of 1851 by dividing the secondary coil into sections for the purpose of better insulation. This division had been previously suggested by Poggendorff. One of Ritchie's instruments was exhibited in England in 1857. It is alleged that Ruhmkorff secured one of these and, copying it successfully, captured the grand prize. See A. E. DOLBEAR in *Proc. Am. Acad. of Arts and Sciences*, N. S., Vol. 23, 1895–1896, p. 359.

[2] *Nature*, Vol. 17, 1877, p. 169.

Returning to Faraday at the Royal Institution in London, we find him soon after 1835 working on electrostatic induction. Coulomb and others had assumed the theory of "action at a distance"; electric charges were supposed to attract and repel each other at a distance without being affected in any way by the intervening medium. Faraday had an idea that this view was erroneous, that electric attraction and repulsion are propagated by means of molecular action among the contiguous particles of the insulating medium, which thereby participates in the propagation of the electric forces. Hence Faraday termed such mediums "dielectrics." Faraday satisfied himself by experiments that induction does not always take place in straight lines, as the theory of an action at a distance without the aid of an intervening medium would lead us to believe; on the contrary, induction takes place along curved lines, and by the action of contiguous particles. These curved lines he termed "lines of force." His experiments showed that the intensity of the electric force between two charged bodies varies with the nature of the insulating medium. He was thus led to the capital discovery of what is now termed "specific inductive capacity." Henry Cavendish had arrived at the same results long ago, but had allowed these pearls of scientific truth to be hidden away. Faraday's apparatus, by which he compared specific inductive capacities, was in principle a Leyden jar in which the dielectric could be changed. It consisted of two concentric spheres. The hollow space between their surfaces could be filled with any desired material. Taking air as the standard dielectric, he found the electric attraction or repulsion for sulphur 2.26 times greater; for shellac, 2.0 times; for glass, at least 1.76 times greater. Faraday's experiments were published in 1837; since 1870 large additions to our knowledge of this subject have been made, but owing to electric absorption the values assigned by different observers for the specific inductive capacity of various substances show a most perplexing disagreement.

In these researches Faraday created a symbolism which has since been universally adopted in teaching physics. We refer to his "lines of force." He used this term for the first time in 1831 in connection with the lines exhibited by iron filings, but the concept of "lines of force" was held by others before him; for instance, by T. J. Seebeck.[1] In Faraday's reasoning "lines of force" took the place of mathematical analysis, a knowledge of which he had had no opportunity to acquire. Being debarred from following the course of thought which had led to the achievements of the French mathematical physicists, Poisson and Ampère, he invoked the aid of "lines of force," which, in his mind's eye, he saw as distinctly as the solid bodies from which they emanated.[2] In recent years Faraday's ingenious symbolism has found its way not only into the technique, but also into elementary instruction. Even in Germany, where the theory of action at a distance in electricity and magnetism has had the strongest hold, Faraday's notions are finding acceptance; for now Hertz has experimentally demonstrated the correctness of the fundamental hypothesis in Maxwell's developments of Faraday's theory of the dielectric.[3]

Faraday was led by speculation to the belief that there existed some direct relation between light and electricity or magnetism. Many experimental attempts to prove this yielded purely negative results, but in 1845 his strong conviction was finally supported by actual experiment. "I have at last succeeded in illuminating a magnetic curve or line of

[1] See SEEBECK's paper in *Ostwald's Klass.*, No. 63.

[2] See CLERK MAXWELL, "Action at a Distance," *Nature*, Vol. 7, 1872–1873, p. 342.

[3] See A. SCHÜLKE in *Zeitschr. f. Math. Unterricht*, Vol. 25, p. 403.

force, and in magnetizing a ray of light."[1] Faraday caused a polarized beam to pass through a piece of "heavy glass," lying in a strong magnetic field, due to a large electromagnet. By means of a Nicol prism, it was found that the wave of light was twisted round by the action of the magnet so that its vibrations were executed in a different plane. He says: "Not only heavy glass, but solids and liquids, acids and alkalies, oils, water, alcohol, ether, all possess this power." Commenting on this relation between light and magnetism, Whewell wrote Faraday: "I cannot help believing that it is another great stride up the ladder of generalization, on which you have been climbing so high and standing so firm."

Faraday's powerful magnets and heavy glass led him to the verification of another of his prophecies. That magnetic properties should be confined to iron and nickel appeared to him too extraordinary to be probable. Knowing that the magnetic strength of iron lessens at very high temperatures, he suspected that other metals might show magnetism at lower temperatures. As early as 1836 he experimented on metals cooled to − 50° C., but without results. In 1839 he repeated these experiments at − 80° C., again without result. In 1845 he added cobalt to the list of magnetic substances. In 1846, at last, he published the general result. On November 4, 1845, he suspended by silk a bar of heavy glass between the poles of his new electromagnet. When the magnet was excited the heavy glass was repelled from the poles so as to assume an equatorial position. Faraday experimented with other substances and found that all liquids and solids were attracted or repelled, provided that sufficient magnetic power was used. Sulphur, india-rubber, asbestos, tissue of the human body,

---

[1] B. JONES, *op. cit.*, Vol. II., p. 195. See also *Experimental Researches*, 19th Series.

were repelled — were shown to be diamagnetic. Says Faraday, "If a man could be in the magnetic field, like Mohammed's coffin, he would turn until across the magnetic line."[1] Diamagnetic phenomena had been observed before, but the experiments were not known to Faraday. Brugmans, A. C. Becquerel, Le Baillif, Saigey, and Seebeck had indicated the existence of repulsive force exercised by a magnet on two or three substances. Wheatstone called Faraday's attention to Becquerel's research on the magnetic condition of matter, and Faraday replied, "It is astonishing to think how he could have been so near the discovery of the great principle and fact, and yet so entirely miss them both, and fall back into old and preconceived notions."[2]

---

[1] In 1853 the London public was greatly excited over the "table-turning" of three skilful performers. Without due inquiry, the effects were referred to electricity, to magnetism, or to some unrecognized physical power able to affect inanimate bodies. Faraday looked into the matter and wrote in part as follows: "I have not been at work except in turning the tables upon the table-turners, nor should I have done that, but that so many inquiries poured in upon me, that I thought it better to stop the inpouring flood by letting all know at once what my views and thoughts were. What a weak, credulous, incredulous, unbelieving, superstitious, bold, frightened, what a ridiculous world ours is, as far as concerns the mind of man." Faraday complains of the great body of men who refer the results "to some unrecognized physical force, without inquiring whether the known forces are not sufficient, or who even refer them to diabolical or supernatural agency rather than suspend judgment or acknowledge to themselves that they are not learned enough in these matters to decide on the nature of the action. *I think the system of education that could leave the mental condition of the public body in the state in which this subject has found it must have been greatly deficient in some very important principle.*" — B. JONES, *op. cit.*, Vol. II., pp. 300–302.

[2] In coining the words "diamagnetic" and "paramagnetic," Faraday consulted Whewell, who wrote in 1850 in a letter as follows: "I am always glad to hear of your wanting new words, because the want shows that you are pursuing new thoughts. . . . The purists would certainly object to the opposition, or coördination, of 'terromagnetic' and 'diamagnetic.' . . .

Beginning about the time of Ampère, several new electric theories came to be advanced.[1] The early theories neglected the action of the dielectric, but assumed the existence of one or two electric fluids and took no account of the principle of the conservation of energy. The recognition by Faraday of the influence of the dielectric medium "is, perhaps, the most important step that has ever been made in the theory of electricity." We have seen that he was led to this by his desire to get rid, as far as possible, of the idea of action at a distance, which was so prevalent in his time, but to which his researches have given the death-blow. Faraday's ideas were expressed in mathematical language and were more fully developed, so as to culminate in the electromagnetic theory of light, by the genius of Maxwell.

James Clerk Maxwell (1831–1879) was born in Edinburgh, enjoyed good opportunities for early development, and soon displayed power for mathematical and physical research. At the age of fifteen he published a paper on oval curves. He attended meetings of the Royal Society of Edinburgh. In 1847 he met William Nicol, the inventor of the polarizing prism, and became interested in the phenomena of polarized light. Professor Campbell[2] says that, to keep their education

Hence it would appear that the two classes of magnetic bodies are those which place their length *parallel* or *according* to the terrestrial magnetic lines, and those which place their length *transverse* to such lines. Keeping the preposition *dia* for the latter, the preposition *para* or *ana* might be used for the former; perhaps *para* would be best, as the word 'parallel,' in which it is involved, would be a technical memory for it." See I. Todhunter, *William Whewell*, London, 1876, Vol. II., p. 363.

[1] Consult J. J. Thomson, "Report on Electrical Theories," *Report of the Brit. Association*, 1885, pp. 97–155; Helmholtz, "On Later Views of the Connection of Electricity and Magnetism," *Smithsonian Report*, 1873.

[2] L. Campbell and W. Garnett, *Life of James Clerk Maxwell*, London, 1882, p. 85; we are using also R. T. Glazebrook, *James Clerk Maxwell and Modern Physics*, New York, 1896.

at the Edinburgh Academy "abreast of the requirements of the day," etc., it was thought desirable that they should have lessons in "Physical Science." So one of the classical masters gave them out of a text-book. The only thing I distinctly remember about these hours is that Maxwell and P. G. Tait seemed to know much more about the subject than our teacher did. In the fall of 1847 Maxwell entered the University of Edinburgh, learning mathematics from Kelland, physics from J. D. Forbes, and logic from Sir Wm. Hamilton. Forbes gave him free use of the class apparatus for original experiments, and he worked without any assistance or supervision with physical and chemical apparatus, and devoured all sorts of scientific works in the library. In 1850 Maxwell entered the University of Cambridge, where he obtained the position of second wrangler. At this time, and later, Maxwell was fond of writing quaint verses which he brought round to his friends, "with a sly chuckle at the humour, which, though his own, no one enjoyed more than himself."[1]   Maxwell became professor of physics at Marischal College, Aberdeen, in 1856; at King's College, London, in 1860; at Cambridge University, in 1871.

In papers on "Physical Lines of Force," published in 1861 and 1862, and in later papers, he translated Faraday's theories into the language of mathematics, and developed the theory according to which the energy of the electromagnetic field resides in the dielectric as well as in the conductors. Faraday had said that "induction appears to consist in a certain polarized state of the particles into which they are thrown by the electrified body sustaining the action, the particles assuming positive and negative points or parts. . . . This state must be a forced one,

---

[1] Read verses in L. CAMPBELL and W. GARNETT, *op. cit.*, pp. 577–651, particularly his parody of Tyndall's Belfast Address.

for it is originated and sustained only by a force, and sinks to the normal or quiescent state when that force is removed." Maxwell changed Faraday's nomenclature; instead of the polarization of the dielectric, he speaks of the change as consisting of an "electric displacement." He looked upon the action in the dielectric as analogous to that of an elastic solid which springs back to its original position when the external force is removed. The change in electric displacement is an electric current, called a "displacement current," to distinguish it from a current in conductors, designated as "conduction current." (Hertz has proved the existence of these "displacement currents" by experiments which are quite free from objection.) In a medium supposed to be subject to such electric displacement, waves of periodic displacement could be set up. The velocity of such a wave was very nearly equal to that of light. Hence, "the elasticity of the magnetic medium in air is the same as that of the luminiferous medium if these two coexistent, coextensive, and equally elastic media are not rather one medium." That electromagnetic phenomena and the phenomena called light have their seat in the same medium, and are, in fact, identical in nature, is the theory elaborated by Maxwell in his great *Treatise on Electricity and Magnetism*,[1] published in 1873. While this theory did not contradict any observed facts, Maxwell himself had only few and indecisive

[1] This epoch-making book has always been found difficult of comprehension. Poincaré writes this: "A French *savant*, one of those who have most completely fathomed Maxwell's meaning, said to me, 'I understand everything in the book except what is meant by a body charged with electricity.'" Hertz expresses himself as follows: "Many a man has thrown himself with zeal into the study of Maxwell's work, and, even when he has not stumbled upon unwonted mathematical difficulties, has nevertheless been compelled to abandon the hope of forming for himself an altogether consistent conception of Maxwell's ideas. I have fared no better myself." — *Electric Waves*, trans. by D. E. JONES, p. 20.

criteria in support of it, but his great prophecy was experimentally confirmed by the illustrious Hertz.

Heinrich Rudolf Hertz[1] (1857–1894) was born at Hamburg. After leaving the gymnasium, he fitted himself for civil engineering. At the age of twenty, he came to a turning-point in his career; he was converted from a man of practice to one of learning. He went to Berlin, and, under Helmholtz, advanced rapidly. He became in 1880 assistant to Helmholtz, in 1883 privat-docent at Kiel, in 1885 professor of physics at the Technical High School at Karlsruhe. There he performed his memorable experiments on electromagnetic waves. In 1889 he succeeded Clausius at Bonn, and thus, at the age of thirty-two, occupied a position usually attained much later in life. In 1892 a chronic blood-poisoning began to undermine his health, and he died in the prime of life.

In 1888 Hertz found means of detecting the presence of electromagnetic waves arising from Leyden jar or coil sparks. This was an accomplishment which Maxwell had feared would never be realized. During the oscillatory discharge of a Leyden jar, or of a Holtz machine, electromagnetic waves radiate into space. Such a wave is called "electromagnetic" because it has two components — an electric wave and a magnetic wave. Hertz was able to observe each separately. If electromagnetic waves fall upon a reflector (a large sheet of tin, for instance), then they are thrown back, and the interference of the two trains of waves, moving in opposite directions, gives rise to places of least and of maximum disturbance (nodes and antinodes). Hertz's detector consisted simply of a circular wire, the ends terminating in brass knobs, which were adjusted

---

[1] H. EBERT in *Electrician* (London), Vol. 33, 1894, p. 272. See also a sketch by H. BONFORT, in *Smithsonian Report*, 1894, p. 719.

at small distances apart. A wave falling upon the wire, under suitable conditions, causes minute sparks to pass between the knobs. Hertz succeeded in reflecting, refracting, diffracting, and polarizing these waves. "The object of these experiments," says Hertz, "was to test the fundamental hypotheses of the Faraday-Maxwell theory, and the result of the experiments is to confirm the fundamental hypotheses of the theory."[1] Electricity has thus annexed the entire territory of light and "radiant heat."

After Hertz had published his results, he learned that English experimentalists had been working in similar lines. He says: "I may here be permitted to record the good work done by two English colleagues who at the same time as myself were striving toward the same end. In the same year in which I carried out the above research, Professor Oliver Lodge, in Liverpool, investigated the theory of the lightning conductor, and in connection with this carried out a series of experiments on the discharge of small condensers which led him on to the observation of oscillations and waves in wires. Inasmuch as he entirely accepted Maxwell's views, and eagerly strove to verify them, there can scarcely be any doubt that if I had not anticipated him he would also have succeeded in observing waves in air, and thus also in proving the propagation with time of electric force. Professor Fitzgerald, in Dublin, had some years before endeavoured to predict, with the aid of theory, the possibility of such waves, and to discover the conditions for producing them. My own experiments were

---

[1] Hertz's papers are collected in a book, *Electric Waves*, trans. by D. E. Jones, London, 1893. A full account of Hertz's experiments is given in Fleming, *Alternate-current Transformer*, Vol. I., in Preston, *Theory of Light*. See also O. J. Lodge, "The Work of Hertz," in *Nature*, Vol. 50, 1894, pp. 133-139, 160, 161; Poincaré, "On Maxwell and Hertz," in *Nature*, Vol. 50, 1894, pp. 8-11.

not influenced by the researches of these physicists, for 1 only knew of them subsequently."[1]

Since the publication of Hertz's experiments, several new detectors of electromagnetic radiation from Leyden jar or coil sparks have been found. The frog's leg, to which we owe the discovery of current electricity, has been tried, but has given poor results. Small Geissler tubes have been used in place of the minute air-gap in Hertz's receiver or resonator. But the most useful and delicate contrivance is the "coherer," the invention of which rests on observations made independently by *Edouard Branly*, of the Catholic Institute in Paris,[2] and *Oliver J. Lodge*, of University College, Liverpool.[3] As usually constructed, it consists of a tube of filings (iron filings are good), placed in circuit with a voltaic cell and a galvanometer. The filings offer a high resistance, but as soon as an electric wave reaches the coherer, the resistance breaks down through a process of electric welding between the filings, the battery current increases and gives a larger galvanometer deflection. Improvements on Hertz's vibrator, or wave-radiator, have been made by *Augusto Righi* of Bologna. A recent patent on wireless telegraphy, which has commanded much public attention, is simply a modification of the apparatus evolved by Hertz, Lodge, Branly, and Righi.[4]

We have seen that Ampère, observing that solenoids act like magnets, proposed a theory of magnetism according to which all magnets were simply collections of currents. He supposed that around every molecule a minute current is flowing ceaselessly. As such an assumption cannot be experimen-

[1] HERTZ, *Electric Waves*, trans. by D. E. JONES, p. 3.
[2] *Comp. Rend.*, Vol. 111, p. 785 ; Vol. 112, p. 90.
[3] *Nature*, Vol. 50, pp. 133–139.
[4] *Electrician* (London), Vol. 39, 1897, p. 686 ; consult also O. LODGE, "History of the Coherer Principle," *Electrician*, Vol. 40, 1897, pp. 87–91.

tally verified, and as it savours somewhat of the fantastic, later
theorists have been content to assume with *Siméon Denis
Poisson* (1781–1840), that each molecule becomes magnetized
when the field begins to act, or with *Wilhelm Weber*, that the
individual particles are permanently magnetic. Weber made
no attempt to explain the origin of this magnetism. He
advanced the view that in hard steel there was some kind of
friction between the molecules, which prevented the molecules
of magnetized steel from turning back into higgledy-piggledy
positions. More recently *J. A. Ewing*, of the University of
Cambridge, has somewhat modified Weber's theory and shown
that a complete explanation of the phenomena can be given
by merely considering the forces which the magnetic molecules necessarily exert on one another. He prepared groups
of little magnets, pivoted like compass needles, so that each
was free to turn, except as each was restrained by the presence
of the others. An electromagnet, whose strength could be
varied at will, was used as the external magnetizing force.
With the aid of this model Ewing was able to imitate the phenomena of the magnetization of iron — how, with a weak magnetizing force, magnetism is acquired slowly, then, as the
external force increases, the iron is gaining magnetism fast
for a while, but is approaching a third stage in which the
rate of increment of magnetism falls off and the iron approaches saturation.[1] If now the magnetizing force is gradually diminished, then the model again simulates a piece of
iron; at first the reduction in the magnetization is slow, then
instability begins and the magnetization diminishes rapidly.
When the external force is entirely removed, a little residual
magnetism remains. As the magnetizing force is applied in

[1] Consult EWING, "The Molecular Process in Magnetic Induction,"
Nature, Vol. 44, 1891, pp. 566–572. Reprinted in *Smithsonian Report*,
1892, pp. 255–268.

the opposite direction, the reversal of the polarity occurs with a rush. "We thus find," says Ewing, "a close imitation of all the features observed when iron or any of the other magnetic metals is carried through a cyclic magnetizing process. The effect of any such process is to form a *loop* in the curve which expresses the relation of the magnetism to the magnetizing force. The changes of magnetism always lag behind the changes of magnetizing force. This tendency to lag behind is called magnetic *hysteresis*." When iron is magnetized, energy is given to it; when it is demagnetized, energy is taken from it. When the magnetization is cyclically altered, there is a net loss, or rather a waste of energy (a transformation into heat), the amount of which is proportional to the area of the loop. This heating Ewing explains thus: "When the molecule becomes unstable and tumbles violently over, it oscillates and sets its neighbours oscillating." Heat is due to these oscillations. When heated, iron is found to be more permeable to magnetization, until a stage is reached, at a high temperature, when the magnetic quality vanishes almost suddenly. This increase in permeability seems to be due to expansion, so that the molecular centres lie further apart, and also to the fact that the molecules are thrown into vibration. Thereby the molecules tumble more easily from one group arrangement into another. As to the loss of magnetic property, Ewing says: "It is at least a conjecture worth consideration whether the sudden loss of magnetic quality at a higher temperature is not due to the vibrations becoming so violent as to set the molecules spinning, when, of course, their polarity would be of no avail to produce magnetization."

The study of the magnetic properties of iron and steel has received a powerful stimulus from the demands of the designers of dynamos, motors, and transformers. The accurate measurement of the relation of various magnetizing forces to the magnetizations produced in a given piece of iron or nickel was first undertaken by Henry A. Rowland.[1] Rowland's were the first experiments on this subject, in which the results were expressed in absolute measure, and the reasoning is carried out in the language of Faraday's theory of lines of magnetic force. Rowland pointed out that the flow of magnetic lines of force through a magnet admitted of accurate calculation, and that the law "is similar to the law of Ohm." The word "permeability," denoting the ratio between the magnetizing force and the resulting magnetization, was proposed by Lord Kelvin.

A concept which is finding wide application in theoretical physics is that of *potential*. Its origin we owe to the mathematicians, Lagrange and Laplace, who applied it to gravitation problems. The first to apply the potential function to a different class of problems was *George Green* (1793–1841), who introduced it into the mathematical theory of electricity and magnetism. His paper of 1828 escaped the notice even of English mathematicians until 1846, when Lord Kelvin had it reprinted. Meanwhile all of Green's general theorems had been rediscovered by Lord Kelvin, Michel Chasles, J. C. F. Sturm, and Gauss. The mathematicians defined *potential* as that function whose differential coefficient with respect to an axis of coördinates is equal to the force acting along that axis. When the ideas of energy and work came to occupy a more central position in the minds of physicists, the term "potential" was interpreted as signifying work done or energy acquired. For instance, "electric potential at any point is the work that must be expended upon a unit of electricity in bringing it to that point from an infinite distance." The notion has

[1] *Phil. Mag.* (4), Vol. 46, 1873, p. 140.

been made use of in elementary instruction, and has often been explained by its analogy to temperature or difference of level.

After the time of Halley, charts showing terrestrial declination were published by Mountain and Dodson, Bellin, and John Churchman (Philadelphia, 1790; London, 1794). The question as to the number of the earth's magnetic poles continued to be agitated. *Christopher Hansteen* (1784–1873), director of the astronomical observatory at Christiania, in 1812 attempted to answer the prize question of the Royal Danish Academy of Sciences, viz. "Is it necessary, in order to explain facts in the earth's magnetism, to suppose more than one magnetic axis in the earth?" He held the affirmative view. Making terrestrial magnetism his life study, he endeavoured to subject to mathematical analysis all observations, with the view of testing rigorously Halley's speculations as to the existence of four magnetic poles in the earth. From secular changes in the lines of equal declination he inferred that there were two northern magnetic poles, moving obliquely toward the west, and two southern poles, moving toward the west; that the shortest time in which all the poles return to the same relative position agreed closely with the period of revolution in the precession of the equinoxes. "By the liberality of the Norwegian government he was enabled to go to Siberia, in company with Due and Erman, to search for the ideal point of the Asiatic pole of magnetism. They started from Berlin, April 25, 1828. . . . Ten magnetic observatories were established in the Russian empire by the recommendation of Humboldt, and great results were reached by Gauss, Sabine, Lamont, and others from the materials collected by Hansteen and Erman. Hansteen ascertained beyond dispute the existence of a magnetic pole in Siberia supplementary to that in British America, and also the biaxal character of the earth's magnetism."[1] The fact that the earth's magnetism in the northern hemisphere reaches a maximum in two places, viz. in the north of Canada and in the north of Siberia, proves conclusively that the earth is not a single magnet. But neither Hansteen's theory nor that of *Sir Edward Sabine* (1788–1883) seem to be in accordance with observations of more recent years. The cause of the earth's magnetism and its secular changes continues to be a mystery.[2]

An important step toward the accurate study of terrestrial magnetism was taken in Germany by *Carl Friedrich Gauss* (1777–1855), who, in conjunction with *Alexander von Humboldt* (1769–1859), organized the German Magnetic Union. Its object was to take continuous observations of the magnetic elements (dip, declination, intensity) at fixed points. Observations were begun in 1834 and were mostly concluded about 1842. Gauss and *Wilhelm Weber* (1804–1891) of Göttingen designed the instruments used in these measurements. Gauss's theory does not aim to investigate the cause of terrestrial magnetism and its changes, but is simply a mathematical presentation of the distribution of magnetism over the earth's surface.

Speculations have frequently been indulged in as to the magnetic and electric relationship between the sun and the earth. As yet, nothing very conclusive has been adduced.[3]

In a paper on terrestrial magnetism, read in 1832, Gauss proposed a system of *absolute units*. Since all forces may be measured by the motions they produce, only three fundamental units are necessary, viz. a unit of length, of time, of mass.

---

[1] *Proc. Roy. Soc. of London*, Vol. 24, 1875–1876, p. v.

[2] Consult further A. W. Rücker, "Recent Researches in Terrestrial Magnetism," *Nature*, Vol. 57, 1897, pp. 160 *et seq.*

[3] Consult the "Abstract of a Report on Solar and Terrestrial Magnetism" by Frank H. Bigelow, *Bulletin No. 21, U. S. Department of Agriculture*, 1898.

The advantage to be gained is this: If all practical units are derived from these three, then all results of measurement are comparable with each other. Gauss took as the unit of force that which gives to unit mass in unit time a unit velocity. As the unit of magnetic intensity he chose that quantity which, acting upon an equal quantity at unit distance, exerts unit force. Gauss's use of absolute units in the measurement of terrestrial magnetism led his colleague at Göttingen, Wilhelm Weber, to introduce absolute units in electricity. His first papers on the subject were published in 1846, 1852, 1856. As practical units of resistance, *Moritz Hermann Jacobi* at St. Petersburg recommended a copper wire of given dimensions, the resistance of which Weber determined in absolute units. As a copper resistance was found to vary in time, *Werner Siemens* (1816–1892) of Berlin, in 1860, proposed as a practical unit the resistance of a mercury prism one metre long and one square millimetre in cross-section, at 0° C. ("Siemens's unit"). Weber determined this in absolute units. In 1861 the British Association and Royal Society of London appointed a committee, with Lord Kelvin at its head, to recommend a unit ("B. A. unit"). Weber's absolute unit of resistance was a *velocity*. The British committee adopted this unit in principle. In 1881, at an international congress of electricians in Paris, Weber's absolute system was adhered to; only, the *centimetre, second,* and *gramme* were selected as primitive units, in place of the *millimetre, second,* and *milligramme,* used by Weber and Gauss. As the *ohm* the congress selected 10^9 times the velocity of one centimetre per second. At this time definitions were given also to the *volt, ampère, coulomb,* and *farad,* along the lines previously marked out by Weber.[1] The subject of

[1] ROSENBERGER, III., pp. 302, 514–519; A. KIEL, "Geschichte der Absoluten Masseinheiten," *Jahresb. d. Königl. Gymnasiums zu Bonn,* 1890.

"dimensional equations" was first systematically presented by Clerk Maxwell.

The securing of a convenient, invariable resistance, equal to 10^9 absolute units, has been a difficult task. The B. A. unit was a little too small. The "legal ohm" was provisionally adopted in 1883 by a committee appointed by the congress of 1881. It was the resistance at $0° C.$ of a column of mercury 1 square millimetre in cross-section and 106 centimetres long. Competent investigators like Rayleigh and Mascart contended that this column was a little too short, but some smaller values obtained by certain experimenters led to the adoption of the mean value 106 centimetres. The "legal ohm" satisfied no one and failed to become legal in any country.[1]

Henry A. Rowland, after pointing out errors in some of the determinations previously made, found the length of the mercury column in question to be 106.32 centimetres. At the meeting of the British Association in 1892, German, French, and American physicists were invited to take part in the consideration of electrical units. The "B. A. unit" and the "legal ohm" were abandoned. The ohm was defined as the resistance offered by a column of mercury at the temperature of melting ice 14.4521 grammes in mass, of constant cross-sectional area, and of the length of 106.3 centimetres. By specifying the mass of the mercury, instead of the cross-section of the column, any error arising from the uncertainty as to the exact volume of a gramme of mercury at $0° C.$ was avoided. A system of *international* units was adopted at the congress held in Chicago in 1893 during the World's Fair. The ohm, as defined in 1892, became the *international ohm.* The other units were defined, including the *joule* as a unit of work, the *watt* as a unit of power, and the *henry* as a unit of self-induction.

[1] H. S. CARHART in *Science*, Vol. 21, 1893, pp. 86, 87.

The electric discharge through partial vacua was carefully investigated after the middle of the century. In 1853 *A. Masson*, of Paris, sent the discharge from a powerful Ruhmkorff coil through the Torricellian vacuum. *J. P. Gassiot* thereupon constructed for experimental study tubes containing a trace of different gases. A few years later, *Heinrich Geissler* (1814–1879), a glass-blower in Tübingen, later proprietor of a manufactory of physical and chemical apparatus in Bonn, began to prepare such tubes with so great skill that they have since been named "Geissler tubes." This designation was proposed by Plücker, who said, "I give them this name and justly so, although the first tubes were not prepared by himself."[1] The discharges through these tubes were of great beauty, but hardly afforded a deeper insight into electricity or the theory of gases. With the improvements in mercury air-pumps and the attainment of higher degrees of rarefaction, the phenomena assumed a wider range. *W. Hittorf*, of Münster, in 1869 noticed that the dark space separating the negative pole from the negative glow increased in width, as exhaustion was carried further and finally filled the entire tube; that the discharge from the kathode caused considerable fluorescence against the glass. More striking and impressive were the experiments which *William Crookes* began to publish in 1878. Crookes was born in London in 1832, and in 1859 founded the *Chemical News*. His experiments on high vacua began in 1873, when, in course of an investigation of the atomic weight of thallium, he attempted to perform the delicate weighings in a vacuum, in order to avoid the effect of the buoyancy of the air. When heated bodies were weighed in his exhausted metallic box, the balance showed irregularities in action which he could not explain by currents of air result-

---

[1] ROSENBERGER, III., p. 521.

ing from differences in temperature. Crookes undertook a
thorough investigation of the phenomenon, and was led in
1875 to the invention of the famous radiometer. At first
Crookes and others inclined to the opinion that the rotation
of the vanes was due to the direct impact of ether-waves.
But Crookes succeeded in carrying the exhaustion of the bulb
to such a degree that the vanes no longer rotated. Hence
Tait, Dewar, and himself invoked the aid of the modern
kinetic theory of gases, and attributed the effect to the molecules of the residual gas. The molecules impinging upon the
heated black surface of the vane rebounded with increased
momentum, and by their reaction propelled the vanes. A
mathematical investigation of this action, based on the kinetic
theory of gases, was given by Clerk Maxwell. In 1878
Crookes touched the line of Hittorf's researches, which were
apparently unknown to him. The thickness of the dark space
observed by him and Hittorf he took to be the "measure of
the mean free path between successive collisions of the molecules of the residual gas." In his highly exhausted tubes
"the molecules of the gaseous residue are able to dart across
the tube with comparatively few collisions, and radiating from
the pole with enormous velocity, they assume properties so
novel and so characteristic as entirely to justify the application of the term borrowed from Faraday, that of "Radiant
Matter." By beautiful experiments he proved that "Radiant
Matter" proceeds in straight lines, casts shadows when intercepted by solid matter, is capable of turning a small wheel,
is deflected by a magnet (shown previously by Hittorf and
others). The state and behaviour of the residual gas in
Crookes's highly exhausted tubes was such that he thought
himself justified in calling this an "ultragaseous state," or a
"fourth state" of matter, differing as much from the gaseous
as does the gaseous from the liquid state. The theory of the

"fourth state" has been much criticised, particularly by the Germans, and is not generally accepted.

While in the days of Gassiot the discharge from the anode was the subject of greatest attention, that from the kathode still monopolizes the interest. Hertz found that the "kathode rays" will pass through metal foil. His assistant, *P. Lenard*, prepared a vacuum tube with a small window of aluminium foil, through which he passed the "kathode rays" out into the air. They still retained their power of exciting phosphorescence, but could not be made to travel through air but a short distance. Lenard held that his rays were not flying particles but "phenomena in the ether."[1] While the discussion over the nature of these mysterious rays was in progress, *Wilhelm Konrad Röntgen*,[2] of Würzburg, in 1895 discovered a new kind of rays which at once caused a sensation throughout the civilized world. He found that a Crookes tube in action emits a radiation which causes a paper screen washed with barium-platino-cyanide to light up brilliantly or to fluoresce. Paper, wood, aluminium, and a great many other substances which are opaque to ordinary rays were found transparent to the new radiation. The fact that animal tissues are transparent and bones somewhat opaque, makes it possible for the skeletons of human beings to be photographed, the resulting negatives being of the nature of shadow pictures. The nature of the new rays being unknown, Röntgen called them "X-rays," but they are usually and more appropriately called "Röntgen rays." They show no perceptible refraction, nor regular reflection and polarization. J. J. Thomson made an experiment which seemed to prove that

[1] See Lenard's papers in *Electrician* (London), Vol. 32, March 23, 1893; Vol. 33, 1894, p. 108.

[2] Röntgen, "On a New Form of Radiation," *Electrician* (London), Vol. 36, 1896, pp. 415–417, 850, 851.

Röntgen rays and kathode rays were different, inasmuch as kathode rays inside a vacuum had no power of exciting the photographic plate.[1] He also found that these rays make insulators conduct and consequently are able to discharge electrified bodies. Improved tubes — the so-called "focus-tubes" — were designed for radiography. An important discovery which appears to be a link towards establishing continuity between the old and the new forms of radiation was made in 1896, in Paris, by *Henry Becquerel*, of the Conservatoire des Arts et Métiers. He is the son and successor of Edmond Becquerel and the grandson of A. C. Becquerel. He observed that certain uranium compounds, after exposure to sunlight, emitted radiations which, like Röntgen rays, could pass through plates of aluminium or of cardboard, but which could also be refracted and polarized. Allied to both of these are the rays emitted by thorium and its compounds, which were discovered almost simultaneously by Sklodowska Curie and G. C. Schmidt. Thorium rays can be refracted, but cannot be polarized by transmission through tourmaline.

We have two methods for producing very high differences of electric potential: one is by induction coils like Ruhmkorff's, the other is by electrical influence machines. These machines have been evolved from the electrophorus of Volta, through the improvements due to *Georg Christoph Lichtenberg* (1742–1799) of Göttingen, *Abraham Bennet, Tiberius Cavallo* (1749–1809) of London, *William Nicholson* (1753–1815, editor of *Nicholson's Journal of Natural Philosophy, Chemistry, and the Arts*, London), *Belli, Varley, Kelvin, Töpler, Holtz, Wimshurst*, and others.

The first marked advance in the design of these machines

---

[1] It becomes more and more clear that kathode rays consist of electrified atoms or ions in rapid progressive motion, and that Röntgen rays are waves or pulses in the ether.

was made in 1865. In that year machines were brought out by *A. Töpler* of Dorpat, later professor at the Polytechnicum in Dresden, and by *W. Holtz*. The latter soon improved his machine, while Töpler, in 1879, united the principles of the two machines into the "Töpler-Holtz machine." A similar one was constructed in 1880 by the mechanic, *J. R. Voss*, of Berlin. The machine with radial strips of tin-foil and contact brushes was described by Holtz in 1881,[1] and again in 1882 and 1883 by *James Wimshurst*,[2] who made his improvements independently of Holtz.[3]

Thermo-electricity was discovered in 1821 by *Thomas Johann Seebeck* (1770–1831). He was born in Reval (Esthonia, Russia). At the age of seventeen he left his native country, never again to return. He studied medicine in Berlin. Being well off, he was free to devote himself to science. From 1802 to 1810 he lived in Jena, and had a personal acquaintance with Schelling, Hegel, Ritter, Göthe, and other prominent men. Unfortunately he allowed himself to be completely dominated by the erroneous anti-Newtonian views on colour, so elaborately and confidently set forth by Göthe in his *Farbenlehre*. Being elected a member of the Berlin Academy of Sciences in 1818, Seebeck took up his residence in that city. Oersted's experiment induced him to enter upon a long series of electric investigation. With the view of verifying certain speculations regarding the magnetic character of the electric current, he established an electric circuit consisting partly of copper and partly of bismuth. One metallic junction he held in his hand.

[1] UPPENBORN's *Zeitschr. f. angewandte Elektr.*, 1881, p. 199.

[2] *Engineering*, Vol. 35, 1883, p. 4.

[3] Consult articles on the theory of recent types of machines, written by Holtz, Wimshurst, and V. Schaffers, in *Electrician* (London), Vol. 35, 1895, pp. 382–388. See also JOHN GRAY, *Electrical Influence Machines*, Whittaker & Co.

He satisfied himself that the resulting deflection of the galvanometer needle arose from the difference in temperature of the metallic junctions, brought about by the heat from his hand. He found similar effects by cooling one of the junctions; the effects varied for different metals, and were greater for greater differences of temperature. He used the expression "thermomagnetic" currents, and later objected to the term "thermo-electric."

Thirteen years after Seebeck's discovery, *Jean Charles Athanase Peltier*[1] (1785–1845), a Parisian watchmaker, who devoted the latter part of his life to scientific pursuits, demonstrated that, conversely, an electric current may produce not only heat but also cold. In copper-antimony junctions he found a heating of 10° where the current went from antimony to copper, and a cooling of 5° where it went in the opposite direction. Greater differences were found for bismuth-antimony joints. *Heinrich Friedrich Emil Lenz* (1804–1865), well known for his law of electromagnetic induction, succeeded in freezing water by the Peltier effect.

After the principles of electromagnetism were established by Faraday and Henry, constant efforts were made in the way of practical application. The early dynamo machines laboured under two defects: the magnetic intensity was not adequate or properly applied, and the electric current generated was not sufficiently steady. The concentration of the magnetic lines of force in a powerful field between the magnetic poles was effected in 1856 by *Werner Siemens* in Berlin through his improved shuttle armature, with its coils of wire wound upon a grooved iron core. Ten years later *Henry Wilde* of Manchester substituted electromagnets for the permanent steel magnets previously employed. He took three Siemens

---

[1] See "Memoir of Peltier" in *Smithsonian Report*, 1867, pp. 158–202.

machines, two of which had electromagnets. The machine with steel magnets generated a current which was used to excite the field magnets of the second machine; the armature current from the second excited the field magnets of the third. The current from the last was used in experimentation. An electric lamp was made to give an intense light, which caused great astonishment among the populace. When passed through a convex lens, the light ignited paper. The electric arc melted not only iron wire, but a rod of platinum 6 millimetres thick and 61 centimetres long. The arc was still a novelty to people, notwithstanding the fact that sixty-six years earlier, in 1800, it was noticed by Sir Humphry Davy, and at a still earlier date by J. W. Ritter. Davy used in his experiments a battery of 2000 cells and rods of charcoal.

In 1866 Werner Siemens demonstrated by the operation of a new machine of his own construction that electromagnets can be used without separate exciters, and that the field magnets may be excited by the current from the armature of the machine itself. This idea appears to have been in the air; for, about the same time and independently, it was advanced by *Murray, Cromwell Fleetwood Varley* (1828–1883), *C. Wheatstone*, and others. In Siemens's armature the coils are wound around a cylindrical core. Another typical armature is that in which the coils are wound upon a ring. This was invented in 1861 by *Antonio Pacinotti* of Florence, and again independently, in 1868, by *Zénobe Théophile Gramme* of Paris. Through Gramme this armature came to be extensively used. Since their day the construction of dynamos for various purposes has been carried to great perfection. Machines of high merit were produced by the Siemens brothers, Charles F. Brush, Thomas A. Edison, and others.[1]

[1] For details see S. P. THOMPSON, "Historical Notes," in *Dynamo Electric Machinery*.

The design of practical dynamos made electric lighting possible. Arc-lighting was never a success until means were thought out for rendering lights placed in series automatic in action and somewhat independent of each other. Such a regulator was invented in 1847 by W. E. Staite; later Werner Siemens and others worked out designs. Among the patterns are clockwork lamps, solenoid lamps, and clutch lamps.

For house illumination arc-lights were not well adapted. A less brilliant light was needed. In the years 1877–1880 inventors arose to the emergency by the production of the incandescent lamp. The names associated with this development of applied electricity are *Joseph Wilson Swan* and *Lane-Fox* in England, *Hiram S. Maxim, William Edward Sawyer, Albon P. Man,* and *Thomas A. Edison.*

In early experiments platinum wire was tried as the substance to be heated to whiteness by the passage of the electric current. In 1878 Edison was thus engaged, but neither platinum nor iridium could be kept from the risk of fusing. In the same year Sawyer and Man of New York tried to prepare carbon fibres from vegetable tissue. They endeavoured to prevent combustion of the fibre by filling the globe with nitrogen, but the process was not successful. Lane-Fox, in 1879, being convinced that platinum and iridium were useless as bridges in lamps, used carbonized vegetable fibres. Swan, in February, 1879, made a public exhibition of a lamp with a carbon filament in a vacuous bulb. Swan's success led Edison to abandon platinum and iridium, and, in October, 1879, he had constructed a vacuum lamp with a filament of lampblack and tar carbonized. In January, 1880, Swan prepared filaments from cotton twine, prepared by immersion in sulphuric acid and then carbonized. Edison sent out explorers into South America and into the far East in quest of suitable fibres for lamps, and in 1880 employed a flat strip of carbonized bamboo for a filament. Most of the modern lamps have filaments prepared from parchmentized cellulose, afterwards carbonized. The race between the several experimenters was indeed close and exciting; numerous lawsuits over the validity of patents followed the commercial introduction of the new lamps.[1]

The discovery that the action of the dynamo is simply the converse of the electric motor, so that the same machine can be used either as dynamo or motor, was made by M. H. Jacobi in 1850. The principle of transmitting power from one dynamo as a generator to another used as a motor was first pointed out and demonstrated at the Vienna Exhibition in 1873 by Fontaine and Gramme. Since then great progress has been made in the details of design of motors.

After much experimentation in the United States and elsewhere on the design of electric railways, the first electric railway was put in operation by the firm of Siemens and Halske in 1879 at the Industrial Exhibition in Berlin.[2]

Up to 1883 the progress made in electric roads was mainly due to Werner Siemens in Germany, but at this time substantial advances were made in the United States by the labours of *C. J. Van Depoele, Leo Daft, F. J. Sprague,* and others.

The first polyphase motor was exhibited to the Royal Society of London in 1879 by *Walter Baily.* It was a mere toy and received no further attention. A two-phase motor was constructed and used by *Galileo Ferraris* in his laboratory at

---

[1] For a fuller account see F. L. POPE, *Evolution of the Electric Incandescent Lamp*, 1889.

[2] In the United States, at this time, Edison, Stephen D. Fields, and Wellington Adams were experimenting on electric roads, and applying for patents. See W. ADAMS, "The Evolution of the Electric Railway," p. 9, reprinted from the *Jour. of the Ass. of Eng. Societies*, of September and October, 1884.

Turin in 1885. He used two independent alternate currents of the same period, but differing in phase and thus producing a rotary magnetic field. Thinking that no motor requiring more than two wires could interest any one but the theoretical physicist, he did not publish his results till 1888.[1] Only a few months later, commercial motors based on the same principles were brought out by *Nikola Tesla*, then at Pittsburg, who had made the discovery independently. A remarkable rotary-field motor, devised by *Dolivo Dobrowolsky*, was used at the Frankfort Exposition of 1891. Many forms of such motors have been constructed since and are meeting with extended application in both Europe and America.

After the principles of electromagnetism were made known through the epoch-making researches of Faraday and Joseph Henry, telegraphy seemed a comparatively easy matter. So many investigators busied themselves with this idea, and performed experiments which were more or less successful, that it is difficult to assign the invention of the telegraph to any one individual. The transmission of signals by electromagnetic apparatus was suggested by Ampère in 1821. Gauss and Weber at Göttingen in 1833 had a crude telegraphic line between the Observatory and the Physical Cabinet, a distance of 9000 feet. Joseph Henry at Albany, in 1831, by the attraction of an electromagnet produced audible signals at a distance. In 1837 Morse of New York devised a telegraph in which the attraction of an armature produced dots and dashes upon a moving strip of paper. *Karl August Steinheil* of Munich discovered that the earth may take the place of a wire for the return circuit. The first commercial line in the United States was erected between Washington and Baltimore

[1] See translation of paper in *Electrician* (London), Vol. 36, 1895, p. 281 ; see also *Nature*, Vol. 44, 1891, p. 617.

through the efforts of Morse. *Samuel Finley Breese Morse* (1791–1872) was educated as an artist, and is the founder of the National Academy of Design in New York. He studied art in the schools of the Continent. While on his ocean voyage homeward, in 1832, the first thought of the telegraph suggested itself to him. He experimented for several years with some success. Finally, his assistant, Dr. Gale, applied the principles discovered by Henry to render Morse's machine effective at a distance.[1] After many discouragements, Morse established, by aid of the American government, the telegraphic line between Washington and Baltimore. On May 24, 1844, the message was sent from the rooms of the United States Supreme Court, "What hath God wrought!" Morse's apparatus is now the most extensively used of all.

In England the telegraph was developed by Wheatstone, William Fothergill Cooke, and Hughes. Methods of duplex signalling (two messages sent simultaneously in opposite directions) were devised by *Wilhelm Gint* (1803–1883; professor at Gratz) in 1853 and *J. B. Stearns* of Boston in 1870; of diplex signalling (two messages sent at once in same direction through a wire), by *Stark* of Vienna and *Bosscha* of Leyden in 1855; of quadruplex telegraphy, by *O. Heaviside* of London in 1873 and *T. A. Edison* of Newark in 1874.

Experimentation on submarine telegraphy began as early as 1837.[2] After some successes with shorter lines, the first Atlantic cable expedition was started in 1857. One of the

---

[1] See "Statement of Professor Henry in Relation to the History of the Electromagnetic Telegraph," *Smithsonian Report*, 1857, pp. 99–106; "Henry and the Telegraph," by WILLIAM B. TAYLOR, in *Smithsonian Report*, 1878, pp. 262–360, containing much detailed information on the history of the telegraph.

[2] For details consult W. E. AYRTON, "Sixty Years of Submarine Telegraphy," *Electrician* (London), Vol. 38, 1897, pp. 545–549.

questions debated some years before was the probable speed of signalling through a cable 2000 miles long. Great vagueness then existed as to the way in which electricity travelled. *Wheatstone* had proved in 1834 with aid of revolving mirrors that electricity travelled with a velocity of 288,000 miles per second; but *Latimer Clark*, from experiments made in the presence of Airy and Faraday on 800 miles of underground wire, came to the conclusion that it took half a second before the current appeared at the other end. Other experimenters obtained intermediate results.

The explanation of these discrepancies was given by a young man, William Thomson, now *Lord Kelvin*, in a correspondence with Sir Gabriel Stokes. This correspondence formed the basis of Thomson's very important paper, published in the Proceedings of the Royal Society in 1855. One of the first conclusions theoretically deduced by him was that electricity has no velocity at all. Just as the time for the flow of heat through a rod depends only on the rod, so the time before the current begins to appear at the other end depends only on the cable — that is, upon the product of its resistance and its electrostatic capacity. The opinion of well-known engineers of the time was opposed to this. Thomson also tried to make it plain that it would take so long for the current to reach its steady state at the end of an Atlantic cable that, if they ever wanted the cable "to pay," they must not wait for the current, but must send messages with currents at the very beginning of their growth. Another important conclusion reached by him was that the retardation of signals was proportional to the square of the length. Thomson estimated the probable speed of the proposed cable at three words per minute, Werner Siemens at one word per minute, Sir Charles Bright at ten or twelve words per minute. The results gave for ordinary recording instruments 1.8 words per minute. On August

5, 1858, England and America had the first cable communica-tion. The President of the United States sent a message con-taining the prayer, "May the electric telegraph, under the blessing of Heaven, prove to be a bond of perpetual peace and friendship between the kindred nations." One hundred and fifty words were transmitted in thirty hours. As time went on the signals grew weaker, and in a month the Atlantic cable ceased to speak. William Thomson calculated what would be the best proportions for the new Atlantic cable, which was suc-cessfully laid in 1866. He designed apparatus to be used in signalling. The astatic reflecting galvanometer was a much improved form of the mirror galvanometer originally devised by Gauss and Weber, and employed on their telegraph line in Göttingen. Thomson's galvanometer raised the speed of cable telegraphy from two or three to twenty-two or twenty-five words per minute. On account of the great fatigue to the eye in following the motion of a spot of light in the mirror gal-vanometer, it was discarded in signalling through cables, and Thomson's "siphon recorder" adopted. The researches of Thomson, as continued by Cromwell F. Varley, showed that the speed can be increased still further by sending a positive current, and then a negative one for a short time.

The earliest record of a theoretical telephone was contained in Du Moncel's *Exposé des Applications*, Paris, 1854, when *Charles Bourseul*, a French telegraphist, conceived a plan of transmitting speech by electricity. The author says, "Sup-pose a man speaks near a movable disk sufficiently flexible to lose none of the vibrations of the voice; that this disk alter-nately makes and breaks the currents from a battery, you may have at a distance another disk which will simultaneously exe-cute the same vibrations." Bourseul did not work out his ideas to a practical end.

The next step in the history of the telephone is told by

D. E. Hughes, as follows: "I was invited by his Majesty the Emperor Alexander II. (of Russia) to give a lecture before his Majesty, the Empress, and court at Czarskoi Zelo, which I did; but as I wished to present to his Majesty, not only my own telegraph instrument, but all the latest novelties, Professor Philipp Reis, of Friedericksdorf, Frankfort-upon-Main, sent to Russia his new telephone, with which I was enabled to transmit and receive perfectly all musical sounds, and also a few spoken words — though these were rather uncertain, for at moments a word could be clearly heard, and then, for some unexplained cause, no words were possible. This wonderful instrument was based upon the true theory of telephony. . . . Its unfortunate inventor died in 1874, almost unknown, poor and neglected; but the German government has since tried to make reparation by acknowledging his claims as the first inventor, and erecting a monument to his memory in the cemetery of Friedericksdorf."[1] Reis's experiments were made in 1861.

For fifteen years electric telephony was neglected, then, in 1876, *Alexander Graham Bell* (born 1847) invented his wonderful telephone, which is still used at the present time as the "receiver." It was first exhibited publicly, but in an imperfect form, at the *Centennial Exhibition*, at Philadelphia, in 1876. Bell was born at Edinburgh, in Scotland, and took up his residence in the United States in 1872. In a lecture delivered at Cambridge in 1878, Clerk Maxwell said that when the news of Bell's invention reached England, he expected the new instrument to surpass the siphon recorder in delicacy and intricacy as much as that excels a common bell-pull. But when the instrument appeared, "consisting, as it does, of parts, every

---

[1] *Electrician* (London), Vol. 34, p. 637. See also S. P. THOMPSON, *Philipp Reis*, London, 1883.

one of which is familiar to us, and capable of being put together by an amateur, the disappointment arising from its humble appearance was only partially relieved on finding that it was really able to talk."[1]

Strange to say, on the very same day (February 14, 1876) on which Bell patented his telephone, *Elisha Gray* applied for a patent for an instrument of a similar kind. Later one company took up the patents of both inventors.

While Bell's instrument seemed perfect as a "receiver," it was defective as a "transmitter." The first step toward remedying this defect was the invention of the carbon transmitter by *Edison* and of the microphone by *David Edwin Hughes*. Edison's invention was brought out in 1877 and consisted of a vibrating plate abutting against a carbon button. The transmitters used in more recent telephony, such as Blake's, Berliner's, Hunnings's, and others are all constructed on the principle of loose contact involved in Edison's instrument.[2]

Hughes's microphone is the same in principle as Edison's transmitter, but its arrangement and action are quite different. In 1865 Hughes had experimented on Reis's telephone. On hearing of Bell's success, he resumed his investigation and produced the microphone. It was first exhibited in 1878 at his rooms to a company including Huxley, Lockyer, and W. H. Preece. The new apparatus was of the most primitive character, "consisting of a child's half-penny wooden money-box for a resonator, on which was fixed by means of sealing-wax a short glass tube, filled with a mixture of tin and zinc, the ends being stopped by two pieces of charcoal to which

[1] *Nature*, Vol. 18, p. 160.
[2] Consult W. H. PREECE, *The Telephone*. The reader will find much information in THOMAS GRAY's article, "The Inventors of Telegraph and Telephone," *Smithsonian Report*, 1892, pp. 639–657.

were attached wires, having a battery of three small Daniell cells — consisting of three small jam-pots — in circuit. The wires were led away to a Bell telephone placed in an adjoining apartment. The money-box, which had one end knocked out, served as a mouthpiece or transmitter, while a Bell telephone was used as a receiver. Sounds scarcely audible . . . to the unassisted ear were . . . delivered with startling loudness through the Bell telephone."[1]

SOUND

In the eighteenth century sound was studied mainly by the musicians and mathematicians; in the nineteenth century it became a regular branch of research for the physicist. The "father of acoustics" is *Ernst Florens Friedrich Chladni* (1756–1827), born in Wittenberg. His father educated him for law, but after the death of his father he devoted himself to science. His reading of several papers on sound brought him to the conviction "that in that more remains to be discovered, because the mathematico-physical assumptions are far more meagre than is usual in science." Euler's and Bernoulli's mathematical papers led him to investigate sounding plates. The necessity of earning a livelihood induced him to travel in order to give art performances and scientific lectures. He invented a new musical instrument, the euphonium, on which he performed during his travels in Germany, France, and Italy. He also made a collection of meteorites. "Inventive power, ready wit, and good nature distinguished him above all."[2]

Chladni experimentally studied the vibrations of strings,

[1] *Nature*, Vol. 55, 1897, p. 497. For the origin and development of the telephone switchboard, "the brain of the telephone system," see *Electrician* (London), Vol. 34, 1895, p. 395.

[2] ROSENBERGER, III., p. 125.

rods, and plates. "Chladni's figures" are celebrated; they are formed by the sand collecting at the nodal lines of vibrating plates. When Chladni, in 1809, exhibited his figures before the French Institute, they created great interest among the members, including Laplace. Napoleon had the experiments repeated for him at the Tuileries, and gave Chladni 6000 francs for the purpose of enabling the latter to translate his *Akustik* (first published in 1802) into French. Chladni discovered the longitudinal vibrations in a string or rod, as well as their application to the determination of sound velocity in solids; he first investigated torsional vibrations in rods, and determined the absolute rate of vibration of bodies. He determined the velocity of sound in other gases than air by filling organ pipes with the gas and then determining the resulting pitch. An elegant method of comparing velocities in gases or in solids was invented in 1866 by *A. Kundt.* "Kundt's method" has been generally introduced into elementary instruction.

A far-reaching discovery, as important in light as in sound, was the *principle of interference of waves,* which we owe to *Thomas Young.* He explained it in a paper of 1800, and later again in his *Lectures on Natural Philosophy.* Wave motion was made the subject of careful study on the part of *Wilhelm Weber* and his brother, *Ernst Heinrich Weber* (1795–1878), who published, in 1825, their work, entitled *Wellenlehre.*

It was long believed that in liquids, sound waves, consisting of condensations and rarefactions, could not travel at all, for the reason that liquids appeared to be incompressible. The compressibility of water had been the subject of experimentation on the part of the *Accademia del Cimento* in Florence, sometime between 1657 and 1667. Hollow spheres of silver were filled with water, closed tight, and then disfigured by hammering. The water was forced through the pores of the metal. Apparently water is incompressible. Boyle believed that water was elastic, but could not establish his view by conclusive experiment. In 1762 John Canton demonstrated before the Royal Society that water is compressible, but his test received little attention. More accurate figures on the degree of compressibility were obtained by Oersted about 1822. Like Canton, he experimented by subjecting the vessel containing the water to the same pressure outside as inside, thereby preventing a change in its capacity. His results indicated a diminution of the .000047th part of the original volume when the pressure was increased by one atmosphere. A somewhat larger value — .0000513 — was obtained in 1827 by *Jean Daniel Colladon*, professor of mechanics in Geneva, and *Jacob Carl Franz Sturm* (1803–1855) of Geneva, who, after 1830, was professor of mathematics in Paris. These co-workers determined also the velocity of sound in water. The experiments were made on Lake Geneva, between Thonon and Rolle, a distance of 13,487 metres. At one station a bell was placed under water and struck with a hammer; at the other station a specially prepared ear trumpet was dipped into the water. The velocity was found to be 1435 metres per second. *Felix Savart* (1791–1841), a teacher in Paris, and later conservator of the physical cabinet at the Collège de France, showed in 1826 that sound waves are propagated in water in the same way as in solids. *Cagniard-Latour* succeeded in imparting sound vibrations to water by means of the siren. This ability of the instrument to cause audible sounds in water led Cagniard-Latour to name it a "siren." He greatly improved the siren and its mechanism for counting vibrations. This apparatus, together with other devices, was used by Savart in determining the limits of audibility. He could hear tones of bodies vibrating at the rate of 24,000 or 48,000 per second. The lower limit he placed at 14 or 16 per second.

A new epoch in the history of the science of sound was created by Helmholtz, who in 1863 published the first edition of his *Lehre von den Tonempfindungen*. The third German edition of 1870 was translated into English by *Alexander J. Ellis* in 1875. New German and English editions have appeared since. Helmholtz attributes musical tones to periodic motions in the air; he distinguishes musical tones by their Intensity, Pitch, and Quality. The Quality of a sound he found to be determined by the "upper partial tones," which are called by Tyndall "overtones." Nearly all musical tones possess these overtones, the number and relative intensity of which determine the Quality. G. S. Ohm was the first to point out that there is only one form of vibration which will give rise to no harmonic upper partial tones, but consists only of the prime tone, viz. the form of vibration peculiar to the pendulum and tuning-fork. Helmholtz made experiments showing the direct composition of vowel qualities, which were "essentially distinguished from the tones of most other musical instruments by the fact that the loudness of their partial tones does not depend solely upon their numerical order, but preponderantly upon the absolute pitch of those partials." "If only the unevenly numbered partials are present (as in narrow stopped organ pipes, pianoforte strings struck in their middle points, and clarinets), the quality of tones is *hollow*, and, when a large number of such upper partials are present, *nasal*. When the prime tone predominates, the quality of tone is *rich;* but when the prime tone is not sufficiently superior in strength to the upper partials, the quality of tone is poor."[1] Helmholtz devised spherical resonators by which he analyzed the human voice and musical tones in general. He also, by synthesis of sounds from tuning-

[1] HELMHOLTZ, *Sensations of Tone*, trans. by ELLIS, London, 1885, pp. 118, 119.

forks, operated by electromagnetic apparatus, succeeded in producing artificial vowels, which were close imitations of the vowels of the human voice. In the same way he simulated the quality of tone of organ pipes, although the "whizzing noise, formed by breaking the stream of air at the lip, is wanting in these imitations."

The study of "beats" led Helmholtz to a new theory of harmony. Pythagoras had made the discovery that the simpler the ratio of the two lengths into which a string is divided, the more perfect is the harmony of the sounds produced by these two parts of the string. Later it was shown by investigators that the strings act in this way because of the relation of their lengths to the rate of their vibrations. Why simplicity should give pleasure remained an enigma, even after Euler had declared that the human soul takes a constitutional delight in simple calculations. Helmholtz, by means of a costly polyphonic siren, which he had constructed, experimented on beats. In the case of two simple tones, the number of beats in unit time is equal to the difference in the rates of vibration. If the number of beats is 33 per second, then the dissonance is intolerable; if the number is smaller or larger, the effect is less disagreeable; if it exceeds 132, then the unpleasantness totally disappears. If each sound has its overtones, then the question of harmony or dissonance is more complicated. Beats arising between fundamentals and overtones, or between the overtones themselves, must be brought into consideration. It is found in a general way that as the difference in pitch of two musical tones is so varied that the disturbing action of beats becomes more and more pronounced, the number expressing the ratio of the vibrations of the two fundamentals becomes larger and larger. Thus, Helmholtz's theory explains how it is that the simpler ratios in music are the more agreeable.

Helmholtz's theory of harmony met with much criticism or, the part of musicians and philosophers, but the attacks were unsuccessful, and the opposition to it has disappeared.

When two simple musical tones are sounded together, there occur two sound phenomena: (1) the *beats* discussed above, (2) *combinational sounds*. The latter are of two kinds: the *summational tones*, discovered by Helmholtz, and the *differential tones*, discovered in 1744 by the German organist, *Andreas Sorge*, and again by the celebrated Italian violinist, *Giuseppe Tartini*. Suppose the two simple tones have, respectively, m and n vibrations per second, then the rate of vibration of the differential tone is $m - n$, and of the summational tone $m + n$. To produce the differential tones it is necessary that the primary tones be of considerable intensity. Helmholtz used for this purpose the siren. The summation tones are much more difficult to observe. They were predicted and discovered by Helmholtz. *Rudolf König*, the celebrated acoustic instrument maker in Paris, entertained views which in some respects were contrary to those of the great German investigator. König held the opinion that when rapid beats set in they themselves give rise to new tones. This theory was not new; it had been held by Lagrange and Thomas Young, but was rejected by Helmholtz. With aid of large tuning-forks of his own make, König endeavoured to demonstrate the correctness of his view. König was not sure that he could detect with his tuning-forks the presence of summational and differential tones, but he claimed to hear tones of the rate of vibration indicated by $m - vn$ and $(v + 1)n - m$, where $m > n$ and v is a whole number, so that vn and $(v + 1)n$ are rates of vibration of those harmonic overtones of the lower tones which immediately enclose the higher tone. *W. Voigt*,[1] in 1890, concludes that both the combinational tones of Helm-

[1] *Wiedemann's Annalen*, N. F., Vol. 40, pp. 652–660.

holtz and the beat tones of König can theoretically be produced, and that the one system or the other will predominate
according to circumstances. If the energy of the two vibrations
approaches equality, combinational tones are more prominent;
otherwise the beat tones will be more easily heard.

König improved an invention by E. Léon Scott of the year
1859, and brought forth the well-known manometric-flame
apparatus for the analysis of sound. The phonograph of
Edison, first described in 1877, has been found serviceable
for the same purpose.

To study the composition of vibrations, *Jul. Ant. Lissajous*
(1822–1880), professor at the Collège Saint Louis, in Paris,
devised, in 1855, a very elegant method. The two vibrating
bodies (tuning-forks, for instance) were supplied with small
mirrors. A ray of light was reflected from one mirror to the
other, and then to a screen. Usually the bodies were so
placed that their planes of vibration were perpendicular to
each other. The curves thus traced by the spot of light on
the screen are known as "Lissajous's figures," but they
had been discovered long before in the United States by
Nathaniel Bowditch of Salem, Massachusetts. In 1815 Professor Dean of Burlington, Vermont, published a memoir, on
"the motion of the earth as seen from the moon," and devised
the compound pendulum for illustration, which is supposed to
have been introduced into science twenty-nine years afterwards
by Blackburn. This paper induced Bowditch to examine the
theory of the motions of a pendulum suspended from two
points, and to make a few experiments to test his theory. He
drew figures which are the same as the curves of Lissajous.[1]

[1] Consult J. LOVERING, "Anticipation of the Lissajous Curves," in
Proc. of the Am. Acad., N. S., Vol. 8, pp. 292-298; for Dean's and
Bowditch's papers see *Memoirs of Am. Acad. of Arts and Sciences*, 1st
Series, Vol. III., 1815, pp. 241, 413.

THE EVOLUTION OF PHYSICAL
LABORATORIES

It would be useless to search Antiquity or the Middle Ages for laboratories devoted to physical investigation. Before the time of Galileo and of Gilbert of Colchester the necessity of experimentation was usually overlooked. Hard thinking was frequently regarded as the sole requisite for scientific discovery. It was not until the time when Gilbert constructed a sphere out of loadstone and showed that our earth behaves magnetically much like his miniature representation of it, that the experimental method secured a firm foothold among physical philosophers; it was not until the young Galileo ascended the leaning tower of Pisa and dropped iron balls of different weights to show that a light ball will fall with the same acceleration as a heavy ball, that the Aristotelian idea concerning physical research was abandoned. The simultaneous clang of those two weights, as they struck the ground, "sounded the death-knell of the old system of philosophy and heralded the birth of the new."

It is amusing to observe that in those days many people reputed for wisdom looked upon experiments as dangerous to intellectual and moral life. In a history of the Royal Society, written in 1667,[1] the author deems it necessary in all serious-

---

[1] Tho. Sprat, *The History of the Royal Society of London*, 1667, pp. 323, 328. Consult also Robert Boyle, *The Usefulness of Experimental Philosophy; by Way of Exhortation of the Study of it*, in three parts, Oxford, 1663, 1671. He argues that experimental science does not lead to atheism.

ness to defend experimentation, arguing that "experiments will not injure education," that "experiments [are] not dangerous to the universities." The arguments were necessary indeed, for the Oxford pulpit declared that Robert Boyle's researches were destroying religion and his experiments were undermining the universities.[1]

The advent of the experimentalist marks the origin of laboratories. We do not mean laboratories of the modern type. Previous to the nineteenth century all of them, with hardly any exception, were private laboratories owned by individual investigators or their patrons.

For chemistry and astronomy, laboratory facilities were established much earlier than for physics. To the present day the word "Laboratorium" carries in Germany the meaning "chemical" laboratory.[2] The Middle Ages had its laboratories for alchemy and astrology. The search for the elixir of life and the key to the transmutation of metals stimulated activity. These were studies congenial to the avarice of the human heart. In the gallery of the Louvre in Paris is a painting by the Flemish artist Teniers, the elder(?). It represents a chemical laboratory of the sixteenth century.[3] The artist portrays a large basement room with forge-furnaces. The floor is covered with alembics, crucibles, and retorts. A group of enthusiasts are seated round one of the tables. Allowing somewhat for the imagination of the artist, this painting probably pictures to us the more luxurious quarters enjoyed by alchemists who commanded the purse and protection of some powerful patron. The majority of alchemists experi-

---

[1] A. D. WHITE, Vol. I., p. 405.

[2] See articles "Laboratorium" in BROCKHAUS's or MEYER's *Konversations-Lexikon*.

[3] See a reproduction of the picture in *Johnson's Universal Cyclopædia*, article, "Laboratories."

mented in secret retreats far from luxurious.   Even after the
complete victory of the inductive method, experimental re
search was usually carried on in rooms intended for domestic
or commercial purposes.   As late as the beginning of the
present century, the laboratory of the most distinguished
chemist of his day, Berzelius, was his kitchen, in which
chemistry and cooking went on together.   When, through the
influence of Gilbert, Galileo, and their successors, physics
began to be an experimental science, it was generally pursued
in the same apartments as its sister science, chemistry.
Formerly specialization was less marked than at present and it
was no uncommon thing for a scholar to be a master in several
branches of science.

The earliest physical experiments were made in private
laboratories.   The investigator usually turned part of his
house or room into a scientific workshop.   When Robert Boyle
at Oxford worked on the elasticity of gases, proving the law
which bears his name, he employed a tube of such length, that
he "could not conveniently make use of it in a chamber,"
and he was "fain to use it on a pair of stairs."   Newton performed his classic experiments on the dispersion of white
light into its component colours at his lodgings in Cambridge.
Benjamin Franklin, after experimenting with the kite, put up
an insulated iron rod at his house in Philadelphia, in order
that he might lose no opportunity to make tests whenever the
air was heavily charged with electricity.

Previous to this century, scientific laboratories existed simply for original investigation; they seldom played a part
in elementary or in higher *education*.   Doubtless, the error
of this practice was felt by many teachers and scientists, and
chief among such men was the Moravian educational reformer,
Johann Amos Comenius (1592–1671), who said: "Men must
be instructed in wisdom so far as possible, not from books,

but from the heavens, the earth, the oaks and the beeches; that is, they must learn and investigate the things themselves, and not merely the observations and testimonies of other persons concerning the things." "Who is there," he cries, "who teaches physics by observation and experiment, instead of by reading an Aristotelian or other text-book?"[1]

Near the close of the eighteenth century, Joseph Priestley, the discoverer of oxygen, expressed himself as follows: "I am sorry to have occasion to observe that natural science is very little, if at all, the object of *education* in this country. . . . I would observe that, if we wish to lay a good foundation for a philosophical taste, and philosophical pursuits, persons should be accustomed to the sight of experiments and processes in *early life*. They should, more especially, be early initiated in the theory and practice of *investigation*, by which many of the old discoveries may be made to be really *their own;* on which account they will be much more valued by them."[2]

In this passage Priestley advances an idea which is finding its practical realization at the present time, since it is only in recent years that there have been established laboratories for pupils of high-school grade, in which the young students themselves practise physical manipulation.

We have seen that experimental research was in vogue earlier in chemistry than in physics. Chemistry again takes the lead in the establishment of laboratories connected with educational institutions and planned for the use of students. Why this lagging behind on the part of physics? There appear to be two reasons. In the first place, chemistry appealed more directly to the needs of practical life. A knowledge of chemistry was indispensable for metallurgy. On the

[1] W. H. WELCH, "The Evolution of Modern Scientific Laboratories," *Electrician* (London), Vol. 37, 1896, p. 172.

[2] J. PRIESTLEY, *On Air*, Birmingham, 1790, Vol. I., p. xxix.

other hand, the age of steam had not yet arrived; electricity and magnetism were sciences still in their infancy. The second reason for the priority of chemical laboratories is that they are less expensive. Earthen vessels, bottles, test-tubes, a stock of ordinary chemicals, are not expensive, yet go a long way towards equipping a chemical laboratory. Physical apparatus, on the other hand, is very costly. Three hundred years ago an air-pump, thermometer, and telescope were expensive luxuries; they are expensive now. One hundred and thirty years ago Priestley wrote, "Natural Philosophy is a science which more especially requires the aid of wealth."[1]

Great educational movements usually begin on top. The laboratory method of instruction was first introduced into the universities and thence descended to the more elementary schools. Lord Kelvin[2] claims that the first chemical laboratory for the instruction of students was established at the University of Glasgow, prior to the year 1831, but the first laboratory of the type existing to-day was apparently established by Liebig, who, in 1824, became extraordinary professor of chemistry at the University of Giessen.[3] Certainly the new movement in the teaching of chemistry was started in Germany with much greater momentum and with more far-reaching influence than in Scotland. Students from all parts of the civilized world flocked to the little university in the small town of Giessen.[4] Chemical laboratories were soon built in Tübingen, Bonn, Berlin, and other places.

[1] JOSEPH PRIESTLEY, *History of Electricity*, 4th ed., London, 1775, p. xv.

[2] "Scientific Laboratories," *Nature*, Vol. 31, 1885, pp. 409–413.

[3] T. C. MENDENHALL, "The Evolution and Influence of Experimental Physics," in the *Quarterly Calendar of the University of Chicago*, Vol. III., August, 1894, p. 10.

[4] IRA REMSEN, "On Chemical Laboratories," *Nature*, Vol. 49, 1894, p. 531.

The earliest American institutions in which students were sent regularly to the chemical laboratory to make their own experiments were the Rensselaer Polytechnic Institute at Troy, New York, and the Massachusetts Institute of Technology in Boston. At the former, laboratory work was required of students prior to 1831,[1] probably from its very foundation in 1824. The movement was independent of that at Giessen. At the Massachusetts Institute of Technology perhaps more systematic courses were given. The laboratory method was in vogue there from the time of the school's foundation at the close of the Civil War.[2]

The transition from private laboratories to those belonging to universities was a gradual one. Usually it took effect in this wise. A few teachers permitted the most enthusiastic and promising of their students to enter their private laboratories. Thus, *Heinrich Gustav Magnus* (1802–1870) in Berlin threw open a few rooms in his residence for physical experimentation. Like Liebig, Magnus, while himself a student, had drawn his inspiration for experimental research from Berzelius and Gay-Lussac. The influence which Magnus exerted in Germany was very great. "He loved youth, and knew how to make himself beloved while imparting a taste for that science to which he had consecrated his life."[3] He began his work at the University of Berlin in 1834 as extraordinary professor of physics and in 1845 was advanced to the position of ordinary professor. Some idea of the work in his private laboratory may be obtained from his students. Says one of his American pupils: "While I was engaged there three other students were present, one occupied by an investi-

1 *Science*, Vol. 20, 1892, p. 53 ; N. S., Vol. 8, 1898, p. 205.

2 *Science*, Vol. 19, 1892, p. 351.

3 "Life and Labours of Henry Gustavus Magnus," *Smithsonian Report*, 1870, pp. 223–230.

gation of acoustics, another in polarized light, and a third in
the measurement of crystals of recently discovered chemical
compounds."[1] Among the greatest of his pupils who experimented under him were G. H. Wiedemann, Helmholtz, and
Tyndall. As the number of students increased, the private
laboratory became more and more inadequate; the university
began to give financial aid and the private establishment grew
into a regular university institution. By this process the
private laboratory of Magnus evolved into the physical laboratory of the University of Berlin, which was opened in
1863. A similar mode of evolution can be traced in case of
Liebig's chemical laboratory at Giessen and Purkinje's physiological laboratory at Breslau.[2]

Physical laboratories for students were gradually established in connection with other German universities. Thus,
at Heidelberg one was opened by *Philipp Gustav Jolly* (1810–
1884) in 1846. It consisted of two rooms in what was originally a private dwelling.[3] In 1850 the apparatus was moved
to somewhat more commodious quarters, in which later Kirchhoff and Bunsen instituted their wonderful researches in spectrum analysis. Referring to these new quarters, Quincke
says: "However modest this institute may appear to the
present generation, it contained the only physical laboratory
in which a German student at that time could do practical
work." If Quincke means to exclude private laboratories,
then this statement may be true, but students had been drawn
to Berlin to work in the private laboratory of Magnus long
before this. Helmholtz was there in 1847.

[1] A. R. LEEDS, "A Laboratory of Experimental Research," *Jour.
Franklin Inst.* (3), Vol. 59, 1870, p. 210.

[2] *Science*, Vol. 3, 1884, p. 173.

[3] G. QUINCKE, *Geschichte d. physik. Instituts d. Univ. Heidelberg*,
Heidelberg, 1885.

The University of Glasgow in Scotland, which was mentioned as laying claim to the earliest student's laboratory in chemistry, is also a candidate for the honour of having first given laboratory instruction in physics. In 1845 Lord Kelvin (Sir William Thomson) became professor of natural philosophy at Glasgow. He invited some of his students to aid him in his original researches; others volunteered for service.[1] " The physical laboratory for many years was a disused wine-cellar in the old university buildings."[2] Thus old Bacchus was superseded by the modern goddess Scientia. Experimental research was carried on for nearly a quarter of a century in this room and in another one, added later. Finally, in 1870, the university was moved into new and palatial buildings. The students' laboratory work under Kelvin was mostly original investigation. " Their interest was excited, was kept alive by their constant intercourse with the guiding spirit of the place, and their zeal was such that . . . the laboratory corps, as it used to be called, has been known to divide itself into two squads — one which worked during the day, the other during the night, for weeks together, so that the work never paused."[3] Neither at Glasgow nor at Berlin were the laboratory courses in physics regular prescribed branches, constituting an integral part of the curriculum; entrance into the

[1] Says Kelvin : "Three-fourths of my volunteer experimentalists used to be students who entered the theological classes immediately after the completion of the philosophical curriculum. I well remember the surprise of a great German professor when he heard of this rule and usage : ' What ! do the theologians learn physics ? ' I said, ' Yes, they all do ; and many of them have made capital experiments.' " — *Nature*, Vol. 31, 1885, p. 411.

[2] *Nature*, Vol. 55, 1897, p. 487.

[3] *Ibidem*, p. 487. Consult also Kelvin's evidence given before the Royal Commission on Scientific Instruction, *Minutes of Evidence*, 1870, p. 332.

laboratory was purely optional. The earliest institution in which laboratory physics was pursued according to a systematic plan for its educational value, and was a required part of the work necessary for a degree, is, we believe, the Massachusetts Institute of Technology in Boston. The institution competing with it for that honour is King's College in London. New England and Old England took the new departure about the same time. Says W. G. Adams: "Professors of physics at different universities have usually selected their best students to assist them in their private laboratories, to the mutual advantage of professor and student, but I believe that Professor Clifton was the first to propose, more than three years ago, that a course of training in a physical laboratory should form a part of the regular work of every student of physics. This system was adopted and at once put in action at King's College, on a very considerable scale for a college with no endowment whatever, and has been working now for nearly three years. Two large rooms adjoining the museum of physical apparatus were fitted up for a physical laboratory, and a third room was built for a store and battery room."[1]

Robert Bellamy Clifton's name is indeed closely identified with instruction in experimental physics in England. He was the first occupant of the chair of natural philosophy at Owens College, Manchester. After his removal to Oxford, he planned the first laboratory in England "which was specially built and designed for the study of experimental physics. It has served as a type. Clerk Maxwell visited it while planning the Cavendish Laboratory (at Cambridge), and traces of Professor Clifton's designs can be detected in several of our university colleges."[2] Maxwell took charge of the depart-

[1] *Nature*, Vol. 3, 1871, p. 323.
[2] A. W. Rücker, *Nature*, Vol. 50, 1894, p. 344.

ment of physics at Cambridge University in 1871, and his laboratory was built in 1874.[1]

Both at Cambridge and Oxford laboratory practice was optional, and the number of students undertaking experimental work was small.[2] But out of this small number rose some of England's physicists of the present time.

In the early part of this century France was the great centre for experimental research. And yet, as Professor Welch says, "France was long in supplying her scientific men with adequate laboratory facilities." "Bernard, that prince of experimenters, worked in a damp, small cellar, one of those wretched Parisian substitutes for a laboratory which he has called 'the tombs of scientific investigators.'" Gay-Lussac's laboratory was on the ground floor and, to protect himself from the dampness, he wore wooden shoes. But in spite of this, French scientists investigated and taught with enthusiasm. Says Liebig in his autobiography:[3] "The lectures of Gay-Lussac, Thenard, Dulong, etc., in the Sorbonne, had for me an indescribable charm. . . . French exposition has, through the genius of the language, a logical clearness in the treatment of scientific subjects very difficult of attainment in other languages, whereby Thenard and Gay-Lussac acquired a mastery in experimental demonstration. The lecture consisted of a judiciously arranged succession of phenomena, — that is to say, of experiments, whose connection was completed by oral explanations. The experiments were a real delight to me, for they spoke to me in a language I understood."

---

[1] R. T. GLAZEBROOK, *James Clerk Maxwell and Modern Physics*, New York, 1896, p. 73.

[2] GLAZEBROOK, *op. cit.*, p. 76; *Minutes of Evidence taken before the Royal Commission on Scientific Instruction and the Advancement of Science*, 1870, pp. 387, 388, 28.

[3] *Smithsonian Report*, 1891, p. 263.

Gay-Lussac invited Liebig to work in his "private laboratory." As elsewhere, there were in Paris no public laboratories for students. Original workers were dependent upon
their own financial resources. Says Arago: "At the end of
the eighteenth century and the beginning of the nineteenth,
no one was a real physicist unless possessing a valuable collection of instruments well polished, well varnished, and
arranged in glass cases." When, in 1806, Gay-Lussac, who
owned only a few instruments of research, was a candidate for
the Academy of Sciences, he had much trouble in overcoming
these prejudices.[1] We know that Dulong expended nearly all
his wealth on apparatus. Fresnel conducted his immortal
experiments privately, and defrayed from his own resources
the heavy expense for apparatus. Foucault carried on most
of his experiments at his own residence. On one occasion
savants flocked to the humble abode of Ampère in the Rue
Fossés Saint Victor to see a platinum wire, as soon as it was
traversed by an electric current, set itself across the meridian.[2]

For many years French scientists complained of meagre
laboratory equipment and lack of room, until, at last, Duruy,
the minister of public instruction (1864–1869), undertook to
meet the requirements. At the beginning of the century,
Germany took lessons from France; at this new period the
process was reversed. Says Professor Welch: "No more
unbiassed recognition of the value and significance of the
German laboratory system can be found than in the reports
of Lorain, in 1868, and of Wurtz, in 1870, based upon personal
study of the construction and organization of German laboratories."

Two decrees of July 31, 1868, affirm the necessity of sup-

---

[1] ARAGO, "Eulogy on Gay-Lussac," *Smithsonian Report*, 1876, p. 152.
[2] HELLER, II., p. 609.

plementing the lectures on science with practical exercises or manipulations. The same decrees provide that besides the laboratories for students there shall be established special laboratories for original research for the use of professors and other savants. The result was the establishment of a large number of laboratories for physics and for other sciences.[1] Referring to these changes, M. Darboux wrote, in 1892: "You know what profound transformations have been accomplished in these establishments [the faculty of sciences] within 20 years. Everywhere the buildings have been reconstructed and enlarged; they have been supplied with large laboratories for the experimental sciences. In some places these are still too small, — the remedy is easy. . . . A barrack on a site not far distant is sufficient. Certainly, we professors of the faculties of Paris will never forget the services rendered to superior instruction by the barracks and halls of Gerson."[2]

A physical laboratory was founded in the old Sorbonne in 1868. J. Jamin was director of it until his death in 1886. In 1894 it was transferred to the new Faculty of Sciences and was reconstructed. At the present time it is celebrated through the researches of its director, G. Lippmann.[3]

In the United States the growth of laboratories during the last 25 years has been surprising. As already noted, the Massachusetts Institute of Technology took the initiative in physics. The idea of giving regular laboratory courses in this subject to large classes was strongly advocated by *William*

[1] *Circular of Information*, Bureau of Education, Washington, D.C., No. 4, 1881, p. 119.

[2] *Report of the Commissioner of Education*, Washington, D.C., 1892–1893, Vol. 1, p. 234.

[3] A. BERGET, in *La Nature*, Vol. 26, 1898, p. 225; *Nature*, Vol. 58, p. 12.

Barton Rogers, the first president of the Institute. In drawing up the scope and plans of the new school, in 1864, he
stated some of the leading objects of such a laboratory.[1]

Edward C. Pickering was put in charge of the department.
In April, 1869, J. D. Runkle, then acting president of the
Institute, wrote as follows: "Pickering has drawn, in quite
full detail, a plan for the physical laboratory, which I will
send you before long. . . . Pickering is very anxious to be
ready by October next to instruct the third year's class by
laboratory work; and if an experience of one year shall be
favourable, as I feel it must be, we can then gradually enlarge
our facilities and take in the lower classes. I am convinced
that in time we shall revolutionize the instruction in physics
just as has been done in chemistry."[2]

After a trial of a little over one year Pickering made the
following statement: "The great difficulty is to enable 20 or
30 students to perform the same experiment without duplicat-
ing the apparatus, and to avoid the danger of injury to delicate
apparatus. Our plan is this: Two large rooms (one nearly
100 feet in length) are fitted up with tables, supplied with gas
and water. . . . On each is placed the apparatus prepared for
a single experiment, which always remains in this place, thus
avoiding the danger of breaking it in moving. A full written
description is also given of each experiment."[3] Several other
institutions, Cornell for instance, were quick to follow suit.
In the article just quoted Pickering says: "There are now
(1871) in America at least four similar laboratories in operation or preparation, and the chances are that in a few years
this number will be greatly increased."

---

[1] *Life and Letters of William Barton Rogers*, Boston and New York,
1896, Vol. II., p. 303.

[2] *Op. cit.*, Vol. II., p. 287.

[3] *Nature*, Vol. 3, 1871, p. 241.

Notwithstanding Pickering's prediction, the vast majority of our colleges and universities failed to make provision for physical laboratories for students until much later. In this matter, the technical schools were in the lead. University instruction, as distinguished from technical, is of more recent date. In 1871 Harvard College had no instruments for electrical measurements, and Professor Trowbridge had to borrow from Professor Cooke's private collection in order to make some tests on his new cosine galvanometer.[1] Most of the large physical laboratories in this country have been erected and equipped within the last 15 years, but now "we have some half-dozen that will compare with any university laboratories in Europe,"[2] with the exception, perhaps, of a few like the one in Zürich, devoted to physics and electrotechnics, which has been built and equipped at an expense of 3,000,000 francs.

The difficulty of arranging laboratory work in physics for large classes, which Pickering endeavoured to overcome, cannot be said to have been removed satisfactorily. Some of our large universities devote a whole building to the purposes of a physical laboratory and yet teach the elementary college physics, required of all the students for a degree, by text-book and illustrated lectures, without giving the pupils an opportunity to experiment for themselves. The teaching force and laboratory facilities are inadequate for classes of, perhaps, several hundred members. Experimental work is done only by the few students who elect more advanced physics, or by those who are pursuing technical courses. If there is any truth in the statement that even Faraday never could under-

[1] *Science*, N. S., Vol. VIII., 1898, p. 204. For comparison of dimensions of several American, English, and German physical laboratories, see *Nature*, Vol. 58, 1898, pp. 621, 622.

[2] A. G. WEBSTER, "A National Physical Laboratory," *The Pedagogical Seminary*, Vol. II., 1892, p. 91.

stand any scientific experiment thoroughly until he had not only seen it performed by others, but had performed it himself, then it is clear that the above method is far from ideal.

There are two distinct methods of conducting large laboratory classes in physics. One is to let all the pupils perform the same experiment (measurement) simultaneously, each student being supplied with all the apparatus necessary for the experiment. The second method is to let each student perform a different experiment, so that, at one time, there are as many different experiments in progress as there are students.

The first method has the great advantage of permitting teachers to discuss, once for all, the theory of the experiment with the classes as a whole, instead of repeating it with each student individually. Moreover, it is easier to superintend a large class when all are working at the same thing than when each is performing a separate task. The great disadvantage of this mode of procedure is that few institutions, if any, have the resources to furnish each student of a large class with the same instrument of precision. Several hundred instruments of the same kind might be needed for each experiment. Wherever this course has been followed, the apparatus has necessarily been of cheap quality and frequently the experimental work has lacked the desired degree of accuracy.

The strong point of the second method is that it necessitates no duplication or multiplication of apparatus, thus making it easier to equip the laboratory with instruments of high quality. Each student is at a different task. The members of the class rotate from one experiment to another on successive days. There is less opportunity for students to compare results, each pupil being thrown more upon his own resources. It is an individual method, calling for a great deal of "elbow instruction." A teacher cannot at one time take care of as many pupils by this method as by the first. Again, the order in which the experiments are taken up is different for each student, making it impossible, as a rule, to take the experiments in a logical succession.

So far as we know, there are few colleges and universities in which either of the two methods has been carried out in its purity with all students. Usually, in large classes, a combination of the two has been found more in harmony with existing conditions; that is, the class is divided into groups, and the experiments, during any laboratory period, are different for each group, though the same for all students belonging to any one group. At the present time the first, or class-method, is the prevailing one in our high schools, while in the universities the advanced laboratory courses are invariably pursued by the second, or individual, method.

During the past decade laboratory courses have been developed and strengthened, not only in our higher institutions of learning, but also in our high schools. Many high schools to-day are better equipped than were some of the prominent colleges ten years ago. The experimentation in our secondary schools was formerly purely qualitative, but now the quantitative work is being emphasized more and more.

At the present time laboratory instruction in physics in secondary schools is, perhaps, more fully developed in the United States than in France and Germany. M. Darboux, dean of the Paris faculty of sciences, reported in 1892 as follows: "There exists indeed in every lycée a physical cabinet, but the instruments to be put into the hands of the students for the manipulations in physics, chemistry, and natural history are wanting."[1] In Germany the desirability

[1] *Report of the Commissioner of Education*, Washington, 1892, 1893, Vol. 1, p. 233.

of letting the pupil handle apparatus and see it in action has been abundantly discussed. Some laboratories have been conducted accordingly, but the new movement is less general there than in America.[1]

The departure in the direction of individual laboratory work, including measurements, for secondary schools took definite shape in the United States when, in 1886, Harvard College changed its entrance requirements in physics. "It was now decided to establish a requirement of laboratory work to be recommended by the College in place of the text-book work, although the latter, considerably increased, remained as an alternative for those who could not command laboratory facilities. It was soon evident, in view of the inexperience of teachers and the very different standards and methods likely to be adopted by them, that a special course of experiments, carefully thought out, . . . was needed to make the new plan a success." A pamphlet was issued by Harvard in 1887, afterward somewhat revised, under the title, *Descriptive List of Elementary Physical Experiments.*

In recent years there has been a growing demand for the establishment of national laboratories for experimentation which is beyond the resources of laboratories connected with educational institutions. But little has been achieved in the way of securing government aid. Yet England, Germany, and France have institutions which in part fulfil these demands. England has the Royal Institution with the new Davy-Faraday Research Laboratory; Germany has its Imperial Physico-Technical Institute in Charlottenburg; France for 100 years has had its Conservatoire des Arts et Métiers

---

[1] Consult E. J. GOODWIN, "Some Characteristics of Prussian Schools," *Educational Review,* December, 1896; also a critical review of this article in *Poske's Zeitschrift für den Physikalischen und Chemischen Unterricht,* X. Jahrgang, 1897, pp. 161, 162.

and, for some years past, also an electrical testing laboratory in Paris.[1]

Of the famous laboratories of the Royal Institution in London an English writer said in 1870: "Probably a greater part than to the universities is to be ascribed in the spread and development of modern science to the Royal Institution, which has been the scene of the teaching and labours of the three by far greatest philosophers of our century, of Young, of Davy, and of Faraday."[2] The Briton of to-day speaks of it as the "Pantheon of Science." The theatre, model-room, and workshops of the Royal Institution were erected in 1800. The aim of the Institution, according to its founder, Count Rumford, was the promotion of applied science. It originally contained a workshop for blacksmiths with forge and bellows. All sorts of models of machinery were brought together. After 1802, when Rumford left England, the industrial element declined, and original research in pure science predominated. When the physical laboratory of the Royal Institution was erected, there was nothing equal to it in England. Nevertheless it was very unpretentious. It became memorable for the brilliant researches of Sir Humphry Davy, Faraday, and Tyndall. For 70 years it remained unaltered, and at the end of that time it was very inferior to the new laboratories in Oxford, Cambridge, Manchester, and Glasgow.[3] When the reconstruction of the laboratories at the Royal Institution came under consideration, the plan was at first opposed by Tyndall. He almost prayed that the place where Davy and Faraday had made their discoveries might be preserved.[4] But improvements were necessary and were made about 1871.

---

[1] A. G. Webster, *Pedagogical Seminary*, Vol. II., 1892, p. 101.
[2] C. K. Akin in *Minutes of Evidence . . . on Scientific Instruction*, 1870, p. 20.
[3] *Nature*, Vol. 7, 1872–1873, p. 264.   [4] *Ibidem*, p. 264.

Through the generosity of *Dr. Ludwig Mond,* the laboratories of the Royal Institution were recently enlarged, and a new laboratory, liberally endowed and equipped with modern apparatus, was erected immediately adjoining the Royal Institution. This new scientific workshop, called the "Davy-Faraday Research Laboratory," was opened December 22, 1896, and is at present under the directorship of Lord Rayleigh and Professor J. Dewar. It is "the only public laboratory in the world solely devoted to research in pure science" and "open to men and women of all schools and of all views on scientific questions."[1]

For many years considerable attention has been given to the standardizing of apparatus at the *Kew Observatory,* England. Meteorological instruments, compasses, photographic lenses, have been tested and verified. Important researches have also been carried on there on terrestrial magnetism.[2] In this work the government has helped but little. It furnished the site and the use of an old building; all other expenses have been defrayed through private benefaction.

Germany has become the envy of other nations because of her magnificent new Imperial Physico-Technical Institute in Charlottenburg, commonly called the *Reichsanstalt,* toward the foundation of which *Werner Siemens,* in 1884, donated about $125,000. The Reichstag voted the necessary additions to this sum. New buildings were provided, and in 1888 *Helmholtz* was made director. On his death, in 1894, he was succeeded by *F. Kohlrausch.* The Reichsanstalt has not only departments equipped for purely theoretical research, but also others devoted to the study of problems useful to industry.

---

[1] *Nature,* Vol. 55, 1896, p. 209.   [2] *Nature,* Vol. 55, 1897, p. 368.

France, for 100 years, has had its Conservatoire des Arts et Métiers. It was founded in the old priory of St. Martin des Champs in 1794, as a public repository of machines, models, tools, plans, descriptions. From time to time free courses of lectures on applied science were given to working-men and artisans. In the physical line a beginning was made by the purchase of the "Cabinet de Physique" owned by *Charles*, and by the establishment of the chair of physics in 1829. The physical equipment has been enlarged from time to time.

Through the participation of 18 nations, an International Committee of Weights and Measures was organized in 1875. A fine laboratory was erected in the Pavillon de Breteuil, in the Park of St. Cloud, near Paris, for the purpose of constructing international standards of the metric system.[1]

[1] A. G. WEBSTER, *op. cit.*, p. 94. For information on the proposed National Physical Laboratory in England, consult *Electrician* (London), Vol. 41, 1898, pp. 778-780.

INDEX